*Socinianism in Poland*

Born in 1885, Stanislas Kot has for the last forty years been the world's foremost scholar on the Polish Reformation. He was founder and editor of the periodical *Reformation in Poland* and is the author of several books on the Polish reform movement and on Polish cultural contacts with the West. Until 1939, when he went into exile, he was Professor of the History of Polish Culture at the University of Cracow. Prominent in political life as well, Professor Kot was a member of the Polish government in exile in London and served for a time as Ambassador to Russia.

# SOCINIANISM in Poland:

*The Social and Political Ideas of the Polish Antitrinitarians in the Sixteenth and Seventeenth Centuries*

Stanislas Kot

*Translated from the Polish by Earl Morse Wilbur*

Starr King Press   Beacon Hill   Boston

# Contents

# *Translator's Preface*

The work here presented to an English-reading public[1] is one
of such significance that it would be a serious loss to students of
advanced political, social, and religious questions if it were
suffered to lie buried in a tongue which comparatively few
western scholars have taken the trouble or had the patience to
acquire. It deals with one important phase of the history of a
religious body (the Minor Reformed Church of Poland, known
to its contemporaries in Poland as Arians, and to Church history
in general as Socinians) which, though its numbers were the
smallest of the Dissident bodies in the Polish Reformation and
its history as an organized body lasted hardly four generations,
was conspicuous not only for its daring innovations in Christian
doctrine and for its outstanding contributions to Polish literature
in its most brilliant period, but also, and even more, for its bold
pioneering in the field of social and political reform, as it sincerely and persistently strove literally to apply the teaching and
the practices of Christianity in all personal, social, and political
relations. The history of this religious movement thus becomes
a sort of laboratory record of experiments in broad fields and
along lines in which the past two generations, have again been
boldly and vigorously exploring. Here we find the record of
early experiments, conducted strictly from the standpoint of
the teaching of Jesus and his Apostles, in every phase of social
radicalism: socialism, communism, anarchism, non-resistance
and pacifism, war, property, taxation, luxury, judicial oaths,
office-holding, crime and punishment, Church and State. As the

---

[1] Stanisław Kot, Ideologja polityczna i społeczna Braci Polskich zwanych
Arjanami (Warszawa: 1932).

effort was made to put theory into practice in the face of often hostile customs and institutions, we see how far their theories were proved practicable, and at what cost; in what respect and for what reasons they had to be modified in practice, and where and why they were abandoned as utopian dreams. We see the main issues ably argued pro and con, and are enabled to pass judgment on the premises and the logic of the arguments. Thus we get some light from the past on the solution of the same problems as they arise today in new situations.

As Professor of the History of Polish Culture at the University of Cracow, the author had singular success in inspiring and promoting the investigation of a wide variety of questions connected with the history of the Reformation in Poland. The results of these investigations are to be found in many important monographs and in the volumes of the journal *Reformacja w Polsce*.

EARL MORSE WILBUR

Berkeley, California

PUBLISHER'S NOTE: This translation, completed during the Second World War, was revised and brought up-to-date for publication with the help of Professor Wiktor Weintraub of Harvard University.

Preserved throughout the text are the German place names Danzig and Elbing, since they are familiar to the English-speaking public. The reader should, however, bear in mind that these towns are now on Polish territory and carry Polish names: Gdańsk, Elbląg.

# *Introduction*

Although as late as the end of the seventeenth century the movement begun by the Polish Brethren—also called Socinians or Antitrinitarians—was causing a turmoil among zealots from the Thames to the Dnieper, stirring up fear, hatred, and contempt, yet with time this movement came to be almost completely forgotten. Indeed, in my youth a comprehensive history of the Polish Antitrinitarians would have constituted an impossible task, for this field was even then unknown. The oblivion accorded the movement was fostered not only by the Catholic and Protestant Church historians who opposed it, but by those others who had appropriated many of the movement's conquests. Free thinkers considered it over-imbued with religiousness. Researchers and scholars were hampered by the dearth of historical data, which are not only rare and widely scattered, but are also in little known languages such as Polish or Hungarian. A thorough study would have required the collaboration of teams comprising theologians, historians, and philosophers.

Though not a theologian myself, I have been fascinated since my early years by this movement as an interesting, unusual, outright audacious phenomenon of religious, intellectual, and social life stemming from the bedrock of sixteenth century humanism. In 1905, the noted Polish slavist, and Berlin professor, Alexander Brückner published in Polish a volume of sketches entitled *The Polish Dissidents*. By perusing some few score very rare and forgotten printed texts unearthed while travelling between Berlin,

Note: Adapted from an address delivered to the Unitarian Historical Society, May 19, 1955, and published in *The Proceedings of the Unitarian Historical Society*, Vol. XI (1956).

Warsaw, Lwów, Cracow, and St. Petersburg, Brückner had'
discovered an unknown world of thoughts, writings, and conflicts.
The sketches were purely literary, highlighting the author's gift
for words and style, but they did to some extent convey some
personal ideas.

This discovery spurred other scholars to further research concerned specifically with various leaders of the so-called Polish
Brethren, and they delved into their lives, dogmatic stands, work,
and influence. In 1919, a Society for the Study of the History
of Reformation in Poland was founded with a membership
including eminent Catholics and Protestants; it had its own review, *Reformation in Poland,* published under my editorship.
In ten fair-sized issues, it offered a wealth of material gleaned
chiefly from archives and manuscripts found in collections as
far apart as Kiev, Wilno, Koenigsberg, Kolozsvár—and Oxford,
Rotterdam, Uppsala, Paris, Basel, Rome. In Warsaw and
Cracow a younger generation of historians plunged with zest
into this sensational research field. Several monographs were
published in Cracow under the auspices of the Polish Academy
of Arts and Letters.

From distant California came the late Unitarian historian
E. M. Wilbur, to visit libraries in Hungary, Poland, Italy, Holland, and England. He acquired a reading knowledge of Polish
and devoted a lifetime's efforts to the completion of his magnificent *History of Unitarianism.* The first of the two volumes
deals mostly with the history of Socinianism in Poland. Wilbur
proved conclusively a theory advanced in the nineteenth century
by R. Wallace and Alexander Gordon, establishing that Anglo-
Saxon Unitarianism had had forerunners—in the sixteenth and
seventeenth centuries—in some Continental countries, and that
it had had an imposing church organization in Poland, Lithuania,
and Transylvania since the middle of the sixteenth century. The
scope of the activity may be measured by the output of printed
texts: the works printed by the Polish Brethren during their
one hundred years' stay in Poland and their thirty years of exile

total nearly five hundred in bibliographies, while the polemical works directed against them from Germany, Switzerland, Holland, France, and England would fill the shelves of a considerable library.

Even though we recognize that Wilbur's task was facilitated by certain early texts of Polish, Hungarian, Dutch, German, and Italian scholars, it involved a tremendous amount of further research and the covering of a lot of ground, with the study of a great deal of material which had to be located, sifted, and evaluated. His book is a unique monument of erudition and research, constructed by an American on European soil; it is a monument to a movement of an exceptional, a universal range.

Professor Wilbur's work was the first broad synthesis ever attempted of the Universal Unitarian movement, and it now must be complemented by works supplying the details, mainly in regard to Poland and Lithuania. The present work endeavors to undertake that task with respect to the social and political trends among the religious innovators of the period, and to rescue from oblivion this rich chapter of the history of the struggle for social equality, for man's freedom from slavery and want, and for the stoppage of bloodshed and intolerance. It may be helpful first to give a brief preliminary history of Socinianism: the birth of the movement in Poland, the chaos and evolution of its doctrine, the non-adorantist trend, the advent of Faustus Socinus, the diffusion of Socinianism and its relation to Anglo-Saxon Unitarianism.

Four hundred years ago, on January 22, 1556, a former lecturer in logic at the Padua Academy stood up, facing the Reformed Synod of Polish Calvinists meeting in the little town of Secemin. This man, Peter Giezek, a Pole from Goniądz in the Podlasie province of the Great-Duchy of Lithuania, then stated his credo, which was recorded as follows by the clerk of the synod: "1. He declared that the Trinity did not exist, and that the word was a new invention. 2. He criticized the Athanasian Credo, and rejected it completely as a 'human invention.' 3. God the Father is the sole God, and there is no other. 4. Christ is inferior to his Father, he is his father's servant. 5. He stated that Logos was The Word, invisible, immortal, transformed at a given time into flesh in the Virgin's womb, and he called this Word the seed of the Incarnated Son. 6. He denied the coexistence of Jesus Christ and God the Father within divinity." Peter supported these statements with quotations from the Scriptures and with excerpts from Ireneus.

There was an outburst of indignation. In a dramatic scene, after tears and adjurations, the synod professed itself incapable of trouncing this obdurate logician and instructed him to present his thesis to the Protestant leader held in highest esteem by the Poles, Philip Melanchthon, hoping that the latter would be able to convince Peter and bring him back into the fold.

But, among the Calvinist pastors attending the synod, some were already receptive to Peter's profession; and it was this group which formed the first nucleus of the Unitarian organization in Europe.

Peter (called Gonesius in theological literature) did not actually take the synod by complete surprise with his statement. While in Padua, he had been reached by the repercussions of Servetus' burning at the stake in Geneva. His master, Professor Matteo Gribaldi, introduced him to Servetus' writings which were being secretly circulated throughout Northern Italy. Gribaldi himself, who happened to be in Geneva on business during Servetus' trial and had freely expressed his indignation at seeing heresy thus punished by death, was at odds with Calvin. Gripped by Servetus' doctrine, Peter Gonesius resolved to spread its concepts by pen and word of mouth. He drafted a huge treatise in which he refuted all *Communicatio idiomatum* and acknowledged in Christ a God created in the shape of a man. He also gave out to a Cracow printer a booklet entitled *De filio Dei homine Christo Jesu.*

On his way back from Italy to Lithuania, Peter crossed Moravia and visited the Anabaptist groups which, escaping from persecution in the Tyrol and Southern Germany, had found a haven in that region and established communistic communities under the aegis of Czech lords. These Hutterians, or Moravian Brethren, as they were known, were pacifists who—in sign of protest against war—wore stout sticks at the side instead of the usual swords. Their tenets appealed to Peter, for they were, in his judgement, in accordance with the Gospels. Henceforth, he too began wearing the wooden stick adopted by the Hutterians, and he also supported their condemnation of the baptism of infants.

Peter's expedition to Wittenberg was fruitless, for Melanchthon detected an echo of Servetus' teachings in his arguments and rejected him. He fared no better at the hands of the Swiss—de Bèze, Bullinger, and Viret. But he remained undaunted.

He gave another work to a printer in East Prussia; and when Prince Albrecht Hohenzollern, a Lutheran, forbade its impression, he continued elaborating his thesis. He went on to Węgrów in Podlasie, where he enlisted the help of a great lady of the Radziwill family to found a community of his coreligionists and establish a printing plant. Out of the pioneer copies then printed, a few Polish ones survived until our time, but they were apparently destroyed in November, 1944—when Hitler's Storm Troopers poured gasoline over all of Warsaw's archives and libraries. One unique Latin edition was preserved at the Bibliothèque Nationale in Paris, the *Doctrina pura et clara de praecipuis Christianae religionis articulis,* acquired three hundred years ago for the collection of the famous Minister Colbert. Another work was lost, Peter's *De primatu Ecclesiae Christianae,* in which he outlined a program taking the first Christian community in Jerusalem as a model of brotherhood and social community.

Peter was not a mere imitator of Servetus' writings. A lucid thinker, dry, logical, devoid of Servetus' emotionalism and gushing enthusiasm but having the sound foundation of a profound erudition, he adduced his own arguments in support of Servetus' thesis. It is he who was really the prime inspirer of the entire

Unitarian movement in Poland and Lithuania, both in regard to
its theological doctrine and its politico-social ideology. Yet he
did not remain recognized for long as the supreme authority in
the matter. While he himself stayed faithful to Servetus' Christ-
ology concerning the pre-existence of the Son of God, he was
shortly superseded by the very men whom he had instigated
and who now were outdistancing him in dogmatic radicalism.

Within a few years of Peter's emergence into the limelight,
debates on the subject of the Trinity were rife at meetings and
synods. Among the participants were Italian newcomers such
as Dr. Giorgio Blandrata, Valentino Gentile, and Gian Paolo
Alciati, who had not felt secure in Switzerland. The majority of
leading pastors took an Antitrinitarian stand and steered their
congregations along that path. The official break with the Reformed Church took place in 1563. It was accompanied by an
outburst of polemical writings in which a few authors shone by
their immense erudition, audacity, and literary talent; such were
Gregory Paulus, Martin Czechowicz, Jan Niemojewski, Simon
Budny, George Szoman, Laurence Krzyszkowski, and Jan
Kazanowski. Though unanimous in their rejection of the dogma,
not all innovators agreed on the formulation of their own
doctrine.

For an adequate idea of the seething of minds, of the abundance of bold personalities and writings proper to that period,
it is best to refer to an account given by Andrew Lubieniecki in
his *Polonoeutychia*. In these memoirs the author narrates the
last years of the reign of Sigismund Augustus (1562-1572), that
tolerant King of Poland and Lithuania. Also, he attributes
Poland's current good fortune—its political, cultural, and literary
expansion—to the safeguarding of tolerance and freedom at a
time when religious wars were raging in Western Europe. This
is what Lubieniecki wrote about the manifold groups and doctrines forty years later, when most of the movements were already a thing of the past:

"Within a period so short, the ten last years only of the Augustian reign, and in a corner of the world so small as this our land, we saw a mass of various worships the like of which could have been seen but in heathen times: Roman Catholics, Greeks or Armenians, Jewish, Tartar, Karaimian.

"There were many tritheists who, rejecting the word Holy Trinity, worshipped three divine beings: God the Father, God the Son, and the Holy Ghost. Such were the Wilno group, the Lithuania and Podlasie groups, and others.

"There were ditheists, who did not recognize the Holy Ghost as a person and claimed the Son and Father were one in essence, out of the Father. Others said that the Son had been born of the Holy Ghost centuries back, and thought him a minor being.

"And those were most markedly split in two.

"For there were those who baptized infants, and whose leaders were Kazanowski, Falconius, Zitinius; and of them, there is no trace. And second were those who did not baptize infants, and whose leaders were Wisniewski, Farnowski, Petricius; they too are gone or have been dispersed among other denominations.

"Then there were those in the Kujawia who held that Jesus had been with the Father for ages; they baptized adults, differed from the ones above in the instruction of exculpation, and followed a rigorous discipline among themselves; their leaders were then John Niemojewski and Czechowicz.

"Besides them were the Dutch Neo-baptists who had come to settle in Prussia, whose ideas they shared and tried to inculcate in the group; they did not fare well either.

"There were those who introduced and propagated Moravian communism and concepts, whom the Moravians themselves were helping to bring in; but they accomplished little, and are not heard of any more.

"There were also those who spoke of the Scripture as a dead letter and a daub of printer's ink and, wishing to imitate Schwenckfeld, held that dreams, visions, and ideas were the things most necessary in religious practice and for salvation; and to them, sins not contravening civil law did not preclude attendance in churches, temples, and synagogues—as offenses committed in body did not matter if spirits were pure.

"There were those who condemned all officiating at any religious service, claiming that nobody was fit to officiate or instruct unless he had had a divine revelation and had either witnessed miracles or performed them. Such were Sleszyński, Biliński, Albinus, John Baptista and many others; and they too were wiped out by the Lord Jesus.

"There were also those who were loutish themselves, walked, lay, and labored in uncouth manner—claiming their ways to be favored by God; and, preening themselves because of them, thought other people undeserving of eternal life. They too are gone, and are not seen any more.

"There were those who incited godly and honest men to relinquish their offices, put away their arms, refuse litigation regardless of the wrong sustained, and who forbade the repeating of an oath. Many decent men left their offices and sold their estates or scattered their possessions.

"But also there were some whose transgression was the worst—and whom Satan strew most thickly throughout Lithuania, White Russia, Podlasie, Wolynia, and the Ukraine—for they did not believe in Jesus Christ. Some mingled together the Old Testament and the Gospel; others placed the Old Testament above the Gospel and introduced Judaism. And of those, some had taken to celebrate the Sabbath, or did not eat dishes not eaten by Jews. But they too were routed by Jesus Christ through his servants, and moreover wiped out so completely that none remained in our lands.

"But God's will was done in the last days of Augustus' reign, sapping the strength of all the sects or else destroying them. For when people got weary of controversies and quarrels, of the public bickering going on in the Diets and in the synods held nearly every year, there were men who came out to say they had sickened of all worldly affairs and wished to go away some place in a band so as to live together, practice their religion, and

await death in peace. At that time, Mr. Sienieński founded
Raków, to which flocked people of the same faith—noblemen,
burghers, ministers, and countless others, foreigners and scholars.
There was no peace, day or night, for three years (1569-1572),
for the various debates went on without respite, until, finally, a
fair number were converted through the arguments propounded,
while the remainder, unconvinced, went on their way and later
perished. The ones who stayed on in Raków were those known
as Christians; they continued to live together in peace, having
elaborated their doctrine and humbled their hearts, or—as they
called it—yielded them to the Lord Jesus. Among them were
scores of ministers later assigned to different places: ten were
brought by Mr. Kiszka to his Podlasie estates in Lithuania, the
Wojewoda Sieniawski took some to Ruthenia, Prince Zbaraski
had others go to Wolynia, and various noblemen also distributed
them throughout their estates."

The religious doctrine which gradually crystallized from among
the vacillations and conflicts derived above was based on the
Unitarian concept of God's unity—a controversial idea provoking clashes of opinion as to the nature of Jesus Christ. Some
recognized Jesus as a man; some as a Saviour entitled to divine
worship; and others, the non-adorantists, as a paragon of life
yet not an object of divine worship, adoration, or invocation.

To date, the genesis and evolution of the Unitarian movement
has not been made quite clear. We know that, following years
of hesitation, it was headed by Simon Budny in Lithuania and
by Francis David in Transylvania (where the germ of the new
doctrine had been brought from Poland by Blandrata). My
own research has led me to the conviction that another man
was the true originator of the movement, a man who was one of
the boldest thinkers of his age and whose personality is not yet
well known. He was Jacob Palaeologus, a Dominican friar born
in the Greek Island of Chios, who had escaped from a Roman
convent. Persecuted as a heretic, he had first fled to France, then
to Prague, and had finally found refuge in Poland—in the city

of Cracow. From Cracow he journeyed to Kolozsvár, in Transylvania. Then, in the years 1571-1574, he conceived his doctrine which, while extremistic in the dogmatic Unitarian sense, rejected the radicalism of the Antitrinitarian group's social ideas. He was an exceedingly prolific writer. When he was arrested in Moravia in 1582 by order of the Hapsburgs, to be returned to Rome, he had an entire case of manuscripts.

The confiscated manuscripts were deposited in the archives of the Holy Inquisition, and Palaeologus was publicly burned at the stake in Rome. Two years ago, I tried to obtain the authorization of the Santo Uffizio to study those manuscripts, which had lain forgotten and unread for so many centuries, but unfortunately my request was rejected. In the archives of the Vatican, which are open to researchers, I found excerpts taken from a single manuscript, a huge work entitled *Contra Calvinum pro Serveto;* they had been collected at the time for the Vatican's use and give evidence of Palaeologus' having authorized another voluminous work, *Contra Institutiones Calvini.* As to the two Palaeologus pamphlets preserved in Poland, they are conclusive evidence of his having been the prime inspirer and leading thinker of the classical Unitarian movement, which was joined by the Pole Budny, the Hungarian David, the Germans Jan Sommer, Adam Neuser, Mathias Vehe Glirius, and Christian Francken.

This group was combated by the majority of Antitrinitarians who advocated divine cult for Jesus Christ; the opposition was voiced in Poland by Martin Czechowicz, John Niemojewski, Alexander Vitrelinus, and others in a series of tracts, and in Transylvania by Blandrata. Blandrata actually brought Faustus Socinus to Transylvania from Basel in 1579 in order to make him dissuade David. But David remained unshaken, and he died in prison without having abjured his faith. Socinus proceeded to Poland, where he spent the rest of his life devoting himself to theological writing.

As we know, the Unitarian movement which had been rising in Poland and Lithuania in the twenty-five years preceding

Socinus' advent, producing numerous writers and a rich literature—mainly in Polish—comprised manifold trends. Though
attempts at some uniformization of the doctrine were pursued
at synods, the task was further complicated by the dissimilarity
of social concepts which increased the general confusion. Opponents, Catholic and Protestant, labelled these innovators after
the heresies of old: Sabellians, Samosatinians, Ebionites—until
the name Arians finally became the one commonly accepted.
Originally, the group called themselves Christians or Brothers,
whence the subsequent appellation "Polish Brethren." Because
of the wide gamut of trends, I personally would rather use a
negative, comprehensive term and refer to them as the Antitrinitarians.

The name "Socinians" was not coined until the seventeenth
century, and even then was adopted only abroad—not in Poland.
In his lifetime, Socinus was not admitted to their ecclesiastic
community by the Polish Brethren, who detected in his ideas
certain differences from their own. He rejected, above all, the
practice of baptism by immersion which the Brethren had started
following under the influence of the Anabaptists. He was accused by some of overestimating the role of Christ as the Son of
God, and condemned by others—erstwhile tritheists and ditheists
—for underrating that role. The main opposition to Socinus was
concentrated in Raków, where the brethren had been drawn by
a yearning for communal life, debate, and meditation. They had
settled in the town, having sold their estates to help the needy,
eschewing the world, the State, the war, public offices, and courts
of law—a group of men consisting of social utopians as well as
mystics, but principally of millenarians. To them, Socinus was
too rationalistic, too worldly, too prone to compromise. However,
his exclusion from the congregation failed to deter him: for
twenty-five years he continued to study, think, write, polemicize,
teach, until at last he attained a position of high authority
among the brethren's younger generation, irked by the persistent
confusion of their elders. Finally, around 1600, Socinus' stand-

ing warranted his being asked to come to Raków to participate in debates on the systemization of the doctrine. The event led to the founding of a local Academy and provided the Raków print shops with a stream of orders.

Socinus died in 1604 in Lusławice, where his tombstone is now enshrined in a monument erected, thanks to the American Unitarians, in 1933. Before his death, Socinus witnessed the initial attempts at disseminating through the Western World the doctrine of the Polish Brethren, later known as Socinianism.

The movement's inspiration stemmed from Servetus, a Spanish exile residing in France, and communicated itself to certain Italians who had migrated across the Alps, namely Camillo Renato, Lelio Socini, Celio Secundo Curione, Bernardino Ochino, Matteo Gribaldi, Valentino Gentile, and Giorgio Blandrata. Yet in no place, not even in hospitable Basel, were these men able to find a field for their teachings or a home for themselves. Wherever they went, they had to cajole, dissemble, and hide.

We can easily imagine the heart-breaking connotations of such an existence: Servetus, who lived in Vienne, near Lyons, under the aegis of Archbishop Palmier as Dr. Villanovanus, was compelled—in his quality of "Prior Physician" of the St. Luke Brotherhood of Apothecaries and Physicians—to attend Catholic Masses. He, to whom the teachings of the Roman Church were the works of the Antichrist, had to lay his hands on a Roman Missal in pledge.

Suffocating in this atmosphere of concealment and terror, the adepts of Unitarianism dreamed of some land at the confines of the civilized world where they could practice their religion in peace. Some were attracted towards Turkey; others sought to enlist patrons in Moravia or in Transylvania.

Yet in Poland and Lithuania they did manage, thanks to the tolerance and freedom reigning in these lands, to set up a large and active church organization possessing schools and print shops. From there, they soon spread into adjacent Transylvania, which was ruled by John Sigismund Zapolya, the son of a Polish princess and the only dynast sympathizing with the Unitarians.

Despite the difficulties raised by their opponents, Calvinists as well as Jesuits, the Polish Brethren succeeded in concentrating their members and securing legal safeguards in the form of the so-called Warsaw Confederation of 1573, which guaranteed "Peace among Warring Creeds." For nearly a century they prospered in Poland. The first generation, bent upon making its way and consolidating its teachings, did not aspire to conquer the world with its doctrine—though they did warmly welcome all who came to them.

But the second generation—thanks to Faustus Socinus—felt strong enough for the propagation of principles to other lands. At its head stood Socinus' pupil Andrew Wojdowicz, who began touring distant universities, circulating the writings of the brethren and recruiting sympathizers—he made some adherents in Wittenberg, among the Germans in Strasburg (Valentin Smalcius), and in Leyden in the Netherlands: Conrad Vorstius and Ernst Soner, who in turn won over two of the movement's luminaries among the German Protestants in Altdorf, John Crellius and Martin Ruar. Ruar became the chief propagandist of the newer generation, spreading the doctrine across the Netherlands, France, and England, making friends for the Polish Brethren. He succeeded in convincing Hugo Grotius, the father of International Law, and a great many Western scholars. In the Netherlands, the Polish Brethren established amicable relations with the Arminians.

As a propaganda weapon, they used the books printed in Raków—the works of Faustus Socinus, of Christopher Ostorod, of John Crellius and, above all, the Raków Catechism, which was to become world-famous. The catechism's author, Hieronimus Moskorzowski, dedicated its Latin edition to James I, King of England. This was motivated not solely by the desire to enlist friends in England, but also by the fact that there actually were numerous secret sympathizers on the Continent, mainly in the Netherlands, as a result of the Polish Brethren's frequent trips.

Proselyting in that area had been started in 1574 by Budny of Lithuania, and English notables were being persuaded to Unitarianism by letters and tracts, or through the British merchants of the Moscovy Eastern Company. In a letter dated 1608 and kept at the London Public Records Office, an English agent in Danzig reports a statement made near Danzig, in the presence of three hundred people, by the Unitarian Christopher Ostorod, who then said that "the Unitarians had friends in England who had advised dedicating the catechism to the King."

The King took the dedication as an insult and ordered the burning of the book—thus only contributing to popularize the catechism. Evidence shows that, besides the several editions printed in 1609 in Raków, one or two were printed in London secretly in 1614 by Humphrey Lownes. They were widely circulated in the country, winning sympathies in behalf of the Unitarians among the Presbyterians and the Episcopalians.

From then on, Unitarianism swept from Poland in a tide, flowing through both Danzig and the Netherlands, carrying the doctrine to England, where it was called Socinianism by its detractors. Twenty years ago, I myself published some highly relevant documents which prove how influential Socinianism actually was in England; the same theme was outlined by Professor Wilbur in his work, in 1952, and elaborated in a book published at the same time by Dr. Herbert John McLachlan, called *The Socinianism in Seventeenth Century England*. The doctrine had to be promoted through underground channels for fear of bloody reprisals, but it did reach many spheres, spreading to the entourage of Archbishop Laud, to the theologians of Oxford and Cambridge, and to the counties. Under Cromwell, there was a real outbreak of literature—chiefly fostered by the efforts of John Biddle, the painter Mann, and the philanthropist Firmin— with reprints from the Latin, and English translations of the Raków Catechism and tracts by Samuel Przypkowski and Joachim Stegmann. The readers comprised John Milton, John Locke, and Isaac Newton, all of whom were gripped by the

subject matter. Following the Polish Brethren's expulsion from
their country in 1660, some of their leaders settled in the Netherlands; among them were Socinus' grandson Andrew Wiszowaty,
Samuel Przypkowski, Christopher Crellius, Stanislaw Lubieniecki, Christopher Sandius. They compiled the group's principal
works into the monumental *Bibliotheca Fratrum Polonorum* and
came to be closely associated with England's religious life.

The extensive theological polemics written at the end of the
seventeenth century, particularly the Unitarian Tracts series,
carried their burning problems through to the eighteenth century,
in the second half of which eminent Unitarian thinkers were still
being branded as Socinians, a name they themselves were proud
to claim.

In the seventeenth and eighteenth centuries, that name con-
noted on one hand a theological concept based on the recognition of a sole God and of his Son the Savior, and on the other
an extremely comprehensive pattern of life and thought, including:

1. Freedom of religious thought.
2. The principle of applying reason to the interpretation of
   the Scriptures, the Revelations, and theological matters in
   general.
3. Absolute tolerance of all creeds.

In respect to freedom of religious thought, the Polish Unitarians had rallied to its banner from the start. As for the
freedom of religion, its principle had been developed to a high
degree by the Polish Brethren. Their first synod resolved:
"And since, in the true Church of God, no man may command
another in matters of faith, nor be compelled himself to yield,
each faction continues obeying that which betokens God's will
at that moment. Everyone has a right not to do things which
he feels to be contrary to the Word of God. Moreover, all may
write according to their conscience, if they do not offend anybody by it. They must bear one another a wise affection, pro-

viding none of them does that which is contrary to the glory of God and outrages the conscience."

They did not think that their doctrine was already perfect, and they endeavored to probe deeper. George Schomann, author of their earliest catechism (1570), gave the following instructions to his sons and grandsons in his testament: "From Catholicism through Lutheranism, Calvinism, and Anabaptism I have come to the true Catholic faith. If a still purer Church should arise at any time, then at once join it."

Thus, opposition to the system of Socinus himself also arose, within forty years of his death; many younger theologians openly insisted that they themselves found errors in the system, and objected to being called Socinians. It was they who were willing to accept the name of Unitarians traditionally used in Transylvania and which was also, let us add, devised by opponents belonging to the Reformed Church. That much is clear from the title of their resolution of 1569, *Consensus ministrorum in Hungaria orthodoxorum contra Unitarios Transylvanos.*

The Polish Brethren represented a humanistic reaction against medieval theology, which was based on unquestioned obedience to authorities and which they themselves rejected along with its entire tradition. They retained the Scripture, stating it might contain something *supra rationem* which transcended human reason, but that nothing, however, should be accepted *contra rationem.* Human reason, *ratio recta atque integra,* is man's tool in learning the substance of the Scripture. This stand was an expression of confidence in man's personal resources. Andrew Wiszowaty, in his work *Religio rationalis,* went furthest of all in the recognition of reason and philosophy in theology, but with the qualification that the true essentials of Christianity must be maintained. The human mind has not been warped by Adam's sin; the real meaning of God's words must be determined through reason, but reason must be sound, free from emotionalism. Reason itself rises to attain knowledge of God, but, without the

Revelations, knowledge of religion's mysteries would be unattainable. In addition to reason, the Polish Unitarians stressed as indispensable the bonds of love, as well as piety and godliness.

The synthesis of rationalism and love made the principle of tolerance mandatory for the Brethren, and they fought for it from the beginning—not for themselves alone, but in behalf of all faiths. Two of their works in particular had wide repercussions throughout the world. First, John Crellius' *Vindiciae pro religionis libertate*, which was translated into Dutch, English, German, and published in France in two editions under the title of *Tolerance de la Religion et de la liberté de conscience*. Secondly, Samuel Przypkowski's *De pace et concordia ecclesiae*, which exhorted mutual love among men, regardless of religious differences. "Dogmas do not constitute the essence of Christianity," wrote Przypkowski, "but devout living; no man is in measure to fathom the nature of God, thus we should allow even those faiths which may seem mistaken to some. We must not impose 'spiritual censure' on anybody, for each of us has a right to his own individual evaluation. . . . We do not grant anyone the liberty to violate, in private or in public, the freedom of conscience, nor the liberty to propagate religion by force and violence." Let us bear in mind that these words were uttered in the year 1628, preceding by over half a century Locke's *Letters on Toleration*. At that time, the reaction aroused was one of shock and of hostility towards the Socinians. The Catholic Bossuet and Jurieu of the Reformed Church were agreed in terming tolerance "that Socinian dogma, the most dangerous of the dogmas of the Socinian sect."

The three above-mentioned principles of the Polish Brethren came to be accepted with the implantation of Socinianism in England in the eighteenth century. The fourth, on which I deliberately do not enlarge, did not evoke much response. It concerned: Relationships towards their fellow-men which, based on the brethren's striving for social equality, enjoined the treating of the lowliest slaves like brothers, the alleviation of their lot, the sharing with them of their own slim portion. It was not until the nineteenth century, in the United States, that this tradition of the Polish Unitarians was revived with the rise of a philanthropic movement against slavery, eventually culminating in ardent abolitionism.

Is it possible to trace in Anglo-Saxon Unitarianism a sequel to the Polish movement? In England, indisputably so, for England was exposed to the active influence of Socinianism during one hundred years and, after that period, to the tradition itself, which lived on. In America, we have no such direct evidence. Yet, in view of the close bonds linking the United States to England's religious, cultural, and literary life, we may draw our own conclusions and assume it is only plausible that some of this influence must have permeated.

But whether this is true or not, the fact remains that the history of the evolution of a doctrine identical with theirs, of its struggles and sacrifices in the course of one century in Poland, cannot fail to interest those who, in the nineteenth century, were able to found their own Churches in an atmosphere of freedom and peace, and who have fostered the magnificent development and scope evidenced today by the American Unitarians.

In conclusion, I will say that I feel duty bound to make others aware of and concerned with the history of the Polish Unitarians. Since my own generation, in which we tried to rescue it from oblivion, a fresh wave of interest has broken out in the movement in postwar Poland, but its aim is not at all the uncovering of true facts. If Polish Communists make a big hullabaloo about the Polish Arians, as they are called over there, it is solely due to the radicalism of the group's social concepts. Even in respect to their genesis and teachings, as in the case of the entire evolution of the Reformation in Poland and Lithuania, the Communist presentation is so distorted as to be actually ridiculous. They eliminate completely the religious factors and,

slanting it to fit in with Stalinist Marxism, treat it as an outcrop
of the conflict between the proletariat and capitalistic feudalism.
Authentic historians who, in the name of truth, have objected to
this distortion, until recently were not allowed to publish works
expressing their own unbiased opinions.

# 1   *The Communism of the Moravian Brethren*

Social and political ideas of the Anabaptists. "Staff-men" and "sword-men." Organization of the Moravian communists. Negative attitude to the State.

The sixteenth century began with indications of a great growth in the authority of the State. The break-up of mediaeval class distinctions, the decline in the power of the Papacy and the Church, the awakening of the idea of a national State and of patriotism, the influence of ancient views regarding the supreme power of the State—all these political and ideological factors contributed, on the one hand, to the acquisition of great actual authority by the States of the time, and on the other, to the fact that both theory, as represented by jurists and political writers, and widespread public opinion saw in the State the most perfect organization of human powers applied to the realization of the highest ends, namely justice and morality. The progress of the Reformation tended at first to increase the power and authority of the State. Lutheranism gave back into its hands without reserve the guardianship of the religious life. Calvinism, it is true, demanded that "ephors," that is representatives of the people, should have influence in the government of the State; but it thus, with Biblical arguments, supported all the more strongly the authority of the State and bound subjects to a religious obedience to it.

The only element which ventured upon a critical considera-tion not only of the supremacy of the State, but also of its

essential, generally recognized functions, was the religious radicalism of the extreme dissenting sects. To be sure, the tradition
of the anarchistic heretical movements of the Middle Ages had
now died out; indeed, the youngest group of the family, the
Bohemian Brethren, had abandoned the radical ideas of Peter
Chelčicki[1] and acknowledged, at the end of the fifteenth century, the State's *raison d'être* and the necessity for a loyal
attitude towards it. The ferment provoked by the revolt of
Luther and Zwingli had, however, tended to awaken forgotten
ideas, this time in the German community and on its border both
in the south in Switzerland, spreading thence to Swabia, Bavaria,
and the Tyrol and exciting the revolted peasantry and the poor
populace of the towns, and in the north in the Netherlands, in
Friesland (the Mennonites) and Westphalia. The ferment was
to be felt also in Silesian towns.

The extreme elements, awakened by the Reformation, gave the
social movement a religious character. They based it on the
teaching of Christ, on the precepts of the Gospel, and on the
standards of the primitive Church, acknowledging as their ideal
a Christian community composed of brethren, free and equal,
independent of any ecclesiastical power whatever except the
leaders appointed from its own members. As an outward sign of
adherence to the community, they submitted to the rite of
baptism at an adult age, whence their name of Anabaptists or
Neobaptists. By refusing to recognize the baptism of infants,
the dissidents emphasized that only a man who had reached
full maturity became a true Christian and chose for himself a
church organization; and that no church had the right to receive ignorant children into membership. This principle unsettled
·the churches, paved the way for religious individualism, and
hence introduced discord into the social organism of the time.
Thus Anabaptism became the symbol of revolution and anarchy,

[1] Cf. Peter Brock, *The Political and Social Doctrines of the Unity of
Czech Brethren in the Fifteenth and Early Sixteenth Centuries* (The
Hague:1957).

although its adherents employed the most peaceable and evangelical language.

Within a few years of the suppression of the peasant uprising, the bloody extermination of the Anabaptist groups in southern Germany was accomplished. The severest punishments fell upon the leaders, who had come from the ranks of the educated clergy, although these were, in reality, a moderate element in the sect. Deprived of their leaders, scattered groups which succeeded in lying hidden in remote places in the mountains, especially in the Tyrol, at length found, in the southeast corner of Moravia, a country where they were permitted to live unmolested. There, in the vicinity of Mikulov (Nikolsburg), they were received by the powerful Lichtensteins despite imperial commands.

The companies of wanderers, composed almost exclusively of artisans, proceeded at once toward the realization of their ideal: the formation of a society of brethren, in which the strictest discipline was imposed, together with manual labor, a common treasury, and a common table. Unhampered discussion, deep study of the Bible, freedom of interpretation carried to the farthest limits, even to prophesying according to the inspiration of the Holy Spirit, brought in their train internal quarrels and divisions. An extreme tendency gained control; hatred of the State, princes, and offices, from which they had experienced so much persecution, grew stronger with the expectation that the Turks would come and shatter the political and social organization of the Empire. They sought arguments in the New Testament not only against the rich and against social exploitation, but also against the authority of the State, the courts and criminal law, the levying of taxes, and compulsory military service. Withdrawing from intercourse with the rest of society, they at the same time ignored the State, in which they rightly saw the chief organization of a hostile and condemned social order. As a sign of protest, they wore at their sides a wooden

sword or staff instead of a weapon, from which came their nick-
name, "staff-men" (*Stäbler*).

These extremes aroused opposition in the sect itself, in the
interests of a certain solidarity with society. One of the few
educated men among the wanderers, Balthazar Hubmaier, formerly Doctor of Theology and Canon of Ingolstadt, gave expression to this opposition. His little book, *Of the Sword*,[2]
critically examined the passages from the Gospels and St. Paul
cited by the "staff-men" against obedience to the State and the
secular power, and opposed to these other passages which expressly bind believers to obedience to the State. "And even
although Scripture said nothing," declares Hubmaier, "our own
conscience tells us that we must assist the authorities, watch,
defend, inflict punishments, perform our labor, go on guard, pay
tribute and taxes, that we may for the time being live together in
peace. You see, dear brethren, that it is a reasonable thing to
punish the wicked and to defend the good."

The attitude which Hubmaier's group, the so-called "sword-
men" (*Schwertler*), held toward the State saved neither him
from death at the stake in Vienna, 1528, nor the Anabaptists,
regardless of their views, from severe persecutions and expulsion
from Moravia in face of the Turkish peril. They soon returned,
however, and even extended their settlements, thanks to the
protection of the families of magnates who appreciated their
labor and their skill as craftsmen. Their chief center now became Slavkov (Austerlitz), where their energetic agent, Jacob,
a hat-maker from the Tyrol, hence named Huter, created out
of diverse elements a uniform organization based on strict
discipline, separation from the world as from unbelievers, community of goods, and absolute direction from above through a
chief bishop and "ministers of the word," that is, preachers.
From then on, the religio-social views of the Moravian Ana-

---

[2] *Von dem Schwert*, 1527. Cf. Johann Loserth, *Doctor B. Hubmaier und
die Anfänge der Wiedertäufer in Mähren* (Brünn:1893).

baptists, who were later also called Hutterites after their organizer, gained ground.

The disorders at Münster in Westphalia in 1534, in which Anabaptist elements took the lead, brought on fresh persecutions in Moravia, despite the fact that the Hutterites broke off all connection with the Westphalian revolutionists, thus emphasizing their peaceableness. Pressure from Ferdinand I forced the Estates of Moravia to banish them. Some hid themselves in the Slovakian mountains; other groups sought shelter in various quarters. After a year the wanderers returned to Moravia. Here years of severe persecutions still awaited them, but they bore them patiently, finding support in the favor of several of the magnates, and in the growing compactness of their own ranks.

Doctrinal quarrels and differences in social views ceased among them; the appearance of "apostles," who at the risk of their lives had made pilgrimages to distant lands to comfort their brethren in hiding, roused a spirit of sacrifice; the affecting "missives" and "words of encouragement" sent from prison, together with hymns, preserved the noble atmosphere of harmonious work for their ideal. Quiet, meek, industrious, patient, they finally won peace and toleration; after the last persecutions had ceased in 1548, and soon afterwards the golden age of their existence began.

They increased and spread, forming several populous communities in southern Moravia, as well as on the Hungarian border in Slovakia. Their number exceeded twenty thousand. Individual dwellings, containing from 300 to 400 persons, were under strict communistic management. They had neither small houses for families, nor separate kitchens, nor distinctive clothes. Private possession of any furniture or even of trifles was not allowed. All the brethren were bound to do manual labor. A man who came from another calling had to learn a trade. Elders allotted and inspected the work. All income from it, even gratuities, went into the common treasury. Their tailors, cutlers,

millers, carpenters, bath-keepers, etc., were famous; as honest
and skillful workmen they were everywhere accepted and well
paid.

There were no persons of education in their communities,
and in general they had an aversion or contempt for learning,
and took pains only to give their children elementary training.
The general level of morals was uncommonly high among them.
Despite the community life of a crowd of men and women,
dissoluteness was unheard of. Marriage was a sacrament; divorce
was allowed only for adultery. Individuals who were wicked or
disobedient they punished by excommunication and excluded
from the community.

At the head of the community stood "ministers of the word,"
preachers chosen for life, from simple brethren, and endowed
with confidence and a despotic-theocratic authority. They followed a tradition, relying upon the doctrine of the martyred
founders of the community. A Silesian named Peter Riedemann
assembled these teachings around 1540, in an extended treatise
which was published under the title *Rechenschafft unserer
Religion, Leer und Glaubens* (Brno: 1565).[3] This was the sacred
book of the Anabaptists, to which they appealed in every case
of doubt. It was founded on the Bible, whose teaching it interpreted after its own fashion.

The doctrinal system of the Moravian communities was simple
and general, not far removed from the Protestant, but doctrine
did not play a very important rôle among them. Reality for
them consisted in a moral problem: the practice of the teaching
of Christ and observance in daily life of the principles of the
Gospel, which they interpreted in their own way. They reproached all the churches with hypocrisy, because their believers,
professing to be Christians, did not in their lives strictly conform to the precepts of Christianity, especially in the matter of
love for their neighbor and for their brethren. They themselves,

___

[3] An English translation: *Account of Our Religion, Doctrine and Faith*
(Bridgnorth:1950).

to be sure, practiced this love of their neighbor in a one-sided way, regarding only members of their sect as neighbors, and being indifferent or even hostile to others, as well as being ruthless to excommunicated brethren.

This attitude is partly to be explained by the fact that the Moravian Anabaptists were treated by all churches, states, and societies as a despised class, with whom there should be no relations, even if it were as yet impossible to exterminate them. The circumstance that they were settled in an environment strange in nationality, language, and traditions—southwestern Germans in the midst of Czechs, who regarded them jealously as competitors in their trades—contributed to their keeping to themselves in their own closed circle and to their isolation.

Under these historical and geographical conditions, the political ideals of the Moravian Anabaptists, based, within the limits possible at the time, upon disregard of the State, could only be confirmed. Here is how they formulated their position in 1545:

As for the authorities, we hold with Paul that they are ministers of God for vengeance, therefore also we pay them tribute, taxes, service, and everything that is not against our conscience. But if they undertake something inconsistent with peace, as a blood tax, a fee to the executioner, and anything that relates to the shedding of blood, that we shall not give, nor shall we assist it, either in word or in deed, believing that vengeance belongeth to the Lord, and that we are not to resist evil, but to love our enemies. Also we shall give no aid nor extra tribute to free ourselves in case of war taxes; also we shall give no labor nor anything as a substitute for blood taxes under any pretext, but shall look to the Lord, who has in his hand the hearts of magistrates, to direct them according to his good pleasure. Nor shall we give the authorities the reverence due only to God, and hence we shall give them no titles: gracious, illustrious, wise or prudent sirs; nor shall we ever bow or bend the knee before them, knowing that the Lord is a jealous God, who will yield his honor to no one. With him alone is favor, since all the powers with all their splendor remain in disfavor with God. Yea, he only is glorious, wise, and prudent, and all men who have no knowledge of his truth live in darkness and improvidence. So then we may not show them divine honor by bowing and kneeling, but may bow the knee only in the name of Jesus Christ.[4]

This brief sketch of the views of the Moravian Anabaptists may suffice to portray the ideals of the only group in Europe, during the first half of the sixteenth century, which extracted all the social and political implications from the Gospel, not shrinking in its radicalism from a rupture with the whole Christian world of the time.[5]

[4] *Geschicht-Buch der Hutterischen Brüder, herausgegeben von den Hutterischen Brüdern in Amerika, Canada.* Ed. Dr. Rudolf Wolkan. (Standoff Colony, near Macleod, Alberta, Canada: 1923), p. 198.

[5] The best account of the internal organization of the Moravian Anabaptists is by J. Loserth, *Der Communismus der mährischen Wiedertäufer im 16. und 17. Jahrhundert (Archiv für oesterreichische Geschichte,* Vol. 81) [1894]). A new edition of the *Geschicht-Buch* was prepared by A. J. F. Zieglschmid, *Die älteste Chronik der Hutterischen Brüder* (Philadelphia: 1943). An accurate picture of their socio-religious ideals is given by Dr. Lydia Müller in *Der Kommunismus der mährischen Wiedertäufer* (Leipzig: 1927). Cf. also F. Hruby, "Die Wiedertäufer in Mähren," in *Archiv für Reformationsgeschichte,* Vols. XXX-XXXII (1933-1935); as well as papers by Robert Friedmann, published in the *Mennonite Quarterly Review,* Vols. XXVIII-XXXI (1954-1957), and in the *Archiv für Reformationsgeschichte,* Vol. XLVI (1955); and Harold S. Bender in the *Mennonite Quarterly Review,* Vol. XXX (1956).

## 2 *First Reactions to Anabaptism in Poland*

Echoes of Anabaptism in Poland. Bernard of Lublin. Edict against Anabaptists. Moravian fugitives in Krasnik. Dislike of Protestants for Anabaptism.

Anabaptism was not an unknown phenomenon in Poland at the time of the rising reformation movement. Groups of persecuted sectarians tried to penetrate into the western parts, into Great Poland and Prussia. Louder echoes must have come from Silesia, where the Anabaptists were winning converts in the towns: the furrier Gabriel Ascherham, one of the leaders of the movement, was active there. Works attacking the Anabaptists were read, for example Luther's, from whom Stanislas Orzechowski, a leading Catholic polemicist, later quoted the contemptuous definition of them as *Schwärmer;* "that is," said Orzechowski, "people with bees in their bonnets." [1] Andreas Frycz Modrzewski was to bring information from Germany about measures against them.[2] The Catholic controversialist Johannes Cochlaeus of Dresden dedicated to the Polish diplomat and bishop John Dantiscus his polemical treatise, *XXI articuli Anabaptistarum Monasteriensium confutati* (1534).

That even at an early period there were those who accepted some of the social ideas of the Anabaptists, is proved by a work

[1] *Orichoviana*, in *Opera inedita et Epistulae St. Orzechowski (1513-1566)*, ed. J. Korzeniowski (Cracow:1891), p. 387.
[2] Letter of June 20, 1536, to Jan Łaski (Johannes a Lasco), in S. A. Gabbema, *Illustrium virorum Epistolae* (Harlingae:1669).

9

by Bernard of Lublin, no longer extant, of whose contents we
know only through the polemics of his opponent John of Pilsen.[3]
Bernard denied the magistrate's right to inflict capital punishment:

The judge, [he argued, according to the summary of John of
Pilzno] may condemn no one to death, for no one has given him
this power. God caused man to live, man may not refuse life,
and so the Creator has given no power to destroy his work; and
man may prevent man from doing evil, but may not deprive him
of life, which is under the protection, but is not the property, of
the government. This writer [John of Pilzno pointed out] does
not allow punishments other than disgrace for the purpose of
correction, and imprisonments for the purpose of preventing further crimes. Finally he demands that a prisoner be not deprived
of liberty longer than fifteen years.

John of Pilzno came out energetically against this humanitarianism and against the denial to the State of the right to put lawbreakers to death, addressing Bernard with an argument *ad
hominem:*

Why do you ask, dear Bernard, who has given leave to take
life? Ask yourself why you killed the brigands at Zywiec who
were trying to kill you. What you are allowed to do is not the
officer for his part to be allowed? It is not becoming in the King
to kill, but he has a duty to our beloved country, where he keeps
guard for us, to have bad men judged, and by putting bad men
to death, to defend us all against them. Dear Bernard, you do
not know our land. You would have us all in danger from knaves.
Do, for Heaven's sake, first make the brigand feel greater pain of
spirit in his disgrace than under torture. Abolish these two reali-
ties, namely that under one lord and law a noble may be pun-

[3] We owe our knowledge of these polemics to T. Czacki, *O litewskich i
polskich prawach* (Warsaw:1801), II, 118. Czacki had a little work of John
of Pilzno, and from it he cited a passage which is our only source in this
case. Bernard of Lublin is known as the father of Polish vernacular writing.
Author of a large volume of fables in verse, he was an independent thinker
and defender of undogmatic religion. Cf. his letter to the Cracow book-
seller Szymon in 1515, published as important evidence of the pre-Luther
religious ferment by M. Flaccius Illyricus in *Catalogus Testium Veritatis*
(Frankfurt:1666), and in Chrzanowski-Kot, *Humanizm i reformacja w
Polsce* (Lwów: 1927), pp. 314f.

ished in one way, a peasant in another; but do not take away the sword from the lord, whom God has commanded to inflict punishment as a matter of duty, but not as a liberty granted out of favor.

Poland therefore feared an invasion of Anabaptists. In August 1535, at the time of the marriage of the Polish King's daughter Jadwiga with the Elector of Brandenburg at Cracow, there was a rumor of the passing of a group of two hundred persons, mostly Silesians, through Toruń (Thorn) and Grudziądz (Graudenz) to Kwidzyń (Marienwerder). It cost great effort to remove them from Prussia.[4]

Sigismund I issued an edict on September 27, 1535, to all officials, ordering the expulsion of Anabaptists from the country:

There arose a few years since the godless and criminal sect of Anabaptists, so universally hated that none of the Christian rulers allows them in his state or possessions, and that justly, for there is no more threatening plague than this, with which those, not men but monsters, are trying to infect the human race. Therefore, since because of their mad rage no one will endure them in his land, they are seeking in various quarters neighborhoods where they may earn their living with their wives and children. Therefore we charge you all, especially the prefects of our cities, towns, and townships, which lie on the frontier of the Kingdom or in Prussian territory, that in case of any chance arrival at these towns of any of this godless race, you forbid them water and fire, and by no means allow them to enter into relations with our subjects. . . . etc.[5]

The language employed in the above edict shows what a dangerous element the Anabaptists seemed to be.

Yet despite this edict, a crowd of Anabaptists from Slavkov came across Slovakia to Poland and wandered far to the east.[6]

[4] B. Schumacher, *Niederländische Ansiedlungen in Preussen* (Leipzig: 1903), pp. 154-156.
[5] *Edictum contra Anabaptistas aliunde passos et ad Poloniam migrantes non recipiendos* (Ms. 168 in Ossolinski Museum), Vol. II, pp. 50f.
[6] Josef Beck, *Die Geschichtsbücher der Wiedertäufer in Oesterreich-Ungarn* (Wien: 1883) (*Fontes rerum Austriacarum*, II, 43), pp. 129, 149.

One group stopped at Kraśnik near Lublin, a second at Włodzi-
mierz. Their leaders were the "ministers of the word" Ulrich
Stadler, formerly employed in the mines in the Tyrol, and
Leonard Lochmair, sometime priest at Freisingen. Stadler, a
prominent leader of the "staff-men" movement, settled at Włodzi-
mierz, and thence in 1535-36 sent letters and instructions to the
brethren at Kraśnik.[7] The wanderers spent a severe winter at
Kraśnik, which belonged to the Palatine Tęczyński; they were
fleeced, oppressed, and imprisoned by the prefects, who appealed
to the King's edict. This oppression is described for us in the
bold letter of Stadler[8] to the persecutors, from which we quote
the most important passages:

The Church of the Lord Jesus Christ, gathered in his name,
makes known to you, both prefects, as follows: God the Almighty
knows your outrages and crimes which during the whole winter
you have inflicted and caused to His poor, miserable exiled little
ones. Again, you have outrageously detained us by force, though
it has never been our purpose or desire to remain. You have also
violently torn away from us our godly elders with no just cause,
and to this hour we know not whether they are alive or dead.
So then you have forcibly taken our brethren from us unfairly
and unjustly. But now you are keeping us also; you have
threatened to burn us all, though we have done none of you any
harm. But the only reason is this, that we will not bow down
or worship your idols which you worship, for you revere the
work of your own hands; also that we will not be obedient to
your Roman Church but to the Lord Christ alone in life and in
death. Moreover, you have no case against us, for we have
lived among you in the full fear of God, and have faithfully
worked for you and used up our goods which we got in our own
land in Moravia by hard work. Again, you have imprisoned us,
and all this on the ground (as we have heard from the mouth of
the Lord Palatine) that we disregard the King's command that
we should leave his possessions or country, to which command we

[7] Four letters are preserved among the manuscripts of the Chapter Library
at Bratislava and published by Lydia Müller, *Glaubenszeugnisse ober-
deutscher Taufgesinnter* (Leipzig:1938), pp. 211-236.

[8] *Geschicht-Buch*, pp. 127-130.

wish to be obedient, and are not, as they falsely slander us, unwilling to obey the authorities and rulers.

You threaten us with further repressions; remember the judgment of God. We have lived among you in peace and have done no wrong to any. But if it is a question of a different faith, then ` only Christ can decide who belongs to the goats and who to the sheep. You persecute us, and wish to detain us by force, to scatter us and grind us to powder. You know that we are not slaves, and have been neither conquered nor bought, and we will not let ourselves be detained. But if—which we do not believe— you have command from the King to detain us, then appoint us a place where we may support ourselves as other free people do. We wish only to work in peace. If you detain us by force and wrong us further, we shall bear it in hope of the mercy of God, but nothing good will come to you from this; your conscience will reproach you and men will condemn you.

We have therefore determined to send you a letter with a reminder and a request that you do us no wrong, else the heavy punishment of God awaits you. You call on us to repent. You are bound to do so yourselves; or do you think that Christianity consists only in fasting on Fridays and keeping holy Sundays? All this we have written in the name of the whole community, praying God to have mercy on you. If our letter displeases you, then remember this proverb: The truth bites and hurts one who is caught in a lie. We have written you in Latin, very simply even if badly, for we could not explain ourselves better; although we would rather have addressed you more clearly and have set forth or related our case more thoroughly in German.

After this letter the wanderers were expelled from Kraśnik[9] in 1536 and withdrew again to Slovakia; but being plundered by robbers, they went back to Moravia. In Great Poland, however, fugitive Anabaptists[10] found refuge with the gentry, while the furrier Gabriel, leader of one of the Moravian groups, fled to Wschowa and there died.[11] Also at the time of the persecu-

[9] From the account of martyrs compiled in 1542 in the *Geschicht-Buch,* it is to be seen that no Anabaptist in Poland suffered death for his faith.

[10] This is confirmed by the records of the chapter at Poznań, July 3, 1537. *Acta historica Medii Aevi (Acta capitulorum,* I, 1408-1530) (Cracow: 1908), XIII, 35.

[11] Beck, *Geschichtsbücher,* p. 71; Moritz, *Reformation und Gegenreformation in Fraustadt* (Poznań:1907).

tions in 1548, the communists sent four brethren to Poland to seek quiet abodes; they went as far as Wallachia, though to no purpose.

Apart from the unusual declaration by Bernard we shall not soon find in Poland another expression of solidarity with the Anabaptist aims. In the later years of the active progress of the Reformation, Catholic writers like Stanislas Hosius, or Martin Kromer in his Polish *Conversations of a Courtier*, made the most of the revolutionary and immoral excesses at Münster in order to frighten the gentry away from Protestantism by the prospect of the extremes to which it may lead. The Polish evangelicals knew the social and political views of the Anabaptists at first hand, but they did not sympathize with their radicalism. Thus, for example, Jacob Przyłuski in his *Statut* says: "It is our just duty to be done with the madness of the fanatics, who make it a matter of doubt whether Christians may hold office or possess anything as property, when the Scripture calls pious rulers gods, and property rightly gained and rightly used yields many good results." [12] That it is necessary to wage defensive war was clear to the pacifist Frycz Modrzewski: "For any king who omitted to wage such a war would encourage the enemy to do such things again. He who sets aside the right to use the sword, which is placed in his hands to punish evil-doers, should not be regarded as the ruler, but as the betrayer of the republic." [13]

The Calvinistic synod at Włodzisław in 1558 considered the fundamental question whether one may forcibly defend oneself against violence. It was voted that defence against violence in a matter relating to property belongs to the magistrate; violence used against a person may be repelled by the person himself. It was added, "We are bound to defend ourselves from the superstition of the Anabaptists, who will not drive off a biting dog." [14]

[12] *Leges seu Statuta ac Privilegia Regni Poloniae* (Cracow:1553), p. 373.
[13] *De emendanda Republica, liber de bello* (Cracow:1551), Chap. ii; *Opera omnia* (Warsaw:1953), I, 242.
[14] Hermann Dalton, *Lasciana nebst den ältesten evangelischen Synodalprotokollen Polens* (Berlin:1898), p. 463.

Moreover, the obligation of pastors and preachers to do manual labor seemed to the Polish Calvinists improper to such a degree that even the Bohemian Brethren had to bear much criticism on this account, for example at the meeting at Chrzczęcice in 1556:

One who wishes to live by the work of his own hands, and thereby to support himself and his household, cannot do enough for his own office, which requires diligent reading, writing, the teaching of others, and much thinking. We also understand therefore that although we shall not perform such work and hard labor with our own hands as others do, but spend this time in study, writing, advising others, and teaching, yet in this we do not sin; and although we were even provided for by others without doing any hard labor of our own, that is not against God, for every laborer is worthy of hire for his work.[15]

[15] Józef Łukaszewicz, *Dzieje kosciołów wyznania helweckiego w dawnej Małej Polsce* (Poznań:1853), pp. 122f.

# 3 The Beginnings of Polish Religious Radicalism

Appearance of Peter of Goniądz. Budny's opposition.
First signs of radicalism. Lublin Diet of 1566. Synod
at Iwie. Triumph of radicalism in 1569. Foundation
of Raków.

Religious evolution towards radicalism began even in Poland
to win sympathizers for Anabaptism. Its first herald was Peter
Giezek of Goniądz (Gonesius) who, as early as 1555, visited the
Moravian Anabaptists and, as a sort of demonstration, following the example of the "staff-men," wore at his side a wooden
sword.[1] Not immediately finding followers in Little Poland, he
began to carry on propaganda in Lithuania against both infant
baptism and the existing socio-political organism. He must have
made converts, for in the Ruthenian-Slavonic Catechism published at Nieśwież in 1562, Simon Budny, at that time Calvinist
preacher at Kleck, indulged in polemics against the social views
of Anabaptism.[2] These are the questions to which his *Katechisis*
tries to reply:

[1] In a speech at the synod of Secemin (quoted in Lubieniecki's *Historia
Reformationis Polonicae* [Freistadii:1685], p. 112, and doubtless written
out, though later, by Peter himself), he speaks of himself as of one known
throughout the whole country only because, "refusing arms, he wears a
wooden sword according to the antimilitary custom of the Moravian
Brethren."

[2] The relevant paragraphs are quoted in Polish translation by H. Merczyng, *Szymon Budny jako krytyk tekstów biblijnych* (*Simon Budny as a
critic of Bible texts*) (Cracow:1913), pp. 16-21. Cf. Stanislas Kot, "Szymon
Budny, der grösste Häretiker Littauens in 16 Jahrhundert" in *Festschrift
für H. F. Schmid* (*Wiener Archiv für Geschichte des Slawentums und
Osteuropa*, II, 1956).

Is it right for a Christian to hold office?

What is a serf or a servant to do, if his master has commanded him to do something wrong?

Is it a sin to kill a robber or any other evil-doer?

If a robber should strike us, are we not to defend ourselves?

Is it right for a Christian to go to war?

Is it right for a Christian to have property or an estate of his own?

The answers to these questions condemn the teaching of the Anabaptists; in abbreviated form, they run as follows: Office is a good thing; it follows from Holy Scripture that God has established kings, princes, governors, and other officials; if an official is bad, the fault is that of the person, not of the office: "Hence it is right for a Christian to hold office, to judge, to defend his goods, to punish the wicked, not only in their possessions, but even capitally, provided only it be done justly." A serf is bound to perform the commands of his master, and to obey him as God himself, insofar as the commands are not contrary to God and his word: "Hence, if his master commands him to go to war or to pay taxes, and eventually even makes him a slave, a Christian must suffer, and pray to God for his master . . . An officer does not sin when he punishes the wicked, not merely by a fine or by flogging, but even by death." A Christian may not attempt another's life, but he has the right to defend himself; if in self-defence he should kill his enemy, this murder should not be punished by the magistrate. It is not right for a Christian to serve in an unjust, aggressive war; but in defence of one's own boundaries "a war is just, and a Christian may take part in it with conscience free." As for private property, Budny taught that "it is right for a Christian to have property, but only provided he has got it by fair means and has given alms from it . . . If a man were to throw away his property outright, or give it to someone, he would then not have wherewith to give alms, and would have himself to ask others for bread."

Thus Budny all along the line declared himself against the innovators and for the existing order. His conservatism went

so far that he even allowed serfdom—in conformity with conditions in Lithuania. He left open the way of disobedience to a
ruler only in the event of the latter's commands being contrary
to the word of God, and even then he did not provide for the
possibility of active resistance.

Shortly after this there came from the press the first booklet
in Poland setting forth the social views of Anabaptism.[3] It was
written by Peter of Goniądz about 1563-1564 and was certainly
circulated secretly, as were also the other writings of Peter of
Goniądz attacking infant baptism, for no more definite bibli-
ographical information about it has anywhere been preserved.
It is therefore from Budny that we learn that the work was entitled *De primatu,* was written in Latin, discussed chiefly the
Sermon on the Mount, immediately called forth the condemna-

[3] Treatises devoted to the Polish Brethren (Antitrinitarians) have more
than once touched upon their socio-political ideas. First to pay attention
to them was Alexander Brückner in the brilliant sketches comprised in the
work *Różnowiercy polscy* (*Polish Dissenters*) (Warsaw:1905). Earlier
symptoms of radicalism occupied Wacław Makowski in a sketch entitled
*Dwójbożcy* (*Ditheists*) in the collection entitled *Wrażenia i studja* (*Impressions and Studies*) (Wilno:1913), and Marek Wajsblum in the article
"Dyteiści małopolscy" ("Ditheists of Little Poland"), *Reformacja w
Polsce* (1928). Budny's views have been presented by H. Merczyng, *Szymon
Budny* (Cracow:1913); those of Gregory Paulus by Konrad Górski,
*Grzegorz Paweł z Brzezin* (Cracow:1929); those of Niemojewski by
Józefat Płokarz, "Jan Niemojewski," *Reformacja w Polsce* (1922); those
of Peter of Goniądz by Józef Jasnowski, *Przegląd historyczny* (Warsaw:
1935). The discussion on war was elucidated by Stanisław Estreicher in
the article "Pacyfizm w Polsce XVI stulecia" ("Pacifism in Poland of the
Sixteenth Century") (Poznan:1930), reprinted from *Ruch prawniczy,
ekonomiczny i socjologiczny.* The views of the Brethren in the last period
of their existence have been discussed by Ludwik Chmaj, *Marcin Ruar*
(Cracow:1921) and *Samuel Przypkowski* (Cracow:1927).

Each of the authors mentioned has contributed toward clearing up particular factors, but the problem as a whole has not thus far been the subject
of systematic investigation; hence neither the origin nor the development
of the social and political views of the Antitrinitarian camp has been
scientifically presented hitherto. There is a general account of the Polish
Brethren and of the Antitrinitarian movement in Europe in the sixteenth and seventeenth centuries in lectures delivered by S. Kot at the
Paris Collège de France in 1935, vide *Le Mouvement antitrinitaire au
XVIème et XVIIème siècle* in *Humanisme et Renaissance* (Paris:1937),
IV, 16-58 and 109-156; also published as a separate pamphlet.

tion of Paclesius, minister at Lublin, and of Krowicki, Gregory Paulus, and Schomann, caused lively discussion in the circle of the first Antitrinitarians, and in time influenced the views of their leaders.[4] Even Budny admitted that "when he first heard what Peter of Goniadz said and read what he wrote against the office of the sword,[5] he did not venture either to accept his doctrine or hastily to condemn it," but "examined it constantly, talked of it, and debated it from one side and the other with any one with whom he happened to be conversing."

The campaign against infant baptism, developing at this period, caused accessions to the camp of the Neobaptists, especially since Italians like Johannes Paulus Alciati and Valentinus Gentile, influential in the Antitrinitarian circles of Little Poland, were describing the life of the Moravian congregations.[6] In the synod at Brzeziny in 1565, at which Neobaptism was advocated, "numerous Anabaptists from Lithuania, Moravia, and other regions" took part.[7] Martin Czechowic, who had returned from Switzerland through Moravia at the end of 1561, knew their life from his personal observation and now at Wilno was very warmly seconding the Anabaptist activities of Peter of Goniądz.

In the preface to his *Office of the Sword* (*Urząd miecza*), giv-

[4] Cf. Budny, *O urzędzie miecza używającym* (lit. *On Office Employing the Sword*), ed. S. Kot (Warsaw:1932), pp. 14, 18, 19, 61, 67, 219. Since Budny is careful about the date and speaks precisely, we must date the work 1563 or at the latest 1564. Paklesius, who died of the plague in 1565, was then still alive and intended to attack it. Its full title was *De primatu Ecclesiae Christianae*, as we can learn from his letter to Palaeologus (Cf. K. Landsteiner, *Jacobus Palaeologus* [Wien:1873], p. 38-39).

[5] The expression has no proper equivalent in English. The reference is to any office having the *jus gladii*, jurisdiction over life and death. It was to holding public offices of this nature that the Antitrinitarians so generally objected.

[6] Alciati, for example, after his sudden departure from Poland, stayed with the Anabaptists at Austerlitz and wrote letters from there in 1564 and 1565 to Gregory Paulus (Sandius, *Bibliotheca Antitrinitariorum* [Freistadii:1684], p. 28). The life of Alciati has been told by M. Wajsblum in the *Polski Słownik Biograficzny* (*Polish Dictionary of Biography*) (Cracow), I, 56f.

[7] Tretius to Bullinger, Aug. 1, 1565 (Wotschke, *Briefwechsel der Schweizer mit den Polen* (Leipzig:1908), p. 251.

ing an historical sketch of the development of anti-State radicalism in Poland, Budny inserted a condensed formulation of the
new slogans, calling it "the doctrine and *theses* of some Polish
brethren." These are probably the theses of Peter of Goniądz,
and they certainly derive from an early stage of the movement:

Of nothing so much as of this do men talk, teach, and even
publish printed books, wishing to prove by Scripture that it is
not right for a Christian to hold an office enjoying the *jus gladii*,
that it is not right for a believer to be king, priest, or prince, nor
commander, governor, prefect, judge, assistant judge, lieutenant,
bailiff, mayor, captain, soldier, infantryman, etc. Moreover,
they maintain that it is not right for this pious man to have an
estate such that from it he may support a war, or to employ any
laws, Polish, Lithuanian, German, provincial, municipal, local
or other, which punish with the sword or even require the taking
of an oath. In short, that it is not right to wear or carry any
kind of weapon, even on a journey, or to defend oneself against
robbers.

This summary gives, it is true, an idea of only a part, though an
important one, of the ideology of the Anabaptists—that concerning their attitude to State authority and to war.

As a considerable majority of the Antitrinitarians of Little
Poland began to lean toward radicalism, those of Lithuania defended themselves against it, and from Wilno warned the Polish
brethren against the "Anabaptist plague" which threatened "to
overthrow the State and to ruin the Church." The synod of
Węgrów in December, 1565, tried to counter these suspicions by a
declaration that no one there had any objective in common with
the Munsterites; that, on the contrary, the congregations, "as
they have up to this time been sincerely obedient to the powers
ordained of God, so wish the more diligently and with the greatest diligence possible to observe this to the end, not in word
alone but also in deed, calling upon the Lord God and praying
him for their rulers, not only out of fear but also for conscience'

sake, as St. Paul teaches in Rom. xiii. 5." [8]  And again from the synod of Brześć in July, 1566, renewed assurance came to Wilno:

We do not here learn violence, nor those abominations of Antichrist, nor the crimes of the Munsterites, but rather the teaching of Christ, respect for the magistrate and obedience to him, not only out of fear but also for conscience' sake. We learn also to live a godly life at home with our wives, knowing that God created woman for one husband, and punished bigamists. We learn to supply from our substance means for supporting the worship of God, knowing that the brethren are free to possess property, since even the Apostle Paul collected alms from rich brethren and gave them to the Church.[9]

It may be seen from these assurances that our Neobaptists wished to allay the fears that the movement might become revolutionary, communistic, and immoral. Even the Italian doctor Blandrata, who pushed the Dissenters of Little Poland towards radicalism in doctrine, warned them from Transylvania to take heed lest by doing away with infant baptism they should become like the Anabaptists: "You know," he wrote to Gregory Paulus, "that the name of Anabaptists is odious to all, and their doctrine generally under suspicion." [10]

The Catholic preacher Herbest triumphantly published a letter, obtained secretly,[11] written from Wilno to Zacius, a Calvinistic minister at Cracow, and containing an accusation against the Neobaptist ministers:

In place of a sermon they prophesy after the manner of the Neobaptists; that is, they tell their dreams and visions, i.e. frightful blasphemies: they introduce plurality of wives, com-

---

[8] In "Najstarsze synody arjańskie," *Reformacja w Polsce,* I (1921), 231; also in the letter of the Superintendent Lutomirski to the brethren at Wilno (Lubieniecius, *Historia Reformationis,* p. 183).

[9] Lubieniecius, *op. cit.,* p. 187.

[10] Alba Julia, Nov. 30, 1565; Wotschke, *Briefwechsel,* p. 268. For Blandrata, cf. M. Wajsblum in the *Polish Dictionary of Biography,* II, 118ff.

[11] He obtained the letter in 1566 at Cracow and published it in *Wypisanie drogi,* appended to *Chrześciańska porządna odpowiedź* (1567), p. Zz 3-4.

munity of goods, contempt of the magistrate, of the courts, and of every rank . . . Serfs writing to masters or to the magistrate use the title of Brother. They turn everything to the levelling of classes and contempt for the magistrate. At the Lord's Supper master sits with peasant in one place. Simple and untaught people conduct religious services. They make decrees according to their own ideas, and venture much in opposition to the magistrate. Here in Wilno it was under discussion whether only those may be admitted to the Lord's Supper who set their serfs free . . . If they rule here longer, not only will there be manifold errors, but we must in the end also fear sedition.

This information comes in fact from George Weigel, a Protestant theologian living in Wilno, who by the end of 1565 prepared a memorial for Calvinist Lithuanian magnates, *De confusionibus et scandalis excitatis in hac Ecclesia Vilnensi.*[12]

Peter of Goniądz made his appearance at Cracow with a wooden sword at his side and argued that a Christian was not free to gird on a weapon with which he could wound.[13] Such displays caused especial irritation among the Protestant magnates, who feared lest the whole reformed movement be thereby compromised and fall under suspicion in the eyes of the King. Meantime, in May, 1566, at Lublin during the session of the Diet, it was stated in the Senate that in gardens in the suburbs Anabaptists were delivering before the crowd sermons "in which disregard of the magistrate was openly taught, for Christians may recognize only one king, crowned with a crown of thorns." [14] Then again the King was alarmed by what had happened at Sochaczew, where the serfs were said to have murdered the nobleman Obierski, having conspired against their master with the

[12] Ms. in the Vatican Library, Ottoboniana, 3076.
[13] Łasicki to Beza, Cracow, May 30, 1566, in Wotschke, *Briefwechsel,* p. 271.
[14] Krajewski to Hosius, Lublin, May 31, 1566, in Ljubovich, *Nachalo Katolicheskoj reakcji v Polshe (Beginning of the Catholic reaction in Poland)* (Warsaw:1890), p. 146.

argument that "Christ has suffered for us, and wished that we might be free." [15]

The senators urged the King to banish the Tritheists and Anabaptists, both recent arrivals and natives, without regard to their rank. Even a section of the Chamber of Deputies consented to the expulsion of preachers who, "disregarding the common law and authorities, wish to bring about confusion of all ranks in the Republic, and with their mischievous doctrine undermine the obedience of serfs to their masters." [16] The Bishops opposed this, lest by the condemnation of some sects the legal recognition of others should follow. The King, incensed against the Anabaptists, "not by reason of the wrong done to God"—which the accounts of the clergy emphasize—"but in defence of authority, lest in time they undermine it in the esteem of the people," issued on the 13th day of June an oral declaration, imposing upon the Anabaptists the penalty of banishment, or else of proscription and death. The threat of punishment hung over even the eminent gentleman Jerome Filipowski, Deputy from Cracow, who "ventured openly to defend the Anabaptists" [17] and in self-defence declared incautiously that the time would come when another King would sit in judgment and take his own under protection. This expression, referring to the King of Heaven, was interpreted to the King as seditious by Filipowski's opponents, especially by the young John Zamoyski. Only the Marshal of the Chamber of Deputies, himself an Antitrinitarian, Nicholas Sienicki, procured favor with the King for Filipowski. This intervention, together with the continued opposition of the Bishops, caused the matter to be dropped, and no formal edict was issued.

Although a crisis had been warded off, widespread public

[15] From a letter of Stanislas Szedziński to Hosius, Lublin, June 6, 1566; in Czartoryski. Ms. 1607, p. 800. Cf. Bodniak, "Sprawa wygnania arjan w r. 1566" ("The question of the banishment of the Arians in 1566"), *Reformacja w Polsce,* V (1928), 57.

[16] *Ibid.*

[17] Letter of Bishop Herburt to Hosius, May 31, 1566, in Ljubovich, *Nachalo,* p. 147.

opinion continued to be aroused by things hitherto concealed in the private discussions of circles professing the new faith, and the public kept a watchful eye on their radical slogans, creating a hostile atmosphere. A. Rotundus, bailiff of Wilno, sent word to Hosius from Wilno on September 13, 1567:

I myself have seen and read a little book printed in Polish at Grodno, containing blasphemies against Jesus Christ than which it is impossible to tell or even to think of greater. In it they deny any authority to all magistrates, extol Christian freedom, and introduce community of all property; they abolish also all distinction of classes in Church and State, so that there may be none between King and people, between rulers and subjects, between the nobility and commoners.[18]

In this time of ferment a curious debate took place at a synod of the Lithuanian Antitrinitarians at Iwie in Wilno province in January, 1568. Budny, in his *Office of the Sword,* quoted the minutes of a discussion as to "whether one may keep serfs or slaves." Two of the ministers, Jacob of Kalinówka and Paul of Wizna, captivated by the humanitarian teachings of the Anabaptists of Little Poland, criticized their brother-nobles for possessing houses and lands and employing serf labor, and some even for keeping "bond-servants," which was contrary to the equality and fraternity of believers. Defense of the existing order was undertaken by Budny, consistent with that which he had already maintained in the Nieśwież Catechism, and he won the majority of the synod to his point of view. He drew from Holy Scripture arguments for a hierarchical structure of society and even proved the lawfulness of serfdom, demanding of masters only that they should not overburden their serfs with labor and taxes. He came forward also against the demand that ministers should support themselves by their own labor and should have no right to hold estates and serfs in their possession.

His opponent, Jacob of Kalinówka, scandalized by the con-

---

[18] Łukaszewicz, *Dzieje Kościołów helweckich w Małopolsce* (Poznań: 1853), pp. 58f.

servatism of Budny and the synod, left Lithuania and went over to the Anabaptists of Little Poland, taking in his train some persons of the nobility, ministers and commoners of Wilno, and the councillor Lucas Mundius. By October of that year we meet them at the Antitrinitarian synod at Pełsznica, where Gregory Paulus as well as Czechowic and his followers in Kujawy province raised the same demands.[19]

It was therefore required of ministers that they resign ministries in which they live by the labor of others, and that they win their bread by their own hands. They also said to the brethren of the nobility: it is not right for you to eat bread by the sweat of your poor serfs, but to work yourselves. Also it is not right for you to live on such estates, which were given to your ancestors for shedding blood. Sell then such estates and distribute to the poor.

This called forth a lively discussion, and they separated without coming to a vote. But some of the nobles felt in conscience bound to obey this summons; also many of the ministers abandoned their posts, which were supported by endowments of the old type, and began to learn trades.

At this synod, during a discussion on social questions, the matter of relations with the Moravian Anabaptists came up:

There was also talk about the Moravian Communists, from whom at this time had come a certain Mundius, a citizen of Wilno, enthusiastically recommending the sect of the communists, both for their government, and for the fact that they were said to be of one mind with our people *de Deo et Christo*, and for their devoutness, whom some believed with satisfaction, but others not much; and therefore there was a dispute among the brethren. Not until Mundius promised messengers from them to the brethren did they become quiet, waiting for the messengers, that they might learn all from them.[20]

The next synod, at Bełżyce in March, 1569, was to discuss the

[19] "Najstarsze synody arjańskie" ("The earliest Arian synods"), *Reformacja w Polsce*, I (1921), 233.
[20] *Ibid.*

social question more thoroughly, for the program included matters "concerning the duties of Christian masters and concerning
Christian servants, the higher authorities, the rich brethren, the
poor brethren, the artizan members of the Church, merchants
and hucksters, the payment of duty and tolls, not bearing arms,
and hunting." But alas, the records of this synod are not extant,
so we do not know what action was taken on these matters. Certainly the discussion was conducted in a very radical spirit, for
all the extremist ministers appeared at the synod: Gregory
Paulus, Schomann, Czechowic, Siekierzyński, the two Kalinow-
skis, Peter of Goniądz, as well as their lay supporters (Filipowski,
Niemojewski, Ożarowski, Brzeziński, Siemianowski, Ronemberg).
There were also (as the fragment of the records testifies) "many
other fiery brethren from the cities, towns, and villages." There
were, however, present energetic opponents of radicalism too, like
Krowicki and Budny.

In 1569, the social ferment reached boiling point in Antitrinitarian circles. Having for ten years undermined doctrines
and traditions step by step, and not shrinking from the most
daring consequences, the Polish Antitrinitarians had attracted
all the most dissatisfied elements of the Reformed camp. There
was no idea too audacious to find among them adherents, and
warmly devoted ones, disposed to put it into practice. On the
one hand, the aspect of this ferment is unpleasant, for it mani-
fests the uncommon extravagance of minds that were often un-
trained, leading to a chaos in organization; but on the other
hand, we are attracted by the uncommon sincerity and self-
sacrifice of men who were really seeking to satisfy their consciences by actions which in their opinion conformed as closely
as possible to the precepts of the Gospel. They did not hesitate
to sacrifice their possessions, their social rank, and their good
reputation in a society which saw in them only heated, distracted
minds. Here is one reminiscence of this chaos, preserved for later
ages by Andrew Lubieniecki in his *Poloneutychia:*[21]

---

[21] Czartoryski Ms. 1370, reprinted in Chrzanowski-Kot, *Humanizm i
reformacja* (Lwów:1927), p. 421.

There were those who disapproved of all attendance at religious worship of any sort, holding that it was not right either to act or to teach anybody unless one had had a revelation from heaven and had seen a miracle, or oneself had had the power to perform them. Such were Sleszyński and Biliński, Tapiński, Albinus, John Baptista, and others not a few. . . .

There were also those who themselves adopted the manner of peasants, labored with their own hands, used to live, sleep, and eat unwashed, and pretended it was pleasing to God, and puffed up with this, debarred all others from eternal life. . . .

There were others who led worthy and pious men to refuse to hold office and to ungird their weapons, and who forbade them to go to law in cases of the greatest injury, or to take the oath in cases of slander. And many men resigned important civil offices, and the King gave them to someone else; others both gave up their estates and distributed the proceeds. And Ożarowski, a distinguished man, came to the King in council at the Diet of Lublin, publicly thanked him for his kindness, but said that he could no longer enjoy it with good conscience nor serve the King nor the Republic hereafter, and resigned to the King his right to Przybysławice in the district of Lublin, asking that the King accept it from him and give it to someone who served him. The King for a long time would not take it from him; but he still insisted, saying, "You can take a thing from me by force, Sir, but you can not give it to me by force." And thereupon Sir John Firlej, Marshal of the Crown, at once asked for it, saying that it had come from his starosty of Kazimierz and asking that the King return it to this starosty; and so the King did.

As in the case of Ożarowski, so in others; the personal sacrifices and renunciations of individual adherents of the Gospel [22]

---

[22] There is, for example, the notable document in which Jan Przypkowski, "recognizing that his serfs in the villages of Upper Przypkowice, Polanka, Mikołajowice, Tarnawa, and half of Stara Wieś in the districts of Cracow and Oświęcim, are with him creatures of one Creator; not wishing, furthermore, that these peasants and serfs of his, as also their sons and daughters in the villages aforesaid, should live henceforth in servitude and bondage according to the general law of the crown, frees these peasants and serfs and their posterity from all burdens. At the same time he gives these his peasants and their sons permission to leave his possessions and go to dwell wherever they will; and moreover he renounces forever his right to prosecute them, or at any time to demand their surrender by judicial means, or to call to account him with whom they are, or to whom one of them goes,

were without influence on the nobility in general. Society considered them eccentrics and treated the noble visionaries with increasing scorn. Jan Niemojewski, Siemianowski, and Brzeziński sold their estates in Kujawy in order to distribute the money among the poorer brethren. General opinion, however, laughed at them as eccentrics:

We saw at the Diet of Lublin in the time of Sigismund Augustus a certain important noble [Niemojewski], a most stubborn adherent of this faith [Anabaptist], in a mean gray garment, without sword, without wallet, without attendant, rebaptized just a few days before. Cardinal Hosius had long conversations with him several times, trying to turn him from this delusion, but he steadfastly insisted that the Holy Spirit taught him that the doctrine that he confessed was true and from God; indeed, that the voice of the Father had been heard from heaven: Whoso shall believe and receive baptism, shall be saved.[23]

No longer having a common language with their neighbors who ridiculed them, the Anabaptists associated mostly with one another, carrying on incessant discussions and disputes. Differences of opinion, errors, and heresies constantly developed among them. They rode without pause to councils, diets, and synods for purposes of defense and to carry on their polemics. Any sort of church organization had vanished. There was no field at hand for cooperative work. "And there were found," relates A. Lubieniecki, "those who said that everything in the world was now loathsome to them; and they deliberated where they might dwell in a community by themselves, practicing their devotions, waiting for death in peace." Thus the decision was made to withdraw from the rest of society and form their own ideal community; and so Raków arose. In the course of the year 1569, on sandy lands belonging to Sienieński, Castellan of Zarnów, in the district

---

or with whom they remain. Instead, he agrees that both they and their sons shall forever enjoy the same freedom." Act recorded in the castle at Cracow, August 2, 1572. Cf. Tadeusz Grabowski, *Literatura arjańska w Polsce* (Cracow:1908), p. 68.

[23] S. Rescius, *De Atheismis et Phalarismis evangelicorum* (Neapolis:1596), p. 255.

of Sandomierz near Szydłów, a company of Anabaptists gathered and there, near the forests, founded a colony for life in common, in the hope that it would be "a sort of New Jerusalem or Zion." [24] Some nobles presented themselves there, especially Kujawians who had sold their estates, many ministers, and a great many plebeians, commoners, and artisans, as well as many foreigners. They came both from Little Poland and from Great Poland as well as from Lithuania and Volhynia. They built themselves cottages and small houses of wood, and some tilled with their own hands as much land as they needed for their support, while others occupied themselves with their trades; but over all still loomed the theological disputes.

The first three years of the existence of Raków seemed like a single stormy synod. As Lubieniecki commented, "there was peace neither by day nor by night, but there were various discussions with various persons, until some, convinced by their reasons, were converted, while others went away remaining as they were." The sharpest disputes were concerned with "taking no thought for the body, with resigning offices and posts of any sort, even those of ministers, as contrary to Christian perfection and equality and, finally, with establishing community of goods." [25]

It was three years before this chaos could be overcome by Simon Ronemberg, formerly an apothecary in Cracow in the building "at the sign of the lizards." For many years he had taken a lively interest in all the doctrinal questions and affairs of the "Minor Church," as the Antitrinitarians were called, and had tried to become acquainted at first hand with all the new ideas. He himself succumbed to the chaos, until at length he reached the conviction that even the most extreme religious confession and the most radical section of society must rest upon some sort of order and organization. Personal acquaintance with

[24] W. Węgierski, *Kronika Zboru ewangelickiego w Krakowie* (Breslau: 1817), p. 10.
[25] Cf. Stanislaus Lubieniecius, *Historia Reformationis Polonicae,* p. 240.

the Anabaptist congregations of Moravia contributed to his clearing up the chaos at Raków.

An eyewitness, the nobleman Sigismund Gierałt, related at a dinner of a Catholic society in Cracow[26] the story of the rapid spread of the Anabaptist sect in the region of Podkarpacie, south of Cracow, especially in the district of Szczyrzyce: the deputy manager of the salt mines of Wieliczka (it was Christopher Morsztyn, who several years later would give his daughter in marriage to Fausto Sozzino) was baptized again, together with numerous inhabitants of Cracow and Wieliczka and their wives. Included were Gierałt's first cousins Adam and Georges, a squire called Bylina who had been recently dipped into the river of Dunajec by Lucławice, as well as a number of common people with their wives, attracted by the gift of new shirts and the exemption from the obligations of serfdom. These were the beginnings of the later famous Lucławice community.

[26] A letter from Cracow to the historian Martin Kromer, dated December 2, 1576; Ms. Br. 17, in Lynköping, Sweden, p. 113.

# 4 *Polish Critics of the Moravian Communists*

Excursions to Moravia. Treatise against the Communists. Critique of the communistic system. Walpot's letter. Moravian Anabaptists and Polish Antitrinitarians.

During the synod at Pełsznica in 1568, Councillor Lucas Mundius of Wilno gave an account of visits and conversations he had had with the Moravians and reported that envoys of theirs were coming to Poland. The Moravian Anabaptists were in fact paying attention to the developments which had taken place in Poland in recent years. At just this time the Moravian congregations were at the period of their most prosperous development, under the direction of Peter Walpot (a cutler by trade), and were carrying on increasing propaganda. They even extended their propaganda beyond German lands and had connections with Italy.

Their *Geschicht-Buch*[1] contains the following record for the year 1569:

After negotiations had been broken off, a zeal for the truth arose in Poland, though with little understanding and quite without result. They already had light in their lamps, but the oil was lacking of which the Lord speaks in the Gospel, and therefore it did not grow into a clear flame, but was bound to be extinguished. They were beginning to abandon the unscriptural wicked bap-

[1] Pp. 338-52.

tism of children, and were rejecting it utterly as an un-Christian doctrine, writing sharply against it and teaching that only those, who believe in the word of God may be baptized. They also wrote powerfully against such a Trinity as the Pope teaches and on the difference between a rich and a poor Christian. This was the reason why the community at their request and desire sent four brethren to Poland, namely brother Ludwig Dörker, a chosen minister of the gospel, with three companions, who were very kindly received there, and caused them also to send four young men to inspect our community.

From the Polish Brethren's records we learn that they conferred with the Moravian envoys, among whom a certain Kaspar attracted attention, and that in September discussions took place at Cracow, after which the guests visited Raków. They in turn sent to Moravia some educated young men who were in future to be ministers, that they might learn trades there, "for the view then prevailed that ministers must learn some trade." [2]

A more numerous delegation of older men followed them to Moravia. "At that time," relates George Schomann in his testament,[3] under the year 1569, "I went with Master Filipowski, Master Simon the apothecary, and many others to Moravia, to confer with the Moravian Brethren about doctrine and discipline." It is not clear whether the following Anabaptist record refers to the same expedition: "On January 25, 1570, there came to Neumühl,[4] where the Elders were then gathered, a numerous company from Poland and Lithuania, namely a Polish gentleman called Jankowski [we know of no such person, unless this should be Filipowski] with three preachers and the apothecary Simon from Cracow, to investigate our community and religion. They also brought a letter from their community to ours, in which they greatly praised our community for its system and organization, for which reason they wished to unite with us."

[2] Dobrowolski, "Nieznana Kronika arjańska," *Reformacja w Polsce,* IV (1926), 168. The manuscript of the chronicle is preserved in Lambeth Palace, London.

[3] Sandius, *Bibliotheca Antitrinitariorum,* p. 195.

[4] On the border of Austria, where the elders then dwelt.

The discussions at Cracow, and yet more the sojourn in Moravia, showed that there were nevertheless grave differences between the Anabaptists and the Racovians. Thus both sides separated disillusioned, and the Polish delegation took away its young men, who had spent the whole winter in Moravia. "Their great worldly wisdom and wit," reads the ironic comment in the *Geschicht-Buch* of the Anabaptists, "in consequence of which the Lord's work seemed to them crude and naïve, could not be suited to the service of the poor and crucified Christ." Later attempts to maintain relations did not improve them. In May, 1570, two Racovians went to Moravia, John Baptista (certainly Święcicki from Lithuania) and John the Italian. The Antitrinitarian congregation at Olkusz, where the radical Daniel Bieliński was minister, added to them its envoy, a man named Järisch Müller, and in a letter[5] of recommendation asked that they be shown the "holy institution of the community . . . They stayed here some time, observing with rather cold hearts; after which they departed. They did not treat the matter very seriously, hence from this also there was no result."

After their departure Peter Walpot sent a letter[6] to the Polish Antitrinitarians, and especially to "certain gentlemen who were here among us," mentioning by name only persons unknown to us: Bartholomew, John the Italian, Lucas Delphinus, Adam Mendicus, Simon Ciechanowski (Tschechonofius), and Jacob Livius. He argued:

Because I wish you well, I cannot conceal from you that in place of the hope that we entertained of you, you have caused us much pain by your mission. They did not come to us to counsel with us and learn from us the organization of the Lord's congregation, but to instruct us and to try to bring us over to their side, which we cannot admit from men who have not yet denied themselves a pagan, worldly life. They reproached us with being too much concerned with or with being afraid (as we are not) of losing

---

[5] Letter from Olkusz, May 25, 1570, inserted in the *Geschicht-Buch,* pp. 340f.

[6] Long letter, *ibid.,* pp. 341-43.

our authority or power if we should follow you. Hence we infer that they thought of themselves perhaps as better fitted for this; while we, as we do not know Latin and many languages, were too mean and contemptible for them at the bottom of their hearts (which matters little to us) . . . Even if we resigned our authority, they should not think that the community would accept them and follow them for their knowledge of many languages or their reputed wisdom, in which in their opinion they far surpass us. They would have first to pass tests and gain experience, as we did, through pain, bonds, imprisonment, and hard work . . . To you, to whom salvation is perhaps of more concern, I send an admonition and request: If there are among you any who desire to save their souls and to conform their lives to this end, let them actively change their manner of life and not be content with knowing how they ought to live.

Walpot concluded his admonition with a warning of the punishments of the Last Judgment and unhappiness in the present life. It may be inferred that the Polish Brethren, when living among the Moravian communities, strove to induce them to change their teaching, chiefly, one may be sure, in the sphere of doctrine, and that it was this which called forth this sharp protest from Walpot.

The exchange of views did not close there, as we shall see. Schomann, mentioning in his testament (after 1590) a visit to the Anabaptists, wrote, "We found a very good discipline of God's people, but all the sects fiercely defended the Triune God." [7] Lubieniecki cites the same doctrine as having been the cause of the break in relations, remarking, moreover, that the Anabaptists showed themselves extremely hostile to those holding other beliefs: "even from them, so despised and condemned throughout all the world, we had to suffer enmity for the name of Jesus." [8]

Meantime, in the light of contemporary sources, the causes of both parties' discontent and of the breaking of their agreements appear rather differently and have less to do with dogmas than

[7] Sandius, p. 197.
[8] *Historia Reformationis*, p. 227.

with the social question. The view of the Moravians is recorded in their *Geschicht-Buch* and is clearly stated by Peter Walpot in his memorial-letter. The view of the Racovians is set forth in a report written on the basis of the discussion at Cracow and the report of the envoys and bearing the eloquent title: *A Treatise not opposed to the Apostolic community such as was once in Jerusalem, which the Scripture of the New Testament mentions and recommends with praise to the disciples of Jesus, and such as disciples of Jesus are supposed to have among themselves, but against such as one of those sects wished to recommend, which have multiplied greatly in the world from the teaching of Jesus after his ascension into heaven—they are called communists in Moravia—and outside of which they say there is no salvation.*[9]

This treatise is a document of first-rate importance, for it is the oldest critique in Poland of the communistic system. Among European anti-communistic polemics (for example Vives' *De communione bonorum*) it is distinguished by the fact that it issued from a camp radical in social respects, from circles for which the problem was of uncommonly vital importance and which were themselves contemplating the possibility of adopting some such system, being restrained not so much by an attachment to private property as by the unfavorable impressions they had received from efforts to put communism into practice. The criticism of the Polish Brethren as well as the move by the Moravians were the results not of economic but of purely religious premises, with their sources in the indications of

---

[9] The contemporary Ms, which belonged to Andrew Dudith, was preserved in the University Library at Leyden, Voss. 331, and published in *Rocznik Towarzystwa Przyjaciół Nauk w Poznaniu*, xv (1887), under the title *Traktat przeciwko "komunistom" morawskim z roku około 1569*, by Jan Karłowicz, erroneously conjecturing that the communists were a Moravian branch of the Bohemian Brethren, and that the Cracovian interlocutor was Jan Rokita. Cf. S. Kot, "Polish Brethren and the Problem of Communism in the XVIth Century Poland," in *Transactions of the Unitarian Historical Society in London,* XII (1956). The following volume of the *Transactions* will include an English translation of *A Treatise.*

the Gospel and references to the primitive Christian community. From these the Anabaptists drew the incentive to establish their "brotherly community"; from these the Racovians found the basis for their criticism of the Moravians. It may be presumed that if the constitution of the Moravian communities had seemed to them agreeable to Holy Scripture, then at their stage of social and religious evolution they would have approved it and tried to put it into practise, at least at Raków.

The treatise begins with a general description of the social organization of the Anabaptists; but this description is already interspersed with critical reservations, relating first to the hierarchical supremacy of the "elders":

And these order, rule, and dispose in everything, and without their will no one does anything, no one speaks in society or goes out or labors; these provide all with clothing; these issue provisions for all to one kitchen at their own will and discretion alone. Whatever these elders order, when they direct or send anyone who dwells among them, be he poorer or richer, to service or to common labor, he does it with great humility and obedience; and they keep no idler, but each performs the labor assigned to him, if not at the trade (which they learn among themselves) to which they direct him (not as if he chose it for himself), then laboring either in the mill or on the land or in the vineyard; then he either threshes or chops wood if he is especially strong (just as they employed our youth also, good in studies and languages, at the flail when they came to them, or at the axe), or they employ them in other services. These elders receive and have under control all the work of these trades, and as landlords they sell whatever remains above their needs.

In the second place, the Anabaptist tendency to gather huge sums of money into a common fund and to use it as capital does not meet with the approval of the Polish Brethren:

Whoever wishes to live in this their community must then contribute landed property or ready money, much or little . . . If he does not like this community of theirs after joining it, it is not too easily permitted to him to withdraw; but if he does withdraw, then they refund to him nothing of what he contributed. In this community, apart from that which is contributed, whether some hundreds or some thousands, there is no small likelihood that there must be great wealth among them, since all work and they do not allow any one to be idle, and since they themselves live only from what they produce, giving nothing to anyone outside their community, either poor or rich . . . And yet because each worker, not wearing fine clothing or squandering, earns more than what he eats and drinks, it is certain that an abundance must remain in the purse or in the treasury . . . In such a community, by laying by from labor and the produce of vineyards and from cattle, and from cash contributed, they will have acquired already no small treasure, of which it is said that no small part is even loaned to the Emperor.

Thirdly, the partners in the community are exploited, burdened with work, and treated as slaves:

As for the food that they give the common people, apart from their own rich and abundant cookery, as we learn from those God-fearing men whom we sent to them, they keep the common people unnecessarily poorly, feeding them only a soup made of water without butter or other fat, putting into it a pig's or a hen's leg. They do not give them beer but only water to drink, while they themselves stuff their bellies full of fish and meat and fill them with wine. And they allow the people scant rest from their labor, and they do not permit them to read the Scriptures, since they have this office from God in themselves. They have so bound the consciences of the people by labor that with them he who works most, as with the Turks he who kills the most infidels, enjoys the most perfect rule. And yet these poor people, so burdened, whom they keep in ignorance, do this with such humility and submission as even to sacrifice their lives while working. Thus they have fenced off pens with partitions for their swine and sheep and other cattle, doing everything in their husbandry with great care; but where they themselves lie with their wives, they are merely screened or curtained off with a sheet. As soon as mothers wean their children, they entrust them to other women, whose strength almost fails because of their miserable food and such hunger that the first wind would blow away another, even a strong person.

Fourthly, the administration is characterized by a want of genuine piety and sincerity, and by hypocrisy:

In their private homes, like the Grand Turk, they allow no one to enter their own rooms except those who have already risen to a certain level, as the Franciscans, Bernardines, and other monks in the Roman sect do. For our brethren, who lived among them for several days, having business with them, they everywhere had escorts, as if for a Tartar ambassador. Plenty of doors and windows were in every corner, out of suspicion, lest some hypocritical deeds of theirs might come to light.

As a whole, the Moravian community appeared to the Poles as "the contrivance of a great enterprise planned for the making of money." They also called them, by a malicious pun, "a sect of communists, or rather of economists."

In the Polish view, this sect was on the high road toward imitation of the institutions of Rome, for it was based upon a principle similar to that which the cloisters formerly had. Their Bishop, however, wished to be a kind of Pope, and like the Pope he offered the community Holy Scripture more seldom than

their own Peter (Riedemann), who established for them this rule, the *Rechenschaft,* and who, although with good intention, yet established a bad foundation, even though taking it from the word of God . . . Thus in the Roman sect the Franciscans and Bernardines and others followed each their own *Rechenschaft* . . . and yet what they came to, we know. And as for them, if one should make a thorough examination and review according to their *Rechenschaft,* not to say according to the Gospel of Jesus Christ, there would be found fullness of deceit and hypocrisy, if one uncovered it. There, beside one in sackcloth, there are a thousand or several hundreds who have a rich table, while another man has vermin and wretchedness and water in his bowl, with hardly an oil-cake, instead of some stew with bread.

The community of the Moravians, in the opinion of their Polish critic, entirely failed to adhere to the principles of the primitive apostolic community. Their leaders commanded the faithful to deprive themselves of property, but they seized it themselves. They forbade others to concern themselves with worldly goods, but they devoted themselves to just that. The money offered to them the Apostles "did not put into the treasury, nor loan to emperors, nor did they themselves live from it more sumptuously, and they did not starve the multitude, but distributed at once to the poor as much as each one needed together with his children or household." The Apostles did not compel believers to gather in "obscure dwellings and secret meeting-places," but charged each to live in his place as a Christian and to carry on a struggle with the world in order to practice in life the teachings of Christ. Believers might have their own houses and property in order to be ready to share them with the poor if there should be need, or to leave their possessions and lay down their lives for the brethren and for the teaching of Jesus. Evil lay not in having possessions, but in failure to practice actively love of one's neighbor; and the Moravians gave nothing to a stranger, however poor, and exploited their own people. "The practice of loving one's neighbor does not consist in shutting up everything in a corner and in giving one's goods to the disposal of another, of whom how can it be known that he will have as good a conscience as God has given me?" The community of Anabaptists was a "wise invention" of leaders who in this way putting fear into men's consciences, exacted their property and labor. "For if the Lord God has taken measures herein to give to one little or nothing and to another much, it is certain that in both cases He does this for His own glory. Let the more wealthy only bear in mind how to dispose of this, and in their abundance of bread let them be mindful of the poor who have nothing; and in their pride in their possessions let them take care not to drift into forgetfulness of God and disregard of the poor."

Thus the treatise deprived the Moravian institutions of their religious foundation, reducing them to a "contrivance" and the "hypocrisy" of those "economists or good managers" who practiced "tyranny and plunder of others' goods and labor. . . .

With this yoke they strive to burden and ensnare men in order to be able to have the more churls; and it was plain to see that they shrank from our brethren when the latter wished to show them by the word of God that such torturing and bad treatment of men is Egyptian bondage rather than Christianity."

And of one thing more the Polish Brethren complained. The Anabaptists confessed the dogma of the Holy Trinity. The envoys from Cracow wished to confer with them about this in the presence of the community, but the elders, "sending the people back to work, would not speak with our brethren."

But those who were sent here to us [i.e. to Cracow] and here recognised our knowledge of God and the other *religionis fundamenta Christianae*, there [i.e. in Moravia] denied it, in which they showed their hypocrisy, in that they were not seeking the glory of God among us but, as if having hit upon dunces, hoping to get silver or gold from us for their enterprise, they laid this trap for us also, in which God did not prosper them and will certainly scatter them there, if acknowledging God and Christ they do not reform.

The suspicion here expressed was doubtless unfair. The Anabaptists could not agree with the Antitrinitarians in doctrine, for then they would have violated the whole tradition established by their founders, theologians by training. At this period, avoiding theology and limiting themselves to the concise principles laid down in the *Rechenschaft* and writings like it, they had no trained theologians and were even unwilling to admit people who knew Latin, but in their simplicity obstinately held to their inherited doctrine; and it was perhaps only through some misunderstanding that it seemed to the Racovians that the Moravian delegates inclined to antitrinitarianism.

The above tract remained anonymous. Its author (most probably Stanislas Budzyński) wrote it for private use, not for purposes of polemics or for publication. Thus the reproaches that he cast upon the Anabaptists were certainly formulated in agreement with the opinion of those who were accurately acquainted with the spirit and institutions of the Moravians.

Confirmation of his severe judgments is to be found in the entry of an unknown Arian chronicler[10] who, speaking of the mutual visits of Poles and Moravians, added significantly, *"Rechenschaft, liber communistarum,* hypocrisy."

The tract about the communists was written after the return of the Polish youths from Moravia, at latest in 1570. It certainly had some influence on the counsels of the Polish Brethren, which resulted in their withdrawal from plans to unite with the Moravians and to take their institutions as a model. The fact of this withdrawal appears from a letter that Simon Ronemberg sent the Moravians on November 1, 1570, though we know its contents only from Walpot's reply. The leader of the communists did not wish to accept this rupture without the expression on his part of critical observations about the Antitrinitarians, and he composed a lengthy document for Ronemberg, a kind of official reply to the Polish Antitrinitarians:[11]

While in one instance [Walpot maliciously observes] you praise us and declare that you desire to learn, ask for admonition and promise to give up all that hinders you on the way to salvation, immediately aftewards you boast of yourselves as God's children, whom God has also enlightened a little, and whom He directs as those possessing the spirit of God. Finally, your work has a kind of meaningless sound so that I wonder at it, and I see in it only empty-sounding words, back of which there is nothing but sounding brass. It is disagreeable to me to have you shower me with praises, and I value them no more than Christ prized praises from the Pharisees. . . . If then I with Christ am to speak to you, who even now call me a noble instrument of the living God . . . then in proof that you have not a covetous heart and one that loves gold, as you boast, as well as that you are aiming at perfection and wish to be saved and lay up treasure in heaven, sell all, forsake and renounce your possessions and temporal riches and set your hearts free from them, for man can not seek both at once. One chokes out the other. But I fear that you will soon be weary of me. . . . You call me the builder of Noah's ark; then if you are not hypocrites,

[10] Dobrowolski, p. 166.
[11] *Geschicht-Buch,* pp. 343-52.

tempters, or lovers of self and disobedient to the truth, why do you not enter this ark, outside of which there is no salvation? . . . Dear Simon, look at yourself, learn to know yourself better. By your own witness you have not yet arrived at the first station of God's will, namely, at real surrender to Him and union with His people.

Here Walpot called on the Poles to join in one common community on the apostolic model:

I do not write this to you, dear Simon, in order that you or any of you may rely on me or on us as on men. If you do not recognize the truth and the apostolic foundation on which one must build, and are unable to believe in our word as in the word of God (which in truth it is), then let it all go, and live in your own place and in your own station. I am writing to you at your own request, for my own peace of mind and for the honor of God, to remind and admonish you, and not in order that you should, by reason of my words, though in truth the words are not mine, turn to the Lord and submit to Him in His and our community. This depends on the will of each one, and the cause is lost if the word of God and the witness of one's own conscience do not drive one to it. No one here is forced into this community, as you imagine; and if we knew of any man of our number that he merely feigned sincerity but fostered in his heart something else, there would be no place for him with us.

Walpot recognized the discreet reproach in the Polish letter, that the Anabaptists saw salvation only with themselves and condemned all who lived otherwise:

I believe sincerely [he replies] that you do not wish to condemn anyone, and that you cannot save anyone, which only God can do. That no man can condemn another is a normal thing, which every one knows; but under cover of this all the false, perverse, and hypocritical hide. . . . We too do not condemn anyone (although as far as possible we should wish to save every one), for that no man can do; but each man is condemned by his own evil deeds. Also all followers of Christ and the community of believers condemn this world by coming out and separating themselves from it, declaring that whoever is not converted cannot partake of salvation. . . . As for you, the fact that you neither proclaim condemnation of the world to the wicked sinners whom you have in your midst, nor lead them to reform, contributes to your peace of mind and serves the flesh. Your little spark glows here like an expiring coal. You have no occasion to worry about banishment. You can expect an enduring place in the world and among your own.

From this Walpot proceeded to a sharper attack:

Hitherto you have not achieved a separation and withdrawal from the world of unbelievers. Where is your community which you may not leave? It lies fallow, unorganized, and you dwell in your beautiful homes to your own comfort, not that of your neighbors and brethren. . . . Where with you is there love of neighbor as of self, even though you declare that all that you have, you have for the benefit and profit of your neighbors? Here I should have to ask your servants, neighbors, and brethren how much you have for their use; and then I should like to try and ascertain whether your justice in this respect surpasses that of the unbelievers and the rich who also gave alms generously. Is love the result of your faith, who, as you assert, do not seek benefit for yourselves, but for your neighbors?

It is true, as you write, that for you thus far all has gone easily and pleasantly. Listen; I wish to tell you something else, really sad. In this country a certain lord,[12] under whose authority more of our brethren and sisters have dwelt than under any other lord, has banished us from his lands. There are a thousand of them, and from three to four hundred children, some of whose parents have withdrawn from this community life: some in prison and distress outside the country have endured unto death for the truth; others are restrained by force under the same enemy, for they lie in chains for the Gospel's sake. If God does not send down special help to us, it may—and that not for the first time—come to this, that we shall go out under the open sky; it will be our lot to lie in the fields or forest, in hunger and neglect. If you had been with us then, with a child or even two, and but once in the course of three days had had a little piece of bread, things would have looked different and would have

[12] Jan Zerotin of Lundenburg. These must have been only threats, for the Anabaptists dwelt on his estates after this and were only subject to annoying taxes.

required much greater patience. Only then would what is in your hearts have come to light and been manifest.

And here is an allusion to the misunderstanding that occurred at the time of the visit of the Polish Brethren:

You know that, when you were with us, it was not your furs, as you got it into your heads, which took away our hope that you might be members of the Christian community. Even with these you could have remained brethren, and they would not have harmed you at all. Nor yet was it your eating and drinking that scandalized us; we willingly granted you these things and did not grudge them; we should only have preferred not to give to you when you used them beyond measure and need. But the trouble was that you opposed the community and persisted in your opinion without any effect or correction, as you do even to this day. And as for the community at once governing itself in your way and learning from you, you are after all not yet confirmed in God and yourselves need to be instructed in the first principles of the words of God. Knowing also therefore that you pretend to be our brethren, although in truth you are not, we have a reason, and that from God, for disowning and shunning you, as Paul commanded . . . from such we cannot even accept greetings, so long as we see no true repentance or understanding. This, dear Simon, I could not forbear to say, in reply to your letter. . . . From my heart I wish for you as for myself eternal salvation; but for this you must direct your ways and counsels quite otherwise, that you may be born again.

After this letter by Walpot the name of the Polish Brethren disappears from the *Geschicht-Buch* of the communists. We have quoted from it the more characteristic passages, especially to show that the question of the Trinity was not the cause of their withdrawal from one another. The essential cause of the disagreement was the matter of social organization and, in particular, the communistic community. The Poles were not willing to give up private ownership of homes and property, as well as a life "in the midst of the world and unbelievers," that is, in the sphere of society. While allowing this as one of the possibilities for those who so wished, they were unwilling to recognize it as a categorical command, on which salvation should be made dependent. From Walpot's letter we feel that Ronemberg was carefully raising just this difference when he reproached the communists for their condemnation of others and at the same time defended his own people's conception of social life as consistent with the indications of the Gospel.

The social structure, as also the political situation, of these two movements was so different that agreement on a common program was a downright impossibility. The Anabaptists were a collection of simple people, artisans and laborers, in large measure refugees from the Tyrolese mining districts. Accustomed to a life of labor, unfitted for other occupations, used to obedience and even to submissiveness, to low wages and poor food, to association with others as poorly off as themselves, they found in the community satisfaction for their elementary needs, ennobled by a feeling that they were a chosen people living according to the Gospel, true children of God, for whom a heavenly reward was waiting after death. There were among them no highly educated persons animated with an ambition to seek new truths and inclined to criticism, who might have allowed themselves to be carried away by confidence in their own powers of reason.

The social composition of the Polish Antitrinitarians was very mixed. The nobility preponderated and, although most charitable and generous, it had nevertheless been brought up with a sense of freedom and of belonging to a ruling class, not to an oppressed one. The numerous ministers, although in the majority of cases of plebeian origin, were by education (as priests or clergymen) and social position (recognized by the gentry as leaders, and respected for their learning) merged with the nobles of the congregation.[13] If they enjoined on themselves self-support by the

---

[13] To be sure, Kasper Wilkowski, in his *Przyczyny nawrócenia od sekty nowokrzczeńców* (*Reasons for my conversion from the sect of the Anabaptists*) (Wilno:1583), i, 148, gives a somewhat different account of the mutual relations of the gentry and the ministers among the Antitrinitarians. "Besides this, they are not free from some private quarrels between

work of their own hands and the rejection of the endowments of the churches, they did this voluntarily, out of idealistic motives, as a result of reflecting on the commandments of Christ, and not under the influence of the social tendencies of any group. They did not even have a democratic tradition such as that in which ministers of the Bohemian Brethren, accustomed to poverty and adopting manual labor as an occupation useful in preventing idleness, were trained. Moreover, there were in this camp a good many plebeians—besides a few individuals of the wealthy bourgeoisie—who were chiefly artisans. These did not, however, give tone to the whole, being satisfied with the fact that both the brethren who belonged to the gentry and the ministers treated them as brethren and respected the work of their calling.

They all met together, not under the influence of discontent with their social condition, not as united by common suffering, not inclined to revolt by their memories of oppression and rebellion, not to reform or change the conditions of their existence, but on the command of conscience for a life and activity according to the Gospel. But on how to put the gospel into practice —on this they held different opinions, since they had among

---

the two classes, on the one hand the ministers and the poor, on the other the gentry. The ministers persist in thinking, and say aloud, that so long as there are gentry in the congregation, it cannot be well nor can there be discipline. For this reason they have stripped many of them of their property and noble rank and made them simple peasants, whereupon many of them now observing it complain, or their wives and children weep. On the other hand the gentry say: So long as these students govern in the congregation, it cannot be well; and they would like to see plain and straightforward men of their own number as ministers, saying that there were such in the Apostolic Church: they were not chosen from students of the schools; men from their own number were chosen for this. In this secret quarreling and secret grumbling or murmuring against one another there can by no means be any good and peaceful conscience."

Wilkowski's information is exaggerated. He has here collected some secret murmurings of persons certainly of second rank, and himself acknowledges that these quarrels were only private and never expressed in public. The Kujawian gentry who sold their estates did not do so in consequence of the insidious intrigues of Czechowic. Niemojewski himself, who is pitied on this account, lived in friendship with Czechowic to the end. For Czechowic, cf. article by S. Kot in the *Polish Dictionary of Biography*, IV, 307ff.

them a preponderance of scholars, who knew theology and languages and reeled off endless discussions, debating and commenting on the Holy Scriptures, which showed them ever new ways according to their interpretation. There could be developed here neither the kind of theocracy represented by the elders among the Moravians, nor a blind and trustful religious obedience similar to that of such simple people.

Apart from these important social differences, a great rôle was played by the difference in their political situation. The Moravian communists were fugitives from distant regions of the Empire, Germans holding together in the midst of a Czech population. Constantly threatened by the sovereign power of the Emperor, they led an uncertain existence by favor of their magnate protectors, who were not close to them in confession but kept them as good and conscientious workmen, out of economic considerations and also to spite the Emperor, to emphasize the inviolability of their privileges. Nothing linked the communists to the community which gave them shelter. They lived not in the midst of it, but outside it; they avoided all contact with it, for it was not of the faithful; they harbored no plans or hopes for propaganda with regard to it. In a political system hostile to them, they felt themselves outcasts; it had brought them only persecution and martyrdom, so that having fled from it, they formed their own completely exclusive community. Their own peculiar system and very strict discipline guaranteed the group compactness and gave a certain sense of independence.

In Poland everything was different. Antitrinitarians were not turned out of society by force. They were not cut off from others by persecution; rather they separated themselves, feeling that they were better and more noble. No one deprived them of their property or personal freedom because of their faith. These they had themselves to resign voluntarily. To have gathered in close communities would not have assured them greater religious freedom nor better material conditions; instead, it would have undermined the foundation of their economic existence at the time and would have rendered impossible any influence of their ideals upon the rest of society, where here and there individuals appeared who were disposed to listen to their teaching. The advantage accruing from the participation of individual brethren in the councils of the Diet of the Republic was obvious. More than once they found protection from accusations made by the clergy and even the Calvinists thanks to the favorable reception given by King Sigismund Augustus to intervention made on their behalf by Nicholas Sienicki, their coreligionist and the popular leader of the gentry. The presence of Antitrinitarians among the deputies made the Diets disinclined to support any resolutions harmful to the brethren.

When, after the death of Sigismund Augustus, the Diet assembled in January, 1573, to fix basic principles for the election of the new King, it decided that among its most urgent tasks was the provision of a guarantee of religious freedom for the citizen. The Protestants feared that a new Catholic King might persecute them. The Catholics wished for the election of the French candidate, Henri de Valois, who had been involved in the Saint Bartholomew's Night massacre, and they therefore felt the need of setting the Protestants' fears at rest. They agreed to guarantee them religious peace. They wished, however, to exclude the Antitrinitarians from this measure, branding them as blasphemers and disturbers of public order. In this they were unsuccessful.

The so-called "Warsaw Confederation," passed by the Diet, embraced all religious confessions without distinction and guaranteed religious freedom to all. In this respect it was unique in the Europe of that time. It was given added force by the circumstance that it was not imposed by a monarch or extorted through war, but freely agreed upon by the representatives of the community, and with such deep understanding that the deputies and senators who signed it bound themselves to defend each other if any man among them were to be persecuted because of his religion—even if the authorities were to do it on some legal pretext. Deputies who were Polish Brethren also contributed to the passing of this act. King Henry, elected a few months later, was obliged to take an oath, against his will, to safeguard freedom of religion. His successor, King Stephen Batory, took a similar oath with good will.

Thus concern for the safeguarding of freedom of conscience also worked against any tendency of the Polish Brethren to cut themselves off from participation in public life, since it was evidently advantageous both for propaganda and for the lawful defense of their own confessional movement. In short, everything combined to prevent the Polish Antitrinitarians from completely cutting themselves off from society; they did not separate themselves into communities based on a system at variance with the Constitution, which would have been unnecessary and unsuitable for them, and they thus did not proceed to the extreme limits of sectarianism.

Hence the Polish Antitrinitarians, even though accepting the formal mark of Anabaptism (the baptism of adults by immersion), could neither unite with the Moravian Anabaptists nor copy the organization of their community, since they could not introduce among themselves a society of the Moravian type, founded on community of labor, property, and living, that is, on communism as understood at the period of the Reformation.

Instead, under the influence of the Anabaptists, within their own circle they observed the custom of calling one another brethren, a custom that the Anabaptists adopted from the traditions of the radical mediaeval sects. In early years this designation was applied territorially, and hence they spoke of Polish brethren or Lithuanian brethren. In time the name Polish Brethren came to mean all those, regardless of descent or nationality, who accepted the doctrinal and social position of the Minor Church, united in Poland, Lithuania, and Prussia.

# 5  *Racovian Pacifism*

The chaos at Raków. Palaeologus' *de bello sententia*. Gregory Paulus' reply. Krowicki's letter. Palaeologus' controversial work. Which is nearer to the spirit of the Gospel?

During the year 1570, accounts of Raków which aroused horror spread abroad. The Polish Calvinists reported them to the Zürich theologians as examples of insanity. "The majority of the Ebionites and Anabaptists," Trecy (Tretius) wrote to Simler,[1] "having sold off considerable estates, have chosen a certain forest for their residence and are there building a town. Meanwhile the more wealthy of them are impoverished, by reason of the community of goods that were formerly held privately. On the other hand, poor fellows like Gregory Paulus with his fellow-ministers are enriched. Many of them have reached such a pitch of madness that they deny not only the immortality of the soul, but even that there is in man any distinct soul whatsoever."

"They are founding a town in the Palatinate of Cracow," writes Łasicki to Wolf,[2] "in which all those of this sort are settling in order that they may perish there together. The very scum are joining this sect, a few of the gentry, none of the magnates so far as I know. This is the manner of contracting marriage among them. A man goes to a woman and asks

[1] From Cracow, Feb. 21, 1570; Wotschke, *Briefwechsel*, p. 319.
[2] From Heidelberg; D. Gerdes, *Scrinium Antiquarium* (Groningen-Bremen: 1760), vi, 651.

whether she will be his wife. If she says yes, he takes her home to become his wife. Some of them have visited the Anabaptists in Moravia and have formed a religious union with them."

But even Antitrinitarians themselves held an unfavorable opinion of the state of things at this time. The greatest chaos was caused when Gregory Paulus with two fanatics, Jacob Kalinowski and Albinus, called on the ministers to abandon their callings, out of a belief that the Holy Spirit would speak through simple men. "You remember," wrote the apostate Kasper Wilkowski,[3] recalling these times, "when you debased yourselves and gave up your ministries, expecting that the Lord God would inspire more worthy men, and you gave place to shoemakers and tailors, highly praising their teaching and marveling at it, and saying that you learned more in one hour while listening to them than in all the ages from books. You can hardly deny this. But being unable to stand it, you had to turn again to books and order the cobblers and millers to keep silence. For you observed to what these dear, strange prophets were leading, and what a confusion they made, of which you are ashamed to this day."

Simon Ronemberg himself (whom Lubieniecki extols as a new Ezra because, thanks to his spirit of grace and his eloquence, he rebuilt a congregation already completely ruined,[4] reintroducing the office of minister), in a letter to Budny, complains of this "spirit of dizziness" and acknowledges that "there was confusion enough at Raków and among us all." From Transylvania Blandrata[5] warned them against confining themselves in a social sect and called on them to "abandon superstition, to live among men and draw them to truth and piety by the example of their lives."

Soon came disillusionment, when the Racovians themselves, listening to sermons "by a gentleman from his farm, a peasant

---

[3] *Przyczyny nawrócenia*, i, 153.
[4] *Historia Reformationis Polonicae*, p. 240.
[5] *Ibid.*

from his plough, a townsman from his last or shop or cask, exclaimed, 'I am bored, and I do not like his talk; it does not edify me.'" The intended "new Jerusalem," instead of developing into a communistic village, developed into a busy town of tradesmen and artisans, in the midst of whom a handful of the more stubborn theologians waited with Gregory Paulus for the end of their stormy lives. Good sense won. The better educated among the youth went as ministers to the estates of nobles (the majority were taken by Jan Kiszka to Lithuania); their elders were already removing to Lublin or Cracow, where they organized the chief congregations of the Polish Brethren (it was not until the next generation, after 1600, that Raków again took the leading rôle in the movement) and tried to dispense with a Utopia and to put up with the existing social system, only reducing its evils by the humanitarian, evangelical life of the brethren.

But here events presented new difficulties, new delicate problems which brought the movement, before it was fully organized, face to face with a great danger. The question of the relation of the brethren to the State and the obligations imposed by the latter on its citizens came to a head. Immediately after the death of Sigismund Augustus, in July 1572, the Senate ordered that the borders of the Republic were to be defended against any attack, and commanded everyone subject to the general levy to be armed and ready. In Antitrinitarian circles, as we know, the use of arms had for some years been condemned: "Under the influence of sermons of this kind, delivered with oratorical passion, many of the gentry, even of famous families, refused to bear arms, lest they act contrary to the Gospel and the teaching of Christ; but for such there was from of old an ancient penalty provided by law, and that the most severe." [6] Then some began to inquire whether Christ really had condemned offices, arms, and laws, and whether preachers had the right to expose citizens

---

[6] J. Palaeologus in his *Defensio verae sententiae*, in the preface to Jan Kiszka, p. 2.

to the loss of reputation and property, as well as to the ignomini-
ous reproach of desertion. Thus it came about that public debates on this matter were held at Cracow, and from there the
cause, still undetermined, was referred to a synod to be held
at Raków.

Staying at Cracow as guest of Andreas Dudith there was an
Antitrinitarian, a Greek refugee named Jacob Palaeologus,
who took part in the discussion, defended the lawfulness of
war, and at the request of Ronemberg and Jacob Kalinowski
put his arguments into writing for the use of the synod, as did
another opponent of radicalism (most probably Stanislas Budzyński). Palaeologus' *de bello sententia,* dated August, 1572, found
advocates at Raków but also very ardent opponents who enjoyed
great influence. It was cried down as though written in blood,
unworthy of any real discussion in view of the words of Christ:
"Resist not evil" and "Whoso taketh thy coat, give him thy
cloak also"—which apparently abolished the magistrate, law,
and the sword.

Palaeologus, in his *de bello sententia,* declares that God does
not condemn every war. It is necessary to distinguish an aggressive war, a war of conquest, from a defensive one. Wars in defense of one's country are "in accordance with the law of God."
A man who refrains from defense of his own goods and inheritance is, from the standpoint of virtue and public justice, a
deserter. Compared to this, death in defense of one's country is
sweet. Since the opponents of war appealed to the Gospel,
Palaeologus also does not have recourse to the Old Testament,
but tries to defeat them with the New. Hence he shows that
the command not to use arms applies only to prophet-priests,
not to secular believers. Christ, who ordered the payment of
tribute to the State, nowhere condemned war in general, still
less a war of defense. Taking possession of his kingdom after
his resurrection, he declared that war to recover one's own was
just. If the power is from God (Rom. xiii), then obedience is
due to the office of the sword. Even the clergy may be called to

exercise government and wield the sword for the public good; still more then may laymen. Christ supported the law of Moses. Did not St. Paul defend himself with the help of soldiers? His opponents recognize—Palaeologus confirms their significant concession in the discussions—that it is lawful for a man to stand on guard, to pay taxes for the support of soldiers, and to hire a substitute for himself. This, however, amounts to the same as being a soldier. A man who discovers a hidden enemy, pays out money for war, or hires a soldier to take his place, surely contributes to the killing of the enemy. Hence Palaeologus' conclusion: "It is lawful for a Christian to bear arms and to defend the boundaries of his country in order to save his own and to exterminate the enemy; whoever acts otherwise and refuses to take up arms in such case, is both wicked and unworthy the name of Christian." [7]

After developing his thesis, Palaeologus proceeds to refute the objections raised by his opponents. As these were drawn from Holy Scripture, the discussion is limited to his own interpretation of the passages cited. Palaeologus explains them all in the sense that they forbid only the private vengeance of wronged persons and arbitrary action by them; they in no way restrict the activity of the government. When a Christian power wages war, it does so as a servant of God. A man fighting with a weapon cannot be godless if God has given him the weapon for the destruction of criminals and the defense of good men, which is the business of justice: "It is true that war destroys men and peace breeds them; but God himself has so ordained that it is better to suffer war than to betray one's native land and lose civil freedom; that it is more honorable to die for a just cause than to be born merely to increase the population." [8] Is it becoming, in time of war, to leave to their fate those who by their work have secured prosperity in time of peace? A man

[7] *Ibid.*, p. 32.
[8] *Ibid.*, p. 45.

who abandons them and hides himself in order not to kill or
be killed himself is a deserter and a traitor. A man who, in time
of peace, enjoys with other citizens the common food, drink,
honors, and other goods, but hides himself when an enemy wishes
to take them, leaving others to defend them and perish for them,
has no right to shelter himself behind a command of God. A
Christian may not even entertain such a conception: he would
sooner take himself out of this world than live in such disgrace.[9]

If an enemy attacks our home, our wives and daughters, shall
we keep silent? May we not cry out and push him away with
our hands or, in such a case, even with a stick, and then why
not with a sword? But if one may not seize a sword to drive
off an assailant, then one also may not cry out and make a
noise. For if because of the word of God, "Resist not evil," one
may not take arms, then is not a man resisting evil when he
cries for help, summons his neighbors, etc.? Either a man may
not resist evil at all, or he may resist it in any way by which
he can repel the evil.[10]

The clear, logical, acute *de bello sententia* placed its opponents
in an uncomfortable position. Palaeologus, though a prominent
Antitrinitarian writer, was unpopular in his own camp because
of his sharp temper, which he also showed in his discussion. Nor
did he for a moment grasp the pacifist and humanitarian intentions of the opponents of war, whom he derided with allusions
to cowardice and desertion. On the question of war, and in-
cidentally also of the power of the State, he adopted without
hesitation a position which the Antitrinitarians had been combating for some years, departure from which, in opposition to all
society, they regarded as a great spiritual advance and an
ethical act.

After writing out his views, Palaeologus made a journey to
Constantinople, returning in 1573 through Transylvania. There

[9] *Ibid.*, p. 47.
[10] *Ibid.*, p. 53.

he found [11] a book composed in the name of the Racovians, *Adversus Jacobi Palaeologi de bello sententiam Gregorii Pauli Responsio*. This reply is very different in structure and tone from the *de bello sententia*. It is not a logical exposition, resting on analysis of arguments and objections, but a kind of speech, saturated with emotion and producing its effect by its feeling.

Palaeologus, argues Gregory, has not presented to us the real Christ, but a fictitious one. Why, Christ was gentle, patient, humble; did not teach war, but prayed for his enemies; promised the Kingdom of Heaven to the humble and merciful; made the harsh laws of Moses mild. He forbade swearing, going to law in courts, seeking vengeance. He commanded a man sooner to run the risk of new injuries, of the loss of goods, of slavery and toil, to give a robber his cloak also. If it is not permissible to demand the return of things taken away, then evidently neither is it permissible to resort to a court for them. Why did Christ command men to offer the other cheek to an attacker if he would have allowed punishment to be meted out by a magistrate? Punishment and vengeance must be left to God, not to men; enemies must be loved not only with the heart, but also in outward act; the greatest evil repaid with the greatest good—that is Christian perfection.

After this presentation of the spirit of Christ's teaching, Gregory asks whether the view of Palaeologus can be reconciled with it. For Christ's sake one should love one's enemies; for the magistrate's, fight with them and overcome them. If one may not pray God for punishment on them, may one demand it from the magistrate? This can not be Christian teaching; the spirit of Christ has departed from it. The essential foundation of Christianity, and the chief difference between the law of Moses and the Gospel, is destroyed. Whoever alters it introduces instead Mohammedanism or paganism.

In the church reigned over by Christ there is no place for the sword nor for torture, apart from excommunication: "Whoever

[11] Dobrowolski, "Nieznana kronika," *Reformacja w Polsce,* iv, 166.

would now try to introduce into the Christian Church—for I am not speaking of civil government—either king or priest, would obviously be depriving Christ of his kingdom and priesthood. If then a king has no place in the Christian Church, how should the sword entrusted to him have one?" [12] Christ commanded men to show obedience to authority by paying tribute, not by handling weapons. The apostolic community at Jerusalem had no officers or judges; but it was obedient to the non-Christian magistrates outside the Church insofar as they did not infringe the glory of God. Paul enjoined obedience to the Roman magistrates, but he did not accept office for himself: "Christians were commanded to obey the government and fear it, but not to exercise it nor to obey its orders when it condemns a man to death or beheads criminals. It [office] is unworthy of a Christian, who is bound to be merciful and to forgive unto seventy times seven, while the government can not be merciful nor forgive any man even once, but must punish him according to his deed, else it injures the other party and does not duly fulfill its obligations." [13]

The Churches of the time at Geneva and Berne had taken government into their own hands, but by the same token had shown that they were not Christian, when they put to death confessors of the one true God (an allusion to such cases as the burning of Servetus): "It is stupidity, not wisdom, to argue that Christians may hold office on the ground that we have commands to be subject to it and to pray for it. Why, we have to pray even for our enemies, from which, however, it does not follow that we have to be enemies to anyone. We are bound to be obedient even to the Turkish government, and yet we do not have to turn Turks." [14]

There is not a word in the New Testament about tortures, imprisonments, crosses, and floggings. Of course, in the world, in

[12] *Ibid.*, p. 72.
[13] *Ibid.*, p. 74.
[14] *Ibid.*, p. 75.

States and towns, there are offices by divine ordinance, for God wishes that order may rule in his creation, so that it may work well for the good, and public peace be maintained. Thus there are officials even in wicked nations, and all must obey them; but a lamb of Christ may not undertake the government of the world with its bears, wolves, swine. Even if he would, he has no means of keeping them under discipline, for the world scoffs at both the Gospel and the pains of hell; in it, therefore, there is need of tortures and floggings, courts and oaths, all forbidden to a Christian. What sort of separation from the world would it be if we adopted the customs of the world, permitting ourselves law-suits and courts, death sentences and wars, and the killing of our enemies? So even the priests of Antichrist (the Romanists) do not sit in judgment on capital cases. It is not permissible today to restore the laws of Moses, which Christ abolished. A man who would bring into the Church of Christ a sword, to fight with or to be killed by it, serves Antichrist and destroys Christianity.

We are not disturbed by the insults heaped upon us as deserters and traitors to our country, for Christ commanded us to bear reproaches for his name's sake. It would be more just to call foes of Christ and traitors to the Gospel men who, under the influence of philosophy and vain hypocrisy, as well as of human institutions, violate the plain commands of God; who for an earthly republic given to the sons of this world overthrow the heavenly kingdom appointed for the sons of God. "If these reproaches are just," concludes Gregory, "then they fall on you, O Christ, who abandoned your own and cruelly betrayed them, who yourself put on no armor in defense of your country, nor commanded your own to do it. . . . Let our opponents heap such reproaches on Christianity and prove to all that they are defenders of Antichrist, or rather of paganism." [15]

We have quoted the *Responsio* of Gregory for its singular interest, since it is (after the lost works of Peter of Goniądz

[15] *Ibid.*, p. 81.

and others) the earliest work authentically presenting the views
of the radical camp, even though we feel a certain disappoint-
ment that Gregory here replies very cautiously, in a rather obscure manner, full of insinuations. To be sure, when we wrote,
at the end of 1572, it was no longer possible to express himself
on such ticklish questions with entire freedom. To have done
so would have been to run the risk of arousing indignation in
various camps, as well as in his own circle, and to draw down
on the already notorious Raków even greater condemnation by
public opinion. Gregory's caution is evident even in the fact
that he avoids any express and direct denial of the warlike thesis
of Palaeologus, but widens the basis of the controversy, thereby
modifying the extreme character of his own position. Instead of
treating clearly the question whether it is admissible to take
part in a defensive war, he strives to make the answer follow indirectly from an examination of the whole relation of the
Christian to the State. Hence he develops an argument on the
question of resistance to evil, of punishments and of courts, of
offices and governments, thanks to which it is possible, in broad
outline, to obtain a picture of the ideology of the Racovians,
undoubtedly less bold and somewhat modified as compared with
the radicalism of its early years.

The State, according to this ideology, is the creature of God,
but is necessary only in view of the existence of evil and of evil
men. Honest, faithful men are here meant by the term "Christians," for the sects do not reckon among them Christians of
other confessions. These men do not need the State for themselves, and could get on without it. They live only with their
gaze directed to the Kingdom of Heaven; they perform all religious duties and practice all the virtues, hence the coercive
power of the State can have no application to them. They
exist rather beside the State than in the State; but despite this
they regard themselves as bound by Christ's command to be
obedient to authority. This obedience is limited to paying taxes
to the State and respecting its agents. On the other hand, they

cannot actively participate in the work of the State, for it is an earthly commonwealth whose aims are not their aims. They cannot accept any office, for attached to it are obligations to punish the guilty, and hence actively to resist evil. Also they cannot appeal to State judges to administer justice, for they are not allowed to seek satisfaction for their injuries.

The existence of a Christian is limited to the sphere of his Church. In its bosom no magistrates are necessary, for the Church employs no punishments beyond excommunication and exclusion. The Church ought not to claim for itself any worldly authority, as the Roman and the new Swiss Churches have done. Palaeologus, it is true, did not assert this; but Gregory debates the matter because he desires in this way to emphasize that Christians can neither imitate the organization of the State nor be assimilated to it, nor in general strive to rule an earthly State. They do not wish to be subject to its influence nor to grant it any influence over them. In other words, they have to exist in as complete separation from the world as is possible, just as the Moravian Anabaptists live. And hence the quite distinct organization of the sect, detached from all external bonds.

In such a system, there obviously exists no problem of war for Christians, nor even of defense. They may not defend anything, and they have nothing to defend. They must give up what an enemy takes from them. They may not have recourse to any court with a complaint of injury suffered. They must obey any foe who conquers them, and not even oppose invasion by the Turk. Whoever should command them to take up arms, they may not go against the teaching of Christ, "Resist not evil." If for this any sort of reprisals should be threatened, the Christian must run the risk rather than deny Christ.

The practical conclusion of this is, therefore, to refuse participation, either direct or indirect, in any way, not out of cowardice, but out of Christian courage, even though it were necessary to atone for it by the most cruel punishments. There is in this no rebellion or revolution, but only a renunciation of civil life.

The author of the *Responsio,* Gregory Paulus, had behind him the whole support of Raków at the time, but in other congregations there arose opposition to so radical a position. A "booklet" arguing against the radical teaching was sent from Cracow by Stanislas Budzyński to the synod at Lutomierz which was to examine the matter in 1573. A reference to this work has been preserved for us in a letter written by Krowicki, from which we learn that Budzyński protested that the Racovians "saw an iron sabre on someone and forthwith condemned him and sent him to hell." Budzyński's outburst was taken in bad part by the synod, which appointed Czechowic to reply to the "booklet." Upon learning of this, the old and ill Martin Krowicki, two weeks before his death, developed his arguments in defense of the magistracy in the form of a letter[16] to Budzyński.

Krowicki does not agree with the brethren's pessimistic view of the State: "Some of our brethren make God a cruel tyrant, as though God were to place in magistracies, in kingdoms, States, principalities, and in all positions of authority such men as he would rather condemn." God has established the magistrate, God has given him a sword; it is not the magistrate who punishes, but God through the magistrate. Krowicki also does not agree with denying salvation to the rich and ruling class. He does not like the Racovian conception of a God who "casts away some persons and repels large classes from him, while he receives into his favor those who go in peasants' clothing, ragged and foul dress, or lousy sheepskins." He does not think that "Christ came to overthrow and corrupt temporal arrangements and the ordinances of God (of the Old Testament) which serve for carrying on this temporal life." He also cites from the Old and New Testaments various texts intended to provide evidence of reverence for kings and governors as well as of the recognition of magistrates and persons of means as pious children of God.

Krowicki is not at all satisfied with emphasis on formal obedi-

---

[16] From Piaski near Lublin, St. Simon's day (Oct. 28), 1573. Letter published by Budny in his *Urząd miecza.*

ence to authority: "that we are obedient to the magistrate and pray God for him." What sense is there in not admitting to the Church of the faithful those who hold office and in thrusting them down to damnation in hell! He regards the development of such teachings by the Racovians as dangerous and compromising: "Much was ordained at Raków that came to nothing, bringing infamy to God, laughter to men, and offence to the Church of God." It provokes him the more that brethren who have voluntarily resigned their offices as ministers put themselves forward as teachers: "And it was a great presumption that the Racovians alone, without other brethren, established a Church for all, being no longer ministers but only mistaken wanderers; and yet others do not wish to recognize this error." This attack is aimed at Gregory Paulus in particular. Encouraging Budzyński to resist him, Krowicki asks whether it is possible in this confusion to rely upon an unnamed "man of God" (he must have been thinking of Palaeologus).

Palaeologus, having obtained the pamphlet by Gregory Paulus, on that very day, August 18, 1573, undertook a reply. It grew to the dimensions of a large work.[17] *Jacobi Palaeologi ad scriptum fratrum Racoviensium de bello et judiciis forensibus Responsio* does not occupy itself immediately with the question of war, but with the fundamental question whether the State is entitled to use the sword, whether the words of Christ about non-resistance to evil annul the right of the State to punish lawbreakers, and that of the citizen to have recourse to the public courts.

Palaeologus treats the Racovian discussion with contempt and mockery, not as a serious examination of an opponent's arguments with the aid of solid proofs, but as a naive piece of verbal declamation for a circle of devoted believers. He alleges that the author had picked a few quotations from the Gospel without regard to their meaning and context, tried to read his own meaning into them, and from three or four misunderstood phrases

[17] In 4o, pp. 83-322.

built up a dangerous doctrine, which he imposed on others as Christian. Would they all let themselves be frightened by what inexperienced and untaught men regard as Christianity? "I should not mention these stupid tales, did not respect for the Poles and the peace of their community, of which all my near friends are members together with me, move me to devote attention to them." [18]

The work of Palaeologus, like that of Gregory, has a theological character. He investigates the degree of support to be found in Holy Scripture for statements made by his opponent and overthrows these by suitable interpretation of the Biblical passages. He discusses at considerable length,[19] phrase by phrase, the Sermon on the Mount in Matt. v-vii, since it was on the teachings of this sermon that the Racovians chiefly based their doctrine. His friend Stanislas Budzyński had long ago asked Palaeologus to make a thorough analysis of this; thus the author now fulfills his promise. The results are as follows.

The office of the sword (i.e. *jus gladii*, the right to condemn to death) was in existence before the time of Christ; Christ did not abrogate it. The sixth commandment does not weaken the magistracy, since it refers to private persons. When the magistrate puts a murderer to death, he is fulfilling his obligation to society and is not committing murder. The removal of a criminal cannot be condemned except by those to whom a surgeon amputating a putrefying hand seems a cruel man. The precept "Resist not evil" has no reference to the magistracy. Properly, a magistrate, as one who is not taking private vengeance, is bound to oppose evil in order that the common man may not alone have to defend himself against an aggressor or recover what has been taken from him.[20] In fact, even the latter is al-

[18] *Ibid.*, p. 247.
[19] *Ibid.*, pp. 100-215.
[20] Rejecting the thesis of non-resistance to evil, Palaeologus touched upon but did not wish to discuss a question which in the sixteenth century forced itself upon humanity: the right of subjects to resist the authorities. He held, however, that in civil war one should not seek revenge for an

lowed a certain measure of defense enabling him only to defend himself, but not to kill an opponent; a magistrate, however, may not refrain from defending private persons. It cannot be a sin to report an injury to the magistrate, nor to bear witness under oath to an undoubted truth. Does a man whose property has been taken away by robbers have to expose himself to infamy also? Does the lawful owner have to surrender his goods to the criminal who attacks him? If Christ had forbidden lawful punishment, he would have overturned the foundations of States. It is therefore lawful to sit in judgment and to decree punishment, but not to dream that God sits by Himself in heaven and does not concern Himself with the world; or if He does concern Himself, that He grasps the sword Himself instead of acting through His servants.[21] Love of one's enemy should not be carried too far, leading to conflict between love of the neighbor who abuses this sentiment, and love of the community wronged by individuals. A government that punishes transgressors wrongs no one.

Palaeologus regards Gregory Paulus as a madman. More absorbed in his own work than in the Gospel, he will not yield lest he lose his reputation, hence he invents commentaries through which "many have already lost their property, and those who before supported the brethren must today beg alms themselves." [22] This fatal stubbornness is a cause "of great disturbance to the Kingdom of Poland." [23] Palaeologus reminds the Racovians that they do not permit the office of the sword, but instead they create an office more contrary to love, for by excommunication a man is deprived of eternal life; they do this evidently to the end that men may apply to them for judgment of their causes instead of to the civil magistrate.[24] Do they not know that by

---

injury, but only not permit (1) destruction of the word of God, (2) changes in ancestral customs, and (3) destruction of public freedom (*Ibid.,* p. 147).

[21] *Ibid.,* p. 243.
[22] *Ibid.,* pp. 235, 275.
[23] *Ibid.,* p. 277.
[24] *Ibid.,* pp. 281f, 320.

denying all authority, they are alienating the sympathy of the people from their cause? For the latter argue that if a man is not permitted to hold office, then he will not be permitted to be a father, a husband, an instructor of youth—for all these are offices of some sort. "Do you not know that because of these dreams there is no discipline in your homes; your sons end by hanging themselves; your daughters end in a dissolute life?" [25] Such decay threatens if abuses are not checked, if even flogging is abandoned. But it is impossible to retain the practice of flogging if arrest, chains, and tortures are abolished. Let the Racovians not be surprised that insults are heaped on them. Those who hewed out huge crosses in the forests and walked around in villages and towns wearily bearing them on their shoulders in order to fulfill the commandment of Christ, "Take up thy cross and follow me," would today be derided for pleading Christ as an excuse for their nonsense; similarly, the Racovians too shelter their crazy dreams behind Christ, but they should understand that the insults falling on them do not affect Christ. [26]

With sharpest irony Palaeologus combats the sectarian spirit of a Church that has cut itself off from the way of life followed by the whole of society. Christ, he declares, nowhere commanded men to "flee from the world." Such a command could be understood only as suicide. He commanded them to shun corrupt manners, not the office of the sword. If a Christian society could not produce out of itself the organs of authority, then Christianity would be reduced to absurdity. The most upright men would then be forced to have recourse to Turkish or Jewish magistrates, or to submit their quarrels to the judgment of ministers of the word (who in this way, having abolished the office of the sword ordained of God, would themselves form an office of the sword), or to see States and countries reduced to deserts because of the increase in crimes following lack of punishment, or else to found monastic societies and persuade

---

[25] *Ibid.*, pp. 317f. Evidently an allusion to actual occurrences at Raków.
[26] *Ibid.*, p. 319.

men that everyone who accepted their doctrines by that very act renounced earthly passions. Let them cease promising men impossibilities, urged Palaeologus, for while wishing to make Christians perfect by abolishing authority and discipline, they produce the most immoral characters.

In acuteness of argument, in skill in drawing conclusions, in political thinking, Palaeologus' reply surpasses Gregory's pamphlet, but Palaeologus offends by his haughty treatment of his opponent and by an unjustified readiness to impute to him wrong intentions. The Racovian work is less a product of logic or of theology than an outpouring of the heart. The statesman finds it naive, vague, and utopian, and it discourages the patriot by its indifference to the native land, yet it is hard to resist the impression that it is closer to the spirit of the Gospel and the teachings of Christ than the arguments of the Greek. Palaeologus does not take anything from the New Testament which could have had a positive influence upon that era of fierce and devastating wars, of political absolutism and social oppression. At that period, a man who was endeavoring to reshape the world and humanity on a religious foundation would sooner have found an incentive in Gregory's interpretation of the Gospel.

From a letter of Stanislas Budzyński to Palaeologus on March 17, 1574 (sent, of course, from Cracow), we learn that Palaeologus' treatise reached the Polish Brethren through him, and that it was Budzyński who tried to counteract with that treatise the radical doctrine of Peter Gonesius:

Your servant Nicholas handed me the manuscript. . . . Having understood from your letter that you were sending it to me in order that I could make a copy, communicate it to other people, and return the original to you, I handed to the leading Rakovians for perusal the discussion of their ideas. Several of them were there, above all George Schomann and Martin Czechowic. Having seen the manuscript, one of them announced that he had no time to waste reading such writings, while other people were so disdainful that they did not even cast a glance at it, saying that they did not want to occupy themselves with vain philosophy, and so on.

I have copied it with my own hand and I am returning the original through Nicholas. I shall distribute it among other people, and I have already given it to Stanislas Lutomirski who will also take care of making another copy in order to study it in Lutomirsk with the ministers and other pious men whose eyes and minds are not so blinded by the Rakovian interpretation.

Martin Krowicki, already eighty years old, and almost the first minister of the Gospel in Poland (from 1547 on), when he was with one foot in the grave—he died a fortnight later—sent me about that time a letter on the same matter in which he fervently urged me not to desist in my work but on all occasions to warn the members of the congregation to keep clear of the Rakovian interpretation in order that the minds of so many distressed and confused people be fortified and not oppressed and deluded by false interpretations of the Holy Scripture. Last September I sent a letter on this matter to the synod in Lutomirsk, but it was not given to everybody for perusal.

How strange that these good brethren took a fancy to the opinion of the Rakovians which they in turn had taken from the writing of a certain Pole, Peter Gonesius, entitled *De primatu Ecclesiae Christianae*, and which, as I see, does not agree with the proper meaning of the words of Jesus Christ, and how strange that they defend and light-mindedly disseminate it among the multitude. Let us hope that they will peruse and reasonably appraise your writing in which you so thoroughly refute this opinion of theirs which has no ground in the Scriptures.

I have also launched among the brethren a booklet in Polish based on your treatise, since not all of them can read and understand Latin easily.[27]

The Racovians hid the manuscript of Palaeologus' work, both because it breathed a spirit which was in their opinion un-Christian and because it was so offensive and contemptuous toward them. In 1574 they held another synod at Raków, at which social and political ideas were discussed, but the arguments of Palaeologus were not brought up. The rôle of opponent to the

[27] Karl Landsteiner, *Jacobus Palaeologus* (Wien:1873), pp. 38-39.

prevailing tendency was assumed by Budzyński; that of defender, as usual, by Gregory Paulus.[28] It seems that it was
Gregory's last appearance in this affair. He no longer replied to
the mockery of Palaeologus. The decline of Raków (thenceforth
for a number of years not a word is heard of it) and also a fear
of exciting public opinion may have contributed to the sub-
sidence of the quarrels.

[28] So at least we may infer from an account, given in Sandius, *Bibliotheca
Antitrinitariorum,* pp. 44, 55, of the existence in manuscript of two letters
of Budzyński, one to the synod at Raków in 1574, in which "he exhorts the
brethren to harmony and defends the use of weapons and the duties of the
magistrate"; the other to Gregory Paulus, in which "he defends political
authorities and the sword, as well as the Christian's right to wage war."
Letters of Gregory in 1574 to Budzyński "on the question of the magistrate
and the use of arms" bear out this inference (Cf. H. Barycz in the *Polish
Dictionary of Biography,* III, 105f).

# 6   *The Establishment of the*
## *Racovian Doctrine*

Schomann's caution.  Czechowic's radicalism.  The
official doctrine of the Church.  Opposition of Budny
and the Lithuanians.  Publication of the controversial
work of Palaeologus.  Ronemberg's reproaches.

In 1574, after the destruction of the "Brog" [1] of the Calvinists
at Cracow, the mob also made for the house of Cikowski, in
which the Anabaptists used to meet.  The attack was indeed
repulsed, but anxiety fell on the little group of adherents of the
"Minor Church."  We feel it when turning over the leaves of a
catechism published at this time by the minister of the congregation, George Schomann.[2]

Already in the preface to the reader, on behalf of "the tiny
and oppressed congregation," he answers accusations made
against the Anabaptists, whose "name, by reason of some criminals, is universally in bad repute and detested, as was the
case with us ourselves a few years ago"; he swears by God
that in the catechism he gives the authentic teaching of the
church and that they deal treacherously in nothing whatsoever,
and ends in mystical fear of a day, soon to come, of dreadful
divine punishments upon the world.  Yet in the same catechism

---

[1] *Brog* (haystack) was the popular name of the Calvinist house of worship
at Cracow, perhaps from its shape.

[2] *Catechesis et confessio fidei coetus per Poloniam congregati in nomine
Jesu Christi.  Typis Alexandri Turobini* (Alexius Rodecki, Cracow:
1574).

he several times strongly emphasizes the duty of subjects to obey the authorities, and of the rich to love the poor.[3] He gives expression to the political and social loyalty of the Church in the following prayer:

Especially do we pray thee, O King of kings and Lord of lords, who thyself dost establish kings and rulers, to vouchsafe by thy holy hand to direct and to preserve the hearts, thoughts, purposes, health, and life, as of all rulers so especially of our most gracious King and Queen of Poland, and of all councillors and magistrates of towns, our lords. Direct them by thy governing Spirit, and defend them from all threatening dangers, for the sake of the due order and public peace of this whole Republic of Poland, miraculously preserved hitherto by thine especial providence, amidst the ruin and desolation of so many flourishing kingdoms; and grant that we, however much oppressed, may under their protection live peaceably and in the fear of God. . . . Have mercy also, O Lord God, on the whole people, even the unskilled multitude, and pardon their dreadful transgressions. By thy Spirit incline all thine elect to render true, sincere, and due obedience above all to thee our God and Lord, and afterwards to all governors and rulers by thee established, not so much out of fear as for conscience' sake.

While the gentle and modest Schomann, avoiding provocation of society,[4] laid emphasis on obedience to authority and prayed for the King, Martin Czechowic, a representative of the more radical congregation at Lublin, carrying out the orders of the synod at Lutomierz, came forward publicly with a justification of a position which coincided with the views of Gregory Paulus. Czechowic's comprehensive Polish catechism, printed at Cracow and designed for less instructed fellow-believers, was composed in the form of conversations between a Pupil and a Teacher, and

---

[3] *Ibid.*, pp. h1, i4, n6, o2-3.
[4] Parallel to Schomann's fervent prayer for purity in the life of married people in the congregation ("that from this no suspicion of any evil may arise," p. o1) is the agitated mention in his Testament (Sandius, p. 191) of "two Bishops who have published libels, as though we, forgetting God and shame, met in our churches to commit all sorts of crimes, and were publicly joined in marriage naked."

hence was entitled *Rozmowy chrystyańskie* (*Christian dialogues*) (1575). The work is brilliantly written, lively, and full of temperament, and in its twelfth chapter "on the Christian life"[5] touches quite boldly on the most controversial problems. His dialogue is by no means dull: in the Pupil's questions the author boldly places the doubts and objections that its lay, and especially its noble, adherents must have raised against the Anabaptist doctrine. *Inter alia* the Pupil adopts all the arguments in Krowicki's letter (cf. above, pp. 61-62).

The discussion embraces three chief problems: (1) resistance to evil; (2) the holding of office; (3) participation in war.

The Pupil does not understand how a man can receive an injury without resisting, for in that case everybody will strike him and it would be better to go at once into the wilderness. The Teacher explains that every calamity is by the will of God, and that even in the wilderness a man cannot escape it. In reply to this the Pupil asks for guidance on Christian behavior in face of three kinds of injuries: (a) "In a matter of his good reputation, which when a man has lost . . . he has nothing more to lose." (b) "In a matter of possessions, whether small or great, without which also no man can live in the world, for now men give each other nothing *gratis* for food and drink, but each must exert himself on his own account, unless it has already come to this: that a man having taken up a beggar's bag, must beg his bread and rouse other peoples' dogs." (c) "In a matter of life or health, which is even dearer than property or renown . . . because it is hardest to bear, if anybody makes an attempt on my health, to have that taken from me." Is it, therefore, lawful to defend these three treasures; is it lawful to strike an assailant or even to kill him?

The Teacher recommends that the Pupil commit himself to the providence and protection of God. "And you," he asks the Pupil, "with what and how would you be willing to defend yourself if somebody intended to deprive you of health, or to kill

[5] Pp. 224-56.

you, or wished to take from you something of your own?" Pupil: "As long as there were any law, then I should act according to the law; but if the law were difficult of access, or did not exist, then only should I use force: that is, he who is the stronger is the better. I am not a dumb stick or a Stoic, hence I should resort to the sword." The Teacher replies that such servants Christ does not wish: a man may kill only with the permission of God, if he has a "kindling of the spirit." A Christian war is permissible only against spiritual or carnal foes, such as our body, our passions, the world; but men who attack our life or goods we ought to disarm and overcome only by the word, "not only not killing, but also not even giving offence, whether by instrument of war, by blows, or even by a word proceeding from an angry heart." Upon his protest that this annuls the natural right of self-defense, the Pupil is informed that a may learns of such a law from a corrupted nature, and that a fornicator or a drunkard abuses it, but a Christian, on the contrary, ought to return good for evil and to leave vengeance to God. In the same way, when defending a near relative, even one as dear as wife or daughter, against a wrong-doer, a man may use only lawful Christian means, "without murder, striking, bloodshed, wrath, and carnal revenge"; if this is of no avail, "then nothing is to be done except to bear it humbly and thankfully to accept it from the Lord as a divine punishment." (Indeed, it is impossible to love one's neighbor better than oneself, and hence in defending him one may not go further than in self-defense.)

The Pupil is willing to be convinced, but thinks that in such wrongs a man ought to seek the protection of the secular power, which is "from God for the defense of the good and for the punishment of the wicked, and beareth not in vain the sword that God himself giveth into its hands." In this way the discussion proceeds to the second great problem: the relation of the Church to the civil power. That Teacher concedes that "all government and all authority is from God, who is now gracious, now wrathful," to punish evil and to show the wrath of God;

but by a special command Christ has forbidden his "faithful" to have recourse to the authorities on account of an injury. The Pupil agrees that it is not really fitting to go to an unbelieving magistrate; but he does not understand why this prohibition has to apply to a "believing magistrate," that is, in a Christian State; in that event why would Scripture command obedience to the magistrate?

"I do not say this," says the Teacher, "nor, please God, will I say that there is no use for superior powers in the world. But I say only this, that a congregation of faithful and sincere disciples of Christ has no need of a magistrate or civil officer with sword, prison, fire, hangman, halter, gallows, which this earthly officer cannot be without, for God giveth not the sword into his hands in vain. Thus it is in the world, not in the Church, that there is need of a magistracy, which would, however, not only be for the alarm and punishment of the wicked—for these do nothing good, save as a result of force and fear—but also for the comfort and defense of the good, who do everything good out of love." The faithful, on the other hand, do not employ means without which government cannot exist, and do not have recourse to government, though they do not reject it, since it is needed to restrain the wicked. "But because wicked men feel the magistrate over them, they refrain from evil, though not willingly; and thus decent people sleep in their homes in peace. And the faithful also praise God in their church and pray the Lord God for authority of every kind, for the King and other superiors, for the country and town in which they dwell, that they may be preserved in peace, that their peace may be joined with the peace of the town." Authority is necessary only because of the wicked; "but for those who, denying themselves, live in piety and holiness, doing no one any wrong, nay themselves humbly suffering all manner of wrong, there is little need of authority, for it is not established for them." Therefore Christians do not interest themselves very closely in the civil authority, "since they gladly wait for a spiritual one in heaven," but they "neither strive for it nor yet despise it" and are concerned that it may "have no trouble or grief" because of them.

"Since the magistracy or authority is from God, does it then follow," asks the Pupil, "that true disciples of Christ may not take this office upon themselves," or may members of the Church hold office and share in its power? The answer is given in the negative. The faithful are "a chosen people," by the grace of God "separated" from the world; in order to share in official power they would have to go out again into the world, which both despises them and is loathed by them; thus it is not allowable for them to accept any kind of worldly office. For them Jesus Christ is King, "beside whom we are to seek for ourselves no other Lord, nor ourselves be placed as lords over others." The believer who is wronged will not resort to another power for justice, nor mete it out for himself, for then "he angers his Lord and arouses him against himself."

To this the Pupil now offers no objection, but raises a third fundamental question: that of war. Since the power of the State reaches everywhere, and the faithful cannot "find for themselves some separate corner to dwell in, in which there would be no secular authority," what is the believer to do "when this authority commands me either to follow it into battle or to kill someone, even as the kings of the Jews did, etc?" Here is the Teacher's reply: "You must be obedient and subject to authority, and render to it what it commands, but only according to the word of God, and nothing beyond that." Even in the Old Testament there are examples of opposition to an authority giving commands contrary to God, but to the "faithful" war has been forbidden by Christ. "I could prove here from both old and new doctors, and even from the popish priests themselves, who call themselves clergy, that it is not becoming in Christian clergymen to fight, and not only to fight, but to condemn a man to death or even to be present at such a trial." In the opinion of Czechowic, this command applies to every member of the Church: "It is certain that it is not right for any faithful regenerate Christian [to fight], whatever authority may command him to do so."

"But if I also," asks the Pupil, "having gone out to war at the King's command, should yet strike no one when others struck, and moreover even bore no arms, should I then be doing wrong?" "It would certainly be wrong," explains the Teacher, "for even then you would, against the Apostle's command, be pulling in the same team with other unbelievers. . . . You would be tempting God, provoking not only the authorities against yourself, but also other warriors athirst for the enemy's blood. . . . And also if you wished to play the hypocrite there, then you would have at once to separate yourself from Christ, for he wants no hypocritical servants." To be sure, there must be wars and soldiers in the world, but it does not follow from this that "the lambs of Christ's Church have to go to war."

If the shedding of blood is so great an evil, asks the Pupil in surprise, how can the government be allowed to do it at all? The Teacher explains this by a divine ordinance that the wicked are to be punished and that a magistrate who bears in vain the sword given him by God is cursed. "It is the authorities of this world who must punish the wicked and shed their blood willy-nilly, but not the disciples of Christ."

"But as to making war"—the Pupil is troubled about rulers —"how can they defend both their dominions and their subjects, if you and I and many others who sincerely adhere to Christ will no longer either fight or go to war?" The Teacher comforts him with the assurance that if God wills, "as soon as he only whistles," at once a multitude of soldiers will assemble from all quarters. "And as for defending their dominions, towns, and common people, it is true that for this, first many people are needed, about whom there will also be no difficulty if there is money." Emphasizing the duty of paying taxes to the State, Czechowic in this way leaves to members of the Church at least the possibility of buying themselves off with money from taking part in a defensive war. Finally, it is his opinion that if God appoints for a State a time of decline, then against this "neither the greatness of a people nor an abundance of money nor wise civil counsel will avail."

At the end of his work Czechowic adds a long Latin appendix entitled *de Vita et Moribus Christianorum Primitivae Ecclesiae* as a supplement to the twelfth Dialogue. He explains to the reader that although in all his Dialogues Holy Scripture was enough for him, yet the brethren have asked that he support this Dialogue only with testimonies from the oldest writers of the Church, on account of complaints that the standpoint of the Church with regard to war is dictated by the Anabaptist spirit. He therefore has to turn to the writers of the Church from whom he had long ago separated, and to choose from them arguments to show that the Anabaptists were not the authors of this doctrine, that the primitive Christians taught and lived thus, having obviously themselves been so taught by Christ and the Apostles. Czechowic, therefore, cites without comment a considerable number of texts, chiefly from the writings of Justin, Tertullian, Cyprian, Athanasius, Basil the Great, Lactantius, and Hilary. These texts, mostly in the form of commands and admonitions, urge abandonment of the spirit of war and vengeance, and are too general to afford complete support for the very categorical doctrine of Czechowic; where, for example, the strictures of Tertullian on the holding of offices by Christians in pagan Rome are in agreement with it, they bear too clearly the mark of their period of history to be applied literally to the conditions of the sixteenth century. Czechowic evidently felt the necessity of citing more convincing proof, for he drew liberally on passages from Erasmus' Commentary on the New Testament, in which Erasmus, indulging his irony as well as his humanitarian and pacifist feelings, attacked his contemporaries for forsaking the spirit of the Gospel. He closed the above citations with remarks of his own, in which he expressed the conviction that men engrossed in riches and transient pleasure would not be affected by these testimonies, and that only the poor, schooled by want in the virtues of the Gospel, were able to follow the word of Christ:

Yet let no one heap slanders upon us, as though we said all this in order to throw off from our necks the yoke of civil office. How would that become us, who in everything adapt our lives to the precepts of our faith and the commands of God, who having abandoned wickedness and earthly desires, wish by our modest, pure, and peaceable life to please God, and not the world? . . . Only if the magistrate should force us to do forbidden things and command something against the word of God, then we are ready to obey God rather than men; but even here we do not permit sedition or outrage, preserving a spirit of peace and good-will to all.

As is made clear in the twelfth Dialogue, Czechowic maintained the whole of the 1572 position of the Racovians, as expressed at that time by Gregory Paulus. Only when writing a popular exposition for a wide circle of adherents, and issuing the *Christian Dialogues* in print (for Gregory's memorial had not been designed for publication), did Czechowic avoid certain phrases from which he might have been suspected of a position hostile to the State. There is no essential difference between Gregory and Czechowic, both views springing from the same ideological stage, which characterized the Racovians at the time of the interregnum.

In the wider circles of the nobility, absorbed in the struggles of parties and candidates for the throne, not much attention was paid to radical Antitrinitarian theories. They were no secret, though care was taken not to bring condemnation upon the Church by provoking public opinion. News of the conflicts of ideas among the Antitrinitarians got about more and more. Not a few things were revealed by Daniel Bieliński, who had at first been one of the most radical ministers himself (according to the Calvinist chronicle at Cracow,[6]), together with others "removing to Raków, a little town where they had thought to establish

<hr />

[6] Cf. W. Węgierski, *Kronika*, p. 28. For Bieliński, cf. article by W. Budka in the *Polish Dictionary of Biography*, II, 45f.

a new colony or Anabaptist society." In 1576, he left the Anabaptists and returned to the Calvinists, having renounced his past in his published *Recantation (Odwołanie)*.[7] There he set forth the internal division within the Church on social questions, as follows:

Some of the gentry keep their property, but others condemn it and leave it for the war, or enter public service. . . . Some disapprove of buying, brewing, and selling beer, while on the other hand others traffic in it. Some assert that it is not right for them to hold office, but others that it is right. But who could tell all the confusion that rules among them? It would be difficult to do so. For there are even such monks among them as wish to enter eternal life, not by the grace of God through faith in the Lord Jesus Christ, but through poverty, axes, plows, hard work, scanty eating and drinking.

But the political relations of the Republic suddenly underwent changes. The election of Batory brought with it an internal growth in the authority of the State government, and several years of military operations. In this atmosphere, neutrality toward the State and condemnation of war, all of which had hitherto had no more than theoretical significance, could not be treated indulgently as the harmless dreams of a handful of utopians. For such views the Moravian Anabaptists had been punished by the State with fire and sword, imprisonment and banishment, though it is true that there, there had been two additional embarrassing circumstances: firstly, social radicalism; secondly, the basing of an anti-State and anti-war attitude on hope of a Turkish victory over the Empire. Among the Polish Anabaptists social radicalism subsided before it had reached the point of an established doctrine and before it could become compromised with any subversive movement, while pacifist theories did not seem so dangerous when they were not linked with fear of high treason.

In the Antitrinitarian Churches of Poland proper the attitude

[7] We know it only from the citations in the *Wędzidło* of the priest Powodowski, pp. 10f, 174.

of Czechowic to State and war became the official doctrine. Krowicki was dead; Budzyński did not express opposition in print and afterwards held his peace; the polemics of Palaeologus remained hidden. The Lublin Church, headed by Czechowic as minister and Jan Niemojewski as elder, took over the intellectual and moral direction of the whole movement; the Cracow Church, with Schomann as minister and Ronemberg as elder, seconded it, and it was there that the publications of all the writers of the Church were printed by Rodecki. With these two churches the declining Raków and the rising Lucławice cooperated.

Opposition to the ruling tendency gradually began to gather strength in Lithuania. Its head was Simon Budny, minister at Łosk, who relied on the protection of the powerful Jan Kiszka, a magnate favoring Antitrinitarianism from his youth, under the influence both of his mother Anna, sister of Nicholas the Black Radziwiłł, and of foreign masters (the Italians at Basel).[8] On his vast estates he introduced one minister of this tendency after another, and together with them he resolved by undergoing immersion to declare his adherence to Anabaptism. His social position, however, did not incline him to accept the extreme doctrine of the Anabaptists, just as the less wealthy among the gentry who favored this sect could not agree to resign their estates and their share in the government of the State. Their ministers—after the radicals had gone with Jacob Kalinowski to Raków, and after the death of Peter of Goniądz—also did not share the radicalism of the Racovians, did not with them pass through a period of confusion, give up their ministry, or resort to manual labor, but used their inherited endowments, parsonages, and residences, peasant serfs and feudal dues. They differed from the Antitrinitarians of Poland proper in doctrine also: were more attached to the Old Testament and questioned the supernatural conception of Christ, arriving eventually at so-called non-adorantism, which refused to invoke Christ or to

[8] St. Kot, "Polen in Basel," *Basler Zeitschrift für Geschichte und Altertumskunde* (1942), Vol. 41, pp. 105-153.

pay him divine honor. Both these views brought them nearer
to Palaeologus. The political situation tended to confirm them
in this standpoint: the wars with Moscow made it impossible
for Lithuania, which was immediately threatened, to treat in
an academic manner the question of obedience to the "office of
the sword." This scandalized the Anabaptists of Poland proper,
and they therefore decided to prepare to go to the Lithuanian
brethren to root out their errors.

Thus in 1578, Martin Czechowic and Alexander Witrelin
arrived at the synod at Łosk and began to censure the attitude
of the Lithuanians. But the leader of the immersed nobles,
Basil Ciapiński, supported by others, declared that it was not
contrary to the Gospel to hold the "office of the sword," or an
estate, to go to war, or to resort to law." [9]

That very year the Lithuanian delegates, Budny and Fabian
Domanowski, were sent to a synod at Lucławice, commissioned
to clear up the questions at issue; but discussion was there
denied them; Niemojewski referred them to the twelfth Dialogue
of Czechowic. In vain they begged Czechowic and Schomann to
lend them the writings of Palaeologus; not obtaining them, they
wrote to the author in Moravia, who sent them in care of
Kiszka.

In a letter from Hluk in Moravia dated Dec. 1, 1579, Palaeologus congratulated Kiszka on his recent appointment to the high
office of Starost of Samogitia (Zmudź) and sought to relieve his
conscience, telling him not to be troubled by the reproaches
which affront pious officials, upsetting the order of the State.
The whole of the discussion of 1572-73 now known to us, i.e. the
treatises of Palaeologus and Paulus, were printed by Budny on
his press at Łosk in August, 1580,[10] at Kiszka's expense. The

---

[9] Budny, *O urzędzie miecza* (Reprint), pp. 22, 231. For Ciapiński, cf.
article by R. Mienicki in the *Polish Dictionary of Biography*, IV, 17; for
his rôle in the development of the White Ruthenian language, cf. A. Mar-
tel, *La Langue polonaise dans les pays ruthènes* (Lille:1938), p. 208.

[10] *Defensio verae sententiae de magistratu politico in Ecclesiis Chris-
tianis retinendo, contra quosvis eius impugnatores nominatim vero contra
Racoviensium scriptum, ex divinis scripturis simpliciter collecta, Jacobo
Palaeologo authore. Habes hic quoque lector scriptum Racoviensium, ut*

work was furnished with some little dedicatory poems: by Budny on Kiszka's coat of arms, and by Thomas Garliński on the treatise of Palaeologus. These two at once set out for Lublin in order to place the book in the hands of their opponents. They were received in the worst possible manner. First they were blamed for publishing it without the authorization of the Church. The year previous, the Lublin synod had in fact established a censorship in order to maintain uniformity of doctrine. Niemo-jewski did not deny to Budny that they would not have allowed him to print it. Not to speak of the fact that they condemned the substance of the arguments of Palaeologus, they were outraged by his mockery and epithets and, most important, they regarded his publication of the whole discussion at that moment, complete with the name of Gregory Paulus and Palaeo-logus' insinuations about desertion and lack of patriotism, as dangerous for the Church and likely to draw down upon them government reprisals. Faustus Socinus asked for a copy, prom-ising a controversy with Palaeologus.

Even Ronemberg, the impartial elder of Cracow, respected by all, wrote Budny a letter reproaching him for attacking "the Lord's poor little band and flock" in so harsh and unfriendly a manner. Budny defended himself in a long reply in which he set forth in detail all his complaints against the Polish Brethren. He showed that their Church had repelled many persons just by its "blasphemy *contra magistratum*," and that this doctrine laid the Anabaptists open to damaging suspicions. Although they commanded "obedience to the King and all in authority, and payment of taxes of all kinds," at the Warsaw Diet (January, 1581, whither King Stephen Batory came from Wielkie Łuki to raise new taxes) the King's anger was stirred up against them on the ground that "they forbid to pay the King tribute"; hence persecutions were in prospect for them. Budny appealed to his own people; and the synod at Łosk in January, 1581, declared, by all votes save two, in favor of the magistrate.

---

*est ab ipsius authore contra sententiam Jac. Palaeologi conscriptum, bona fide editum.* Copy in the Czartoryski library, Cracow.

# 7  *Faustus Socinus on War and the State*

Socinus against Palaeologus. His motives in enter-
ing the discussion. Contents of his work. Defense of
the Racovians. He tones down the extremes of their
position. The Transylvanians are not satisfied. Batory
is displeased. Powodowski attacks Czechowic.

The brethren in Little Poland could not allow the opinions
of Palaeologus and Budny to go unanswered. It was a question
not only of defending their own teaching, but also of shielding
themselves from the anger of the royal power and of refuting
an argument which shifted emphasis from the New to the Old
Testament, round which their opponents (Palaeologus, Budzyński, Budny) were ever more plainly rallying. The discussion with
the menacing Palaeologus they entrusted to Faustus Socinus,
who had for a year been living in Poland and was a man famous
for his thorough knowledge of theology, his immense learning,
and his uncommonly subtle and acute understanding. It is true
that he was divided from the Churches of Little Poland by his
dislike of immersion, in consequence of which he was not formally
received by them as a member; despite this they had such a
degree of confidence in his orthodoxy that both the Lubliners
and the Cracovians actually asked him to ward off the danger.
At first he hesitated, the more since in certain particulars he
did not share the attitude of Gregory Paulus. He demanded
that they first appeal to Gregory himself for an answer. It

appeared, however, that the latter was now unequal to the task: oppressed by poverty and material cares, he had laid down his pen, a fact to which the bad state of his health and poor eyesight contributed. Moreover, Gregory declared that he considered, that not he but the Raków congregation was the author of the pamphlet attacked by Palaeologus; this congregation now barely existed or had suffered such a change that there was no one to reply in its name.[1] Socinus then resolved to undertake this task. At a synod at Chmielnik in January, 1581, he sought for an opinion of what he had written.[2] As the work progressed, the manuscript was sent to press, of course with Rodecki, in sections, until at last in August a considerable volume appeared, without the author's name however.[3]

In the preface to Palaeologus, the author explains why he has come forward: the controversy about the magistrate is being taken amiss by kings; the view of the Racovians is presented by Palaeologus in such a light that it may expose the author of the Racovian argument to loss not only of his property but also of his life. Why does Palaeologus, when conducting a discussion on war, bring forward the question of the magistrate in the title of his book? Why does he not pass over in silence the names of the Racovians and Gregory in his discussion? It looks

[1] To say nothing of the politico-moral question, the brethren were in fact not much inclined to subscribe to the Racovian tradition. At this time Czechowic, in his *Respons na script Stanisława Farnowskiego* (Reply to writing of Stanislas Farnowski), 1579, expresses anger with Farnowski on this matter: "Bringing the hatred of all men upon us, and laughing at us in contempt, he calls us *Racovians*. He never shows, however, that all of us whom he thus attacks lived at Raków and, if there were some mistakes at Raków, that we agreed to them, and did not oppose them. . . . Of all this, Daniel, not the prophet of God, but the modern Jew (Bieliński) may be witness" (K. 40).

[2] Letter of Socinus to Jan Balcerowicz, Cracow, January 30, 1581, in *Bibliotheca Fratrum Polonorum*, i, 424; cf. also his letter to Dudith, December, 1582, i, 497.

[3] *Ad Jac. Palaeologi librum, cui titulus est Defensio verae sententiae de magistratu politico* etc., *pro Racoviensibus Responsio. Ex typographia Theophili Adamidis*, 1581, 4o, pp. 8-371. Second Edition, Raków, 1627; Third Edition, in *Bibliotheca Fratrum Polonorum*, 1656; detailed description in Estreicher's *Bibliografia*, vol. 28 (1930), where the works of Socinus are for the first time listed and described with extraordinary care.

as if he wished to bring down hatred upon his opponents and to ingratiate himself with the rulers. Perhaps, however, he only published those names without thinking. Socinus intends to defend the Racovians against unjust reproaches, all the more since Palaeologus wrongly explains the meaning of the Racovians' arguments and often does not even understand them correctly: "If they sometimes accidentally stumbled, whether in argument or in the interpretation of Holy Scriptures, and you criticize them for this fairly, it is not to be wondered at, especially since you yourself so often stumble in both that it is impossible even to mention all your mistakes." It especially provokes the author that Palaeologus loads Gregory, "a brave and learned man, who has long and zealously toiled in the Church of the Lord," with so much malice and invective. He, Socinus, will try to confute Palaeologus by arguments, not by insults; but let him not be surprised if sometimes the blows may fall rather sharply.

The work of Socinus keeps closely within the bounds of theological argument: there are for him no other considerations. He draws proofs only from Holy Scripture, interpreting passages and refuting the interpretations of his opponent in his own way. In his arguments Socinus is exceedingly exact and particular; he debates each of his opponent's theses in unusual detail and fullness. We shall not go here into the apparatus of his citations, explanations, and demonstrations, but present his leading ideas, some of them in greater detail, in view of the great historical importance of the work and its author.

Socinus's *Reply* is divided into four parts. The *first* is devoted to supporting and defending the argument of Gregory Paulus. The Racovians justly complain of Palaeologus that he represents Christ falsely, that he introduces regulations contrary to his teaching, and that he puts the Gospel and Christ in the background in favor of Moses. It is not permissible to appeal to the fact that Christ himself punished his enemies; he was infallible, while a magistrate may easily do wrong both in war and in exercising the right of the sword. When two kings go to war

against each other, one is certainly a wrong-doer. Despite this,
we do not deny the magistrate the right of the sword; but though
he may use it, a private man never may. The government will
always find enough who are willing to go to war, apart from true
Christians. It should not compel the latter to take up arms.
Indeed, to overwhelm his Jewish enemies, Christ used Gentiles,
not Christians. The teachings of the Sermon on the Mount were
proclaimed to all and are binding on all men. Christ forbade his
disciples to seek punishment and vengeance by way of the courts.
Meanwhile, according to Palaeologus, a man who does not seek
vengeance sins; no barbarian religion commands this. The
command to love one's enemies means more than an express
forbidding of war. The Old Testament did not bid a man to love
his enemies but commanded the avenging of public wrongs lest the
State be flouted, for God placed the happiness of the Jews in the
maintenance of a temporal State. In the Kingdom of Christ no
man may hate another, for the enemy there is not man, but
Satan, and the fight should be against him, hence with spiritual
weapons.

And what if war should break out by the command of God?
There is no such war. If people and government in concert
command a war, then it is said that God stands behind them. On
this view, almost all wars would be by command of God. Frequently the stronger part of the nation desires war, and the
government with it—are we to regard that part with which
the government goes as thereby the better? In that case it
would be better simply to acknowledge that the government itself is predominant and decisive. A command of the government
is not a divine mandate; how many times has a government
declared an unjust war! Nothing has ever become just by
government decree.

The result of concession in favor of an allegedly just war is
that today a people takes up arms even against its sovereign,
and they (the allusion here is through Palaeologus to the Calvinists) give encouragement to this and even publish books in

this spirit.[4] France and the Netherlands especially bear witness to this, being imbrued in the blood of brothers because the people, or a part of them, were persuaded that it was right for them to wage war against their own government. They glorify those who fell in these wars as martyrs of Christ. Excellent defenders of the magistrate are those who arm the people against the magistrate, proclaiming kings to be tyrants! If they imitated those whom they brand as revolutionists, the power of the magistrate would not be overthrown, and instead of a multitude of secret fighters, plunderers, rapers, murderers, we should have at least a handful of true martyrs for Christ's sake.

If Christian people only waged wars commanded by Christ, then they would certainly undertake no war. Christ did not show Christians earth, but heaven, so why should they kill men?

The *second* part is taken up with an analysis of the reply of Palaeologus and supports the attitude of the Racovians against his criticism. The Racovians justly affirm that only the magistrate may punish an injury; but private persons may not claim from the magistrate punishment of wrong-doers. It is a calumny when they affirm that a believer may not take oath on the command of the magistrate. A man may do this, if it is a question of discovering the truth; it is a different matter, however, if a private party is to take oath in connection with carrying an injury to law for his own advantage. The authorities are not forbidden to inflict punishment for injuries, insofar as they take action officially, or upon the complaint of anybody who is not a true disciple of Christ.

To love and to punish are not always mutually contradictory,

---

[4] The reference is to the published writings of the so-called anti-monarchists, especially famous works like Junius Brutus' *Vindiciae contra tyrannos* (1579). Simultaneously Czechowic was attacking the Calvinists in his *Rozsądek na wykład katechizmu Gilowskiego* (*A Judgment on the interpretation of Gilowski's Catechism*) (1591), K. 3f: "Does not his Church defend its faith, even as the Roman Church does, with sword, fire, and halter? Does it not have within itself fights, battles, defeats; and besides, subjects opposed to its own authority, as is proved by affairs in France, and all under the cover of religion."

but if a man prays God for punishment of an enemy, does he do this out of love for him? That would be a strange love of his neighbor. According to Palaeologus, a man should not ignore an injury, still less pardon it, in which case a Christian would be worse even than those famous pagans, who forgave injuries out of innate mildness. If, for the glory of God, we have to take care that injuries are punished, then every man ought to inform against himself when he does something wrong. What a torture-chamber the Christian religion would become! The words of Christ do not, however, exclude every form of punishment, but relate to capital punishment, with which the Racovians are concerned.

To withdraw from the world, at which Palaeologus so scoffs, means to avoid the companionship of ungodly and carnal men. If in consequence of love of a higher order, love of God, a man is not attached to temporal things, then it is not desertion.

The Racovians are accused of not permitting the holding of offices. This is not an absolute prohibition. A Christian may even be King; but two reservations bind him: (1) only Christ may be the King of the Christian Church; (2) a Christian may not shed blood, even if he should hold office (whether the second is right, Socinus adds, does not come into the question, for it does not affect the present discussion). The first principle the Racovians are bound to emphasize, for if there is not another, a terrestrial, King of the Christian Church, then, in the first place, the Christian kingdom and estate are superterrestrial, and for the sake of defending them a man should not cause loss to his neighbor; in the second place, there is no earthly power that can permit what Christ forbade, and hence no power can command revenge. Thus, understanding that a Christian is not free to do everything that others do, and especially to shed blood, they do not allow their members to accept office, so that they cannot send their neighbors to death. If it were possible to hold office without violating Christ's commands, then a Christian might rule. Government itself the Racovians do not condemn *per se;* its unpleasant functions result only from the sins of the world. A man may therefore not serve as magistrate among non-Christians, though nothing would hinder his being King or an official among Christians or God-fearing people. Socinus indignantly repels the insinuation that the Racovians themselves wished to grasp in their own hands the authority of the magistrate.

The *third* part refutes the chief arguments adduced by Palaeologus against the Racovians. First, in the matter of war. Palaeologus calls a man who does not take part in a defensive war a deserter, but for the Racovians such courage is inferior to Christian courage. Palaeologus goes with the world. Would to God that he went on from worldly prudence to heavenly; for in comparison with heavenly goods earthly ones are worthless.

The Racovians command the payment of taxes: do they thereby countenance the war to which the tax-money is applied? As the tax-money belongs to the government, a man may not refuse to pay it; it does not matter what the government does with it. In speaking of prohibition against war, we do not refer to the government but to the private man. What is forbidden to a Christian is yet of itself alone not necessarily bad. So, then, if a private man goes to war (insofar as his action is not limited merely to frightening the enemy away), he must be excluded from Christ's kingdom; but if the war is just, he does no wrong provided only he does not pretend to be a disciple of Christ. Christ did not need either to approve or to condemn war; he only forbade his disciples to take part in it.

A Christian has to obey the magistrate as God, though the magistrate be wicked or a pagan, and not to spare his own life at the summons of the magistrate, provided his commands do not conflict with Christ's. For in that event it is impossible to obey the official, though the world were to fall. Meanwhile today they erroneously assume that for the glory of God a man may act in opposition even to his own King.

Palaeologus suggests that the Racovians consented to act as guards in war and to furnish hired soldiers. As to being on guard, Socinus is of a different opinion; a man cannot so act without killing the enemy. It is permitted to hire soldiers provided the hiring is not done directly, i.e. if the matter amounts to a tax from which the government enlists its soldiers.

A Christian does not fight in defense of frontiers, for he is a pilgrim in a foreign land, who has to fight only for heaven; nor does he fight in defense of peace, for a man may not put love of peace above love of God. Should a man kill his neighbor to fulfill the command of love? He should let himself be killed rather than kill others. Let us leave concern about peace to God. A man can always find a way to avoid breaking the commands of God. Those who take up arms against their kings in defense of religion proceed unlawfully; they merely show their own disregard of God; a man should suffer death sooner than repulse violence by arms, for in the latter case he is in reality defending not God but his own life and property.

Palaeologus charges the Racovians with desertion, as if they avoided war out of cowardice. It is impossible to make such a charge, for their position, even if it be mistaken, is founded on religious commands. A Christian has no native land on earth; he sees no difference in the country to which he belongs as compared with other lands; he may prize it somewhat more highly than others, but he may also prefer another country to his own. For it is one thing to be a political man, another to be a Christian; to the latter, a god-fearing foreigner is his true fellow-citizen and may be nearer to him than his whole earthly fatherland.

Is it right to go to war if a man does not kill or wound anyone there? Yes, if he thereby saves himself from greater danger, for example loss of life, which must not be risked too lightly, but only when God or a neighbor's good requires it. But before this a Christian must declare to the official that he will not kill with a weapon. He may, however, hold a weapon in his hand. He may not approve of those fanatical foes of arms who do not strike a dog or a wolf, even when the beasts do not scruple to

rend an innocent flock. Such superstition is a menace to true
piety. It is quite the same when it comes to defending wives
and daughters from attackers; it is permissible to frighten off
the latter, provided one does not strike them or return evil for
evil. Not all resistance to evil is forbidden, but only punishment and revenge, hence shouting, railing, and frightening are
not forbidden.

On the second fundamental point of doubt, the punishment
of wrongs by the magistrate, Socinus judges that the injured
person may have recourse to a court for the return of things
taken from him, provided he does not demand punishment. If
the Racovians understood otherwise, he would not have undertaken to defend their view. Christ only forbids the injured
party to seek punishment of the wrong-doer by the court. Only
the authorities may take measures for punishment, officially,
or when someone informs them of an injury. A man may, however, make a complaint before a court without threatening his
opponent with punishment. Thus he may, for example, demand
repayment of a loan, for this does not bring punishment upon
the debtor. It is more dangerous to demand the return of things
that have been stolen, for there are heavy punishments for
robbers; today the magistrate hangs them even for small thefts.
It is therefore permissible to demand restitution only if this does
not bring down punishment on the wrong-doer. It is another
thing if the magistrate himself calls the wrong-doer to account;
then the judge may punish him, for the court metes out punishment for the satisfaction not only of the injured person but also
of the State.

The *fourth* part Socinus devotes to attacking subsidiary statements by Palaeologus, with especial violence when it is a question of nailing down Palaeologus' inclination to give the
legislation of Moses precedence over the teaching of Christ.
Socinus admits that he comes forward against Palaeologus lest
anybody should suspect the Racovians of sharing the Greek's
errors, and also denies him the right to call the Racovians

brethren, which is an affront to them, since they are not included in one Church with Palaeologus.

The above summary elucidates the thought of Socinus as faithfully as possible without, however, giving a complete picture of his work, which is a tedious theological discussion, only rarely enlivened by outbursts of irony or indignation, or again by the effects of his keen logic.

On the whole, Socinus supported the fundamental ideas of the Polish Anabaptists. The State is not a Christian organization, and true members of the Church do not enter its service but have to realize the teaching of Christ in the life of the Church. War, even when defensive, cannot be reconciled with the duties of a Christian: the Church must be absolutely pacifist. The law of the sword, insofar as it expresses itself through the punishment of transgressors by the government, is not a Christian institution. Believers can neither take advantage of it nor cooperate with it. For a Christian it is inadmissible to hold any office with which this law is linked. In support of these theses Socinus employed immense theological learning and a talent for penetrating logic. He defended the conception of relations with the State to which the Racovians gave expression—a conception which fundamentally separated them from the rest of society and from all other confessions, making out of them architects of a different society.

And yet in the work of Socinus there breathes a spirit different from that felt in the arguments of Gregory Paulus, which in a marked degree breathe the atmosphere of a radical sectarianism. Socinus had a deeper understanding of vital reality, a greater practical sense, which he derived from Italian social conditions and life at the court of the Medicis of Tuscany. He also took into account the duty of defending the Anabaptists from the danger that was gathering around their heads.

Socinus therefore moderates extremes of doctrine which now bordered on the absurd, now threatened the Racovians with the anger of the government. He avoids whatever might smack

of social revolution, does not bring forward the problem of
the poor and poverty, does not complain against wealth, does
not undermine property but rather recognizes it, permitting the
possession of money, the loaning of it at interest, and reminders
for its return. He does not proclaim unconditional avoidance of
courts and refusal to take oaths. He does not advocate absolute
passivity before an aggressor and strict non-resistance to evil,
allowing milder, bloodless means of defense. He does not
approve a too easy disposal of one's life, and permits of certain
compromises to save it. He commands the payment of taxes,
even though they undoubtedly go to pay for war and mercenary
soldiers. At that period, when general military service was
unknown and even those bound to it personally were allowed to
substitute other persons for themselves, this concession made
it possible to avoid conflicts with the authority of the State even
at critical moments.

And what is most important, while fundamentally upholding
the pacifism of Christians and their passive or neutral relation
to the organization of the State, Socinus binds them to an unlimited obedience to the State authority: that is, he forbids
any manifestations of rebellion or resistance in a matter which
loosened the hands of all the confessions of the time, even the
most monarchist, and justified action against their rulers—the
religious question. If king or government violated consciences
and compelled men to profess a religion they regarded as false
or blasphemous, both Catholics and Calvinists felt absolved
from obedience and flew to arms. According to Socinus, in such
a case Christians must remain passive and rather risk death. All
"sedition," which was thought to be threatening from the side of
the Anabaptists and was so alarming to kings, was thereby pre-
cluded.

Socinus' work, issued secretly and anonymously, was not
destined to achieve immediate fame, but it attracted the attention of persons actively interested in this important question.
The author himself sent a copy immediately after its appearance

to his benefactor, the aged Dr. Blandrata in Transylvania. There the work made an unfavorable impression. Another emigrant from Italy, Marcello Squarcialupi,[5] also an Antitrinitarian and a physician, having read the book through at one sitting during the night, wrote to Socinus on his own and Blandrata's behalf, reproaching him. They did not consider that the controversy undertaken by Socinus was required. The matter of the magistrate was not necessary to salvation; more important was true knowledge of God, and a holy life. Why did he attack such an influential writer as Palaeologus in defense of the chimaeras of the Racovians? Their crazy dreams ought not to be identified with the Christian Church. Socinus, as a foreign immigrant, should not discourage government. Finally, Squarcialupi blamed him for being aggressive and presumptuous, and considered it tactless in him to attack anonymously an author who signed his name.

Socinus defended himself in a long letter,[6] emphasizing chiefly the fact that he was called into the controversy by those most concerned in it, and that it was very injurious to the Church to leave Palaeologus' calumnies unanswered. He had not spoken hastily, but had entered the controversy only when it was shown that there was no one else to defend the right view. To be sure, the majority of persons from the old Raków were living, but away from Raków, and on more than one point they thought differently and had completely changed the view that once attracted them to Raków. Moreover, he was not defending the acts of the old Racovians, but only one view of theirs in which they were in the right. If a man should avoid running risks, this caution did not extend to divine affairs. The question of the magistrate was not unimportant, not window dressing, but a wall in the building of Christendom. He entertained the hope that

[5] Letter from Alba Julia, Sept. 15, 1581, in *Bibliotheca Fratrum Polonorum, Socini Opera*, i, 359f.

[6] From Cracow, Nov. 20, 1581, *op. cit.*, pp. 361-68. The original is in the Chapter archives at Alba Julia (Gyulafehérvár); cf. *Sprawozdanie z poszukiwań na Węgrzech* (Cracow:1919), p. 131.

posterity would not disapprove this work of his. If his tone seemed harsh, then Palaeologus was to blame; the reply was rather mild, considering the damage done by Palaeologus, who had spread the infection of his judaizing from Transylvania and Hungary into Lithuania where, under the influence of Budny the churches had already almost torn themselves away from the Polish Brethren. As to his writing anonymously, he made no secret of his authorship and was aware from the beginning that his name would be known to Palaeologus.

Socinus deceived himself if he expected that by his arguments he would dispel the suspicions against the Anabaptists. His work was complained of to Batory as being hostile to the authority of the State. The priest Jerome Powodowski declared to the King in 1582, "Both in the Tribunal at Lublin and also here in my native place [Poznań] where I dwell among these poisonous scorpions, I could no longer endure it when certain exiles from other lands made bold to run in haste to your Royal Majesty's kingdom." He ascribed to them "a certain offense against worldly authority, a certain work about which, openly published and sent through me, Your Royal Majesty deigned to have in his hand."[7] Batory did indeed take notice of Socinus' book and gave ear to its accusers. Warned of this, Socinus left Cracow and took refuge in the country with Christopher Morsztyn, owner of Pawlikowice near Wieliczka. Rumor of the King's anger spread widely. In Vienna, for example, it was reported that Socinus had fled from Poland on account of his book against the magistrate. To clear himself from blame, therefore, Socinus sent an explanation to the Duke and Duchess of Tuscany.[8]

[7] *Wędzidło na sprosne błędy a bluźnierstwa nowych arjanów . . . i pokonanie ich w Rozmowie Marcina Czechowica opisanych* (*A Check upon the obscene errors and blasphemies of the new Arians . . . and refutation of those contained in the* Dialogue *of Martin Czechowic*) (Poznań:1582), p. 63. To Batory, who did not know Polish, Powodowski certainly sent not the *Rozmowy* of Czechowic but the Latin book of Socinus.

[8] Cf. his letter to Dudith, March 6, 1583, in *Bibliotheca Fratrum Polonorum*, i, 509.

He also took advantage of the kindness shown him by the Chancellor of the Prince of Transylvania, Martin Berzewiczy, who was staying with the King, and asked him to conciliate Batory.[9]

I should have been glad, he writes him, to set out to thank you, but I decided not to leave my friendly hiding-place as long as the King (whom I honor most after God and my lord Francesco, Duke of Tuscany) does not change his opinion (which he has taken from malicious men) that I have written a book in favor of destroying the authority of government. It is not true. There the discussion is not of the authority of the government, but of the duties of private Christians, which certainly strengthen the government. On the basis of Holy Scripture, indeed, I grant government more than anybody else, more than the law of nations, or the civil law, more even than the general opinion of the theologians. Socinus therefore begs Berzewiczy to convince the King of this and to appease his anger; to this end his friend Resmini will point out to him paragraphs in the book testifying how high Socinus places the magistrate.

The situation began to grow threatening for the Anabaptists when the Catholic Church, which hitherto had taken little account of the very extreme sect, came out against them. A learned theologian, the priest Jerome Powodowski, who as deputy of the clergy at the Tribunal had opportunity rather frequently to observe the Lublin Church, studied Czechowic's *Rozmowy Chrystjańskie* thoroughly, debated at Lublin in 1579 with Jan Niemojewski, and at Smigiel with Jan Krotowicjusz, the minister there, and at the end of 1582 published the large volume entitled *A Check upon the Obscene Errors and Blasphemies of the Neo-Arians*. He dedicated it to the King, and the primate Karnkowski himself furnished it with a warm recommendation. Powodowski with unusual passion attacked the Lublin Church, and especially Czechowic, heaping insults upon him and repeatedly calling him a beast. Branding

[9] Letter of March 12, 1583, *ibid.*, i, 493.

Czechowic's arguments on the question of the deity of Christ as blasphemous, he called for the avenging hand of the government against nonsense so obscene and absurd, that "such heads would be worthy not of Holy Scripture or its arguments, but of the rope, prison, and after that something worse." [10]

He constantly insisted that the rejection of ecclesiastical authority by the Anabaptists contained signs of revolt against the authority of the State as well:

The Pope acknowledges the temporal authority of emperors, kings and others appointed in their places, and himself grants them his confirmation or blessing on these stations. But the Anabaptists, wherever and however they can, free themselves from this authority, themselves transferring it to their little church, even on the little spot where it sits among the reeds. [11]

How far this disobedience to the authorities, now not only spiritual but also temporal, has spread, especially in this Anabaptist sect [he complains in another passage[12]]; this and other shameful things Daniel Bieliński recalls, and describes their recent course in the books of his *Odwołanie* [*Recantation*]. But they themselves, not by oral and secret teaching now but in a work openly published,[13] prove that it is not necessary for a subject to listen to the authorities when they wish to employ him in war, but this has to be submitted to each man's conscience.

They irritated Powodowski the more since in general the Anabaptists were not nobles—he was evidently here thinking of the two congregations which he knew, Lublin and Smigiel—but "peasants, turners, planers, skinners, linen-weavers, blockheads, and other dregs of the human race." [14]

---

[10] P. 11.

[11] P. 4. The allusion is to the site of their church building at Lublin: "But these Neo-Arians, having abandoned the fertile lands of their native places, are removing to the sandy ground in the wilderness at Raków . . . , also under Lublin wall near the water and almost by the reeds, where their master Lucifer dwells."

[12] P. 174.

[13] Powodowski here has in mind the Latin supplement to Czechowic's *Dialogue, De vita et moribus primitivae Ecclesiae.*

[14] P. 178.

## 8 Budny's Dispute with the Anabaptists of Little Poland

The Little Polanders versus Budny. Synod at Lubecz. Budny's work. Confession about the authorities. Wilkowski's attack. Czechowic's defense. Niemojewski supports the doctrine. Budny condemns it.

Socinus' work reached Palaeologus in Moravia. Being attacked, he intended to prepare a reply, but was delayed for lack of a copy of his own work; the only one which he obtained from Budny he had given Dudith, hence he sent to Lithuania for another. Before it arrived, however, Palaeologus was sent under arrest to Italy, where he never left the Papal prison.[1]

The Anabaptists of Little Poland, relying on Socinus' book, resolved to force the Lithuanian brethren to abandon their position or to remove refractory members from the Church. They therefore called on them to convoke a synod at Iwie in January, 1582, although they themselves did not attend it. The matter did not come to a debate until March, at the synod at Lubecz near Nowogródek, in the presence of Kiszka. From Lublin came the ablest representatives of the Church: Niemojewski, Czechowic, Nicholas Zytno, Peter Domaniewski, Peter Lubieniecki, and several of the younger members. The debate on the magistrate began March 6. Budny proposed to take into

[1] This information, as well as what follows, is taken from Budny's *Urząd miecza*.

97

consideration the limited question: "Whether it is fitting for a Christian man to hold an office with the right of the sword, or not." The Little Polanders broadened the scope of the discussion, demanding a general debate on the theme: "What is a Christian life supposed to be?" This is in accordance with the already mentioned Dialogue of Czechowic, who was the chief defendant of the Raków thesis at Lubecz also. Czechowic supported the view hostile to the magistrate with his old arguments, but his opponents were not satisfied by them. To facilitate the discussion, they demanded written arguments, while Budny also wrote down his own. The whole day following was filled with stubborn discussion. The Little Polanders were forced to seek for new arguments and finally, being unable to convince the Lithuanians, they broke off the discussion and departed, having first taken steps for removing from their position Lithuanian ministers who seemed to them suspect both in their doctrine about the magistrate and—this certainly above all—in their doctrine about the deity of Christ. Indeed, Budny's group inclined to non-adorantism, i.e. non-payment of divine honors to Christ.

After the departure of the Polish Brethren, Budny decided to come out publicly in defense of his position. Foreseeing a complete break with the Little Poland Church, perhaps upon hearing that the synod of Lucławice regarded him as unworthy of the title of minister and brother, he proceeded to an open discussion with his opponents. He did not shrink from revealing a fundamental difference and, to illustrate the dispute, he gathered the extensive material which affords us such a precious historical picture: the minutes of the synod at Iwie in 1568, Krowicki's letter to Budzyński in 1573, his own reply to Ronemberg, together with the confession of the Lithuanian Church on the sovereign power (undated, but certainly freshly drawn up).

The substance of the publication was to be "a defense of the magistrate," divided into two parts, corresponding to the course of the Lubecz synod. The first part contained "the arguments of those who say that it is unfitting for a Christian to hold office," arguments taken from the *Rozmowy chrystjańskie* of Czechowic, with the additions brought forward at Lubecz, all, obviously, accompanied by criticism. The second and positive part embraced the "chief arguments from Holy Scripture, that a Christian may hold an office enjoying the right of the sword," that is, proofs of the author's thesis developed in detail with the assistance of corroborative evidence for each one in turn. To the whole Budny prefixed a foreword to the reader, in which he traced the historical course of the controversy from the appearance of Peter of Goniądz up to that moment. To this were added some dedicatory verses by Alexander Chomętowski (on the magistrate and on Budny's book), by Fabian Domanowski, and by Budny (on the arms of Christopher Lasota, Cupbearer of Lublin). In a letter dated January 23, 1583, the author dedicated the whole book to the same Lasota, whose guest Budny was on his return from Lucławice in 1578, and who surely sympathized with his views. It is significant that although the work *O urzędzie miecza używającym* came out in the type of the press at Łosk,[2] this was not indicated on the title page nor did Budny dedicate the work to Kiszka. Undoubtedly, the Little Polanders had already been able to shake the confidence of his patron. The book was published at the cost of Alexander Chomętowski, January 28, 1583.

Socinus' treatise did not discourage Budny. Mentioning it, he conceded that though "learned, it is written not so much against Palaeologus' opinion as against Palaeologus himself, as an attentive reader can easily perceive." He had thus noticed the deviation of Socinus from the rigor of the Racovian doctrine. For him, however, these concessions were not enough. He desired to defend the clear position to which he had already given expression in his catechism twenty years before. He did

[2] In 4o, unnumbered pp. 8+136+12 of index.

not, to be sure, claim to possess adequate talents, but he believed in the justice of his thesis: "I am aware of the fact that
there was need of a writer with a better turn for this rôle, and
more polished in his Polish, but where shall we get these
Italians?" He was angered by the absoluteness of the Little
Polanders, who in such a difficult matter allowed no freedom
of opinion but imposed their own view: "Do not let us introduce
the Papacy anew into the Church of God, or dig pits for one
another . . . do no let us lord it over anyone's faith."

Budny expressed his teaching concisely in the confession of the
Lithuanian Church on the sovereign power. Starting from the
basis that all power, whether good or evil, is derived from God,
he asserts that all kings and sovereigns are servants and anointed
of God. Hence also "all citizens of any country, without ex-
ception, but especially Christians" are absolutely bound to
render them obedience and honor. They may not rebel, even
though the ruler were to govern them tyrannically and take away
their property and life. Hence he condemns the peasant revolts
in Germany and the riots at Münster. One must pray for one's
rulers, even though they be non-Christians, and not only pay
all kinds of taxes but even perform service in war . . . faithfully and without making complaint." Only if they were to command something against God, must one not obey, but rather
suffer death. If office is a good thing, then a ruler or lesser
official may belong to the Church. It is fitting for a faithful
Christian to hold office, even that of king. Only adherence to
the Church binds a king to obey the Christian ideal. And here
Budny points out those kingly virtues discussed by political and
hortatory literature, ancient and renaissance, especially com-
mending the counsel of Modrzewski's *de Emendanda Republica*,
of which Budny himself had published a Polish translation
(Łosk, 1577). A Christian king is allowed to have wealth, money,
jewels, "but must be on his guard lest he have it through over-
working his serfs." He is bound to read Holy Scripture, to up-

root idolatry from the hearts of his serfs, and to take care lest "needless drones eat his bread in vain while poor folk and orphans miserably suffer distress from hunger or cold under hedges, or even die." These instructions call for the combating of the Church and clergy of Rome. The final conclusion is that a man of any calling or office may be admitted to the Church if he accepts the true faith, "be he King, Emperor, Prince or Duke, Hetman, Palatine, Count, Starost, Lieutenant, Burgomaster, Bailiff, even a soldier." In short, all the exclusiveness which gave the Church the character of a protest against the existing structure of the political and social world of that time is abolished.

Budny does not proceed to break with the ideology of the Anabaptists to the point of defending war, but he champions the right of the Christian to seek from the authorities punishment for a wrong-doer. He reproaches the Church with giving too broad an application to Christ's command not to resist evil. On the one hand, this command cannot refer to the magistrate, who punishes transgressors on a divine injunction, nor on the other to a man who in a private sphere checks abuses—such as a landlord chastising a servant or a father reprimanding a child. Otherwise both Church and the social and political organism must decay. If in such cases it is permissible to resist evil, it is impossible to condemn the government and the magistrate. A man who has been wronged and resorts to the magistrate is not returning evil for evil, "for it is not evil that anyone thus receives according to his deserts from the magistrate or the law, since it is not evil, but sacred justice, which cannot be considered as evil; but it is evil when a man takes anything of mine from me and I take from him as much or twice as much, as generally happens."

Regarding the law of the sword as a deposit from God in the hands of the government, Budny criticizes the dislike of the civil government sown among the Anabaptists by Peter of

Goniądz and countenanced by Czechowic.[3] Both men, appealing
to the history of the giving of a king to the Jews in the person of
Saul, when Jehovah did not at once gratify the Jews' demands,
had given it to be understood that "God does not like the so-
called office of king." According to Budny, God was offended
only by the fact that the Jews desired a change of rule although
Judge Samuel was living. Even at present the acknowledgment
of a king in Christ does not prevent resort in temporal affairs
to an earthly king; that would amount to the same as not being
allowed in illness to call a physician because Christ is the
physician of the faithful. From these arguments it is evident
that in the last analysis Budny, in contrast to other Anabaptists, recognizes the great importance of temporal affairs
and does not regard concern about them as opposed to the
obligations of Christians. We also learn from Budny that Peter
of Goniądz was the author of the statement that "to put a
believer in office is nothing else than to bring him into the world
and commend him to the world." Budny does not consent to
lessen the authority of the royal office by such teachings: God
himself had ordered David to be anointed as king; if many kings
and officials live in a worldly way, having no care for eternal
life, it does not follow that this is the fault of "these holy offices";
it is the fault of the men.

On social matters also, Budny opposes the traces of Anabaptist doctrine which, through Peter of Goniądz, had pene-
trated to the Racovians. He does not agree that poverty alone
is the condition of salvation. If God has called a man to a
higher station in society, then "indeed it may be better that such
a one rather than another in rags should bear and know such

---

[3] Exalting the greatness of Christ as sovereign of the world, Czechowic
contrasts him with earthly kings: "He has from God the Father his power,
sovereignty, Kingdom, and whatever he has; but they arrive at this by
craft, treachery, jealousy, force, and other wicked devices, but meanwhile
with the wrath of God (as Saul in his kingdom)." From *Rozsądek na wyk-
lad katechizmu Gilowskiego* (*A Judgment on Gilowski's exposition of the
catechism*) (Cracow:1581).

duties and honors, for the Lord God does not take into account either brocades or rags, but looks on the pure heart and the one that loves him." As twenty years before, so also now, Budny regards the existence of serfdom in Christendom as a natural condition, and in particular holds that in Poland "a noble, though a private citizen, may inflict capital punishment on a slave, and also on a serf." He regards it as an Anabaptist superstition to forbid a minister to hold serfs: "they would rather have the ministers of the Church of God both wander about and beg than live honestly like the Apostles, having both houses and servants."

The public airing of troublesome disputes, the uncovering of internal differences, the emphasis upon the aversion to civil and social order which existed in the Church, the suspected prevalence of a doctrine advocating appropriation to the Church of the attributes of sovereign power, the calling of attention to Czechowic as head of this trend and an Anabaptist Pope, must all have called forth among the Little Polanders indignation against Budny—all the more since what he said made Powodowski's charges seem more credible and furnished new material against the Anabaptists, whom he described outright as "anarchists," that is, opponents of civil authority and social order. The most recent apostate from the Church at Lublin, Kasper Wilkowski, drew freely from Budny in his book published at the end of that year, *Przyczyny nawrócenia do wiary powszechnej od sekt nowokrzczeńców* (*Causes of my conversion to the Catholic faith from the sects of the Anabaptists*); he took him as witness that the Church was appropriating to itself "the power of government, punishment, law-making, and teaching." From the *Urząd miecza* Wilkowski extracted the Anabaptist canons against war, courts, and offices. To these he added sneering charges that members of the Church acted hypocritically: that they did not sell and distribute their estates to the poor, and that they winked at the holding of offices by influential nobles but on the other hand did not allow a poor man even to accept a bailiff's office or a clerkship in a market town.[4]

It was impossible to leave unanswered attacks falling from so many sides at once. The Anabaptists did not wish, however, to begin a controversy with Budny, perhaps in order not to enter into a detailed discussion of so many ticklish and dangerous questions. Instead they replied to him indirectly in their controversy with Powodowski and Wilkowski.

In his *Epistomium na Wędzidło* (*Epistomium to the Check, etc.*), Czechowic charged Powodowski with want of good faith, with intentional and deliberate defamation of the Anabaptists before King Stephen, as though they opposed secular authority. In the first place, argues Czechowic,[5] nothing of the sort is found in his writings. If either the King himself or any honest judge were to read these writings through, "he would not say that there was anything in them which would lead *ad seditionem*, to riot and rebellion in the Republic, and not rather to all kinds of Christian submission to every earthly authority according to what the word of God teaches." Czechowic here appeals above all to his work, *Trzech dni Rozmowa* (*A three days' conversation*), today unknown, in which he had gathered "in brief all that we hold about authority,[6] so that he who despises it and exalts himself above it (although already our false brother [Budny], having abjured the truth, now slanders me together with others and distorts my words) for this will render account to God." Czechowic further appeals to the testimony of outsiders, who sometimes drop in at the Lublin church, as well as to "some little songs of our own in our catechisms, written by us."

Czechowic is provoked yet more by the suspicion that the

---

[4] *Przyczyny nawrócenia*, p. 36f.

[5] *Epistomium* (1583), p. 55f.

[6] Of this work we know only from Sandius (*Bibliotheca Antitrinitariorum*, pp. 50, 174), who gave its title in Latin: *Trium dierum colloquium* (*in quo Christianus, Evangelicus et Pontificius introducuntur loquentes*) *de quibusdam articulis fidei, praecipue vero de Paedobaptismo*. It was written, at Nieśwież, January 6, 1565, for the use of Nicholas the Black Radziwiłł, but was not published until 1578 at Łosk at Kiszka's expense.

Anabaptists have broken away from secular authority, "themselves transferring it to their little church, even on the little spot where it sits among the reeds":

> He speaks against reason in thus declaring something which contradicts all the senses, which show something else to those among whom we dwell, opposed to the many calumnies which assail us without shame from many of them. Among the latter there are [again an allusion to Budny] those who would wish to drag the office of the sword into their Church, apparently calling themselves also our brethren; but we are resisting them, wishing always to show that we are gladly content with the magistracy given of God to us together with the others; God is witness of this, we are not setting up another for ourselves, for that under which we live is good for us. . . . He speaks also even contrary to experience and himself. . . . Insulting us in his own way, he mentions that some of our brethren, having abandoned the fertile lands of their native places, are removing to the sandy ground in the wilderness at Raków. I know not whether they serve the kingdom or now serve the appropriation to themselves of authority and oversight, which others, who enjoyed them before they did, freely let go, showing notable humility . . . For it is no small thing to call a man king, and to accuse him of taking sovereignty upon himself, and nevertheless to affirm of him that he, having abandoned the fertile lands of his native place, yes even the magistracy, takes refuge on a patch among the reeds or in the wilderness on sandy ground, having withdrawn from men, and founds a new kingdom in Raków.[7]

In the *Odpowiedź na potwarzy Wilkowskiego* (*Reply to the calumnies of Wilkowski*),[8] Jan Niemojewski refutes Budny's charge that the Church had passed laws forbidding holders of secular offices to belong to it, as well as prohibiting the faithful from engaging in war and lawsuits. Such laws the Church has not passed, but only conforms to the teaching of Christ; adhering to its spirit, his members avoid "quarrels, going to law, wars,

[7] p. 405f.
[8] Appended to *Okazanie, iż Kościół rzymski papieski nie jest apostolski ani święty ani jeden ani powszechny* (Demonstration that the popish Roman Church is not apostolic nor holy nor one nor catholic) (1584), printed by Rodecki at Cracow.

and murdering one another." "As sons of God true Christians do not trouble themselves overmuch about temporal damage and loss, nor the division of their property, for they know that they have a better inheritance in heaven, nor do they too much fear those who kill the body, knowing that they cannot kill the soul."

Niemojewski tries to discuss relations to the civil power in greater detail. Secular authority is established by God to ensure justice, to punish the wicked and their crimes, and to protect the good. Christians respect the authorities for this, yet themselves, "being called to something greater and more perfect, do not concern themselves with such things." "Although it befits those who are in the world, and have not yet tasted true fellowship with Christ the Lord in his holy spirit, to hold office and use the sword, but justly, yet it is not worthy of those who are already called to something else and to greater perfection." The first Christians observed this; but with time, when they began to mingle too much in the affairs of the world, their customs changed, they admitted kings and emperors to the Church, were unable to explain the Christian customs to them, and "knowing that it was hard to put the meek and lowly yoke of Christ on these bisons, they consented to the existence of officials in the Church and confined the prohibition against the holding of offices of the sword to the clergy only. In this way they introduced two kinds of Christians: the one bound to cherish the spirit of Christ, and these they called the clergy, and the other kind, "who have not the spirit of Christ, who are entangled in worldly things, and who are called men of the world." Already by this division it was indicated that a man who wants to be a clergyman and to employ spiritual armor (which should apply to all Christians) may not hold office or make war with carnal weapons. If the Roman Church does not care about carrying out this rule of Christ and allows its lay faithful to do what it forbids to the clergy, it does not follow from this that those who conform to it should be condemned.

It appears from the above that Niemojewski wholly supports

the doctrine of the Church on the incompatibility of the office of the sword with Christianity, and that the arguments of Budny had in no wise been able to weaken it. Everything that could savor of disobedience to the authorities or arouse a suspicion of the appropriation to the Church of any of the functions of government is removed from it; but the irreconcilable position, declining to allow the State the character of a Christian institution and its functionaries the name of good Christians, is maintained.

But as a sincere man, Niemojewski cannot conceal the fact that their doctrine is opposed to the demands of actual life; hence he admits that the Church cannot observe it absolutely, and it does not dismiss members who do not conform to it:

We (he declares with regret), although we should gladly see that all our brethren were advancing toward perfection, entirely observing their Christian duty, also showed our brethren how dangerous a thing it is to hold secular offices, for such men must often neglect and omit Christian duty and be occupied and involved in worldly affairs. Moreover, without this violation of conscience and profanation of the name of God they cannot hold office, for they are obliged frequently to countenance unjust laws and statutes such as are found among us in Poland and to witness an unjust and idolatrous oath. However, we do not forcibly press or constrain anyone to such perfection. There are among us many of those who, not having yet attained Christian patience, go to law for redress of their injuries. Finally, we still suffer among us even such as hold offices, and though we do not seek to win their favor, nor approve these things in them, yet we expect that they will do what they ought to do, not to please us but for God and Christ and their Christian duty.[9]

It is also worth noting how Niemojewski answers the charge that they did not follow the Gospel strictly in that they did not sell their estates and distribute to the poor. "This," he replies to

[9] Niemojewski inserted this polemic on the subject of the attitude to the State in reply to the seventh and eighth chapters of Wikowski's *Okazanie*, pp. 202-16, settling matters apparently with Wilkowski but really with Budny, whose criticisms Wilkowski merely quoted.

Wilkowski, "does not mean that those who have property, having sold all, should give to the poor, for they would soon have to beg for themselves, and those poor would soon grow rich and proud." In these words Christ only taught true kindness, which. does not grudge personal sacrifice in order to help a neighbor in need. Commanding men to feed the hungry, clothe the naked, take in the stranger, he showed that "he does not wish that those who follow him, being rich before, should at once become beggars," but only instructed them how to dispose of their property. But here also Niemojewski acknowledges in all simplicity that he is not satisfied with the existing practice of active brotherly love in the Church: "Although it is idle to excuse onself here, one must acknowledge the fact that as love is weak, so also there is not much kindness among us; but in this it is idle to throw the blame on the teaching of the holy Gospel, which is sincerely preached among us, but only on our weak faith and carnal coldness." Being himself of truly evangelical spirit, he does not mention that he personally sold all his estate in Kujawy in order to give to the poor, and that for this reason he was the object of false pity and derision.

Both Czechowic and Niemojewski treat Budny as an apostate. The Synod of 1584 condemned him anew and expelled him from the Church. As a reason they must have given in the first place his judaizing (also evident in his work *O urzędzie miecza*), for Kiszka, who had been his patron for many years, removed him from his ministry, which, as Starost of Zmudź,[10] he would not

[10] Budny's opponents, on the other hand, maintained relations with Kiszka. Czechowic turned to him in his great work *De paedobaptistarum errorum origine,* printed by Rodecki without a date, with a dedicatory preface dated April 7, 1575. This date is either given falsely or is a misprint for 1585.

This preface to Kiszka is very characteristic of Czechowic. While praising the Starost of Zmudź as the only one of the magnates who not only favors their Church but shows this publicly without regard to jibes and scoffing and even intends to submit to immersion, he at the same time reproaches him for thus far not entirely breaking with the world, and calls on him to withdraw from worldly affairs (certainly from the magistracy), lawsuits, quarrels, and wars. Hence, instead of the powerful Senator and

have done merely in defence of the magistracy. From then on, Budny disappears from the stage. But the thesis for which he fought was not smothered by his personal defeat. It sprang from the necessity of life, from a desire to remove from the Antitrinitarian Church the character of a closed sect, and to adapt it to the social situation of the time; thus it was slowly and imperceptibly to clear a way for itself, to make breaches in the rigorous doctrine of the Church, and to gain at first timid and then increasingly open adherence.[11]

influential defender, he would prefer to see in Kiszka a simple member of the Church. Kiszka, lord of 70 market towns and 400 villages, did not heed Czechowic's summons and did not resign the starosty of Żmudź, from which indeed he went on to the castellany of Wilno. To the end of his life, however, he remained faithful to Antitrinitarianism, and when he felt death approaching, July 6, 1592, he wrote with his own hand a confession of faith to prevent any false rumor that he had abandoned it (cf. J. Jasnowski's article "Peter of Goniądz" in *Przegląd Historyczny* (1935), p. 36.

[11] For Budny's role in the development of Unitarianism, cf. articles by S. Kot in the *Polish Dictionary of Biography*, III, 96-99; and in *Wiener Archiv für geschichte des Slawentums und Osteuropas*, II (1956), 63-118.

# 9  *Faustus Socinus Retracts*

Life in the Antitrinitarian community. Tendencies
toward revision. Concessions of Socinus. Discussions
at Raków in 1601 and 1602. Relaxation of ethical
and social severity. Ostorodt's separation from Anabaptism. Smalcius' dispute with Franz.

Thus after twenty years' opposition, Budny had lost the
struggle. The Church had sided with the radical tendency,
moderated, to be sure, and with the men who for twenty years
had pleaded for it, that is, Niemojewski and Czechowic. Vic-
torious, no longer having any opponent, and not attacked by
any, the teaching of the Church unexpectedly began to be
weakened and transformed.

Unfortunately we do not have a sufficient number of sources
to be able to trace this slow evolution in its beginnings. The
decade after Budny's *On the Office of the Sword* is the least
known period in the history of Antitrinitarianism. And at just
this time it went through a multiple internal crisis. Those who
had shaped the movement from its foundations died off with the
years, and with their passing the face of the Church changed.
Anabaptism, still defended against attacks from the outside, is
the object of stubborn internal quarrels which lead in the end to
questioning its reality and importance. The Church, hitherto
led exclusively by Poles, begins to be subject to the influence of
prominent foreigners, who submit more than one of the doctrines
of the Niemojewskis and Czechowices to re-examination. Socinus,

though not admitted to the Church by the old members, exercizes an increasing influence on the young adherents of Antitrinitarianism, both Polish and foreign; the new generation is somewhat less sectarian and more realistic, and under its influence the Antitrinitarian movement is transformed from Anabaptist to Socinian.

How strict life in the Antitrinitarian community in Poland appeared was described by Ostorodt, minister at Smigiel in Great Poland, in an epistle[1] to the group of Anabaptists at Strassburg in 1591:

We admit no one to our company who does not first receive baptism, cease to do evil and learn to do well, live not after the flesh but after the spirit, love not only his brethren but also his enemies, suffer violence and wrong, cease from war and quarrelling and not only do nothing of the sort but also not give any cause or support thereto. In this respect the Mennonites err not a little, who will not dress handsomely themselves but make handsome gowns for others, paint pictures, manufacture guns and like objects which the world needs for use and display.

If a brother or a sister has anything against a brother or a sister, they become reconciled to each other according to the teaching of Christ. If they do not succeed, then they call for the mediation of two or three more; and if these fail, then they are brought before the church, not in order to excommunicate them but to correct and reconcile them. But if a member is obstinate before the church, then he is excommunicated.

If a man causes offense by his sins, no account is taken of his rank, but he is punished publicly and is required to make a public repentance; or if he is stubborn, he is excommunicated, and that not to destroy him but to put him to shame, for no one shares food or drink with him until he comes to himself and sincerely repents, and then he may be saved.

We have elders, that is, teachers, overseers, and also ministers of the poor according to the tenor of Holy Scripture. Exhortations take place, as far as possible every day, together with public prayer, thanksgiving, and songs, according to the teach-

---

[1] Cf. Theodor Wotschke, "Ein dogmatisches Sendschreiben des Unitariers Ostorod," *Archiv für Reformationsgeschichte* (1915), pp. 137-54; from a Ms. in the Stadtbibliothek at Bern.

ing of Paul in a tongue that can be understood, for Poles in Polish, for Germans in German (I. Cor. xiv, 26).

Besides, we live at peace with all men. Indeed we should be glad to have fellowship with every man who calls on the name of the Lord Jesus and is obedient to him, so far as he wishes to live with us. For we well know that all who fear the Lord, work righteousness, and call on the Lord Jesus will be saved. Why should we not regard them as our brethren, though as yet they do not understand something? Only those who insolently oppose the truth, though in other respects they lead honest lives, we do not count as of our number.

For the community at Smigiel, composed predominantly of townspeople, it was comparatively easy to hold to the teaching of the Church. The demand for revision came from the nobility. A chronicle[2] ascribed to Radecke speaks of this:

In the years 1595, 1596, and 1597, someone explained to the brethren, especially to the nobility, that they could with clear conscience possess the estates, rights, and privileges of nobles, and bear arms, whereupon the aspect of the Church completely changed, especially among the nobility. They quite ceased to be different in appearance from the rest of their contemporaries, especially the women, who began to dress up, to take part in the wedding feasts of persons from the world and in other festivities. This gave rise to great unrest in the Church. The common people complained that they were treated with contempt. Though this was all evident and not to be denied, yet no one would admit being responsible for the change; the ministers especially tried to cast the blame on one another, but nothing did any good. They several times tried to find a remedy for this evil, but to no avail: the longer it went on, the worse it grew.

In the correspondence of Faustus Socinus we find confirmation of the evolution that took place in these years. He had increasingly often to reply to doubts expressed to him, and to questions from persons who found it burdensome to persist in extreme strictness; and each time he proceeded to certain in-

---

[2] Cf. Kazimierz Dobrowolski, "Nieznana kronika arjańska 1539-1605" ("An unknown Arian chronicle"), *Reformacja w Polsce,* IV (1926), 169.

dulgences and mitigations. Certainly his contact with the actual
conditions of Polish life during his four years at Pawlikowice
with Christopher Morsztyn, whose daughter he married in 1587,
had not been without influence upon him. Firstly he was asked in
1594 by Peter Stoiński, minister at Lucławice, about the question
of taking a complaint to the civil court. In a lengthy reply,[3]
Socinus developed views that he had already indicated in the
controversy with Palaeologus. Christ only forbade the seeking
of punishment for an injury; he did not forbid claims in court
to what is one's own, that is, to money, property, and compensation for injury, in cases where one seeks no damage to one's
neighbor, but simply one's own goods. If through the indemnifi-
cation the defendant suffers some unpleasantness, this is nevertheless not the intention of the complainant. It is permitted to
sue for one's own even should the guilty party receive some
penalty from the court, provided it is not beyond reason.

A further concession by Socinus is more important. As to
holding office, he argues, coming very close to Budny, that there
is nowhere any evidence or proof that this as such is forbidden
to Christians. Indeed, it follows from Paul that believers may
hold as slaves, over whom they have the right of life and death,
brethren and nonbrethren. Hence the flimsy argument that it
is not fitting for sheep to govern wolves falls to the ground. In
that event it would not be possible to hold slaves or, in Poland,
serfs; which would be a ridiculous paradox and a scandal.
*Imperium* and *dominatus* are not forbidden to Christians in
Scripture, but moderation is recommended in exercising them.

It appears from Socinus' letters that already at the previous
year's synod at Lublin he had, at the request of the brethren,
prepared an argument on this matter, but the synod had no
time to consider it;[4] hence it came up again this year at the

[3] Dated Cracow, May 19, 1594; cf. *Bibliotheca Fratrum Polonorum,* i,
434f.
[4] Letter to Völkel, June 16, 1594; *Bibliotheca Fratrum Polonorum,* 1,
452.

synod of Lublin. Because of illness Socinus was, however, un-able to be present, and he therefore sent some hints in writing to Stoiński. If Ostorodt is at the synod, he advised him, then consult with him, for he is of our opinion, before you begin the discussion with Niemojewski. Thus it appears that Niemojewski was still at the head of the uncompromising party.

Shortly after this, Elias Arciszewski, joint owner of Smigiel (whose son Christopher became famous in the next century as a soldier in both hemispheres[5]), turned to Socinus for explanation in some matters that were giving the nobility trouble. It is permitted, Socinus replied briefly,[6] to hold even the highest office, provided Christian love is not thereby violated, that is, provided a man does not condemn guilty persons to death or to mutilation of their members. It is a more difficult matter with war and whether a Christian ruler may enlist men for it. A private Christian may not kill anyone in the course of war, even though the government commands it. To take arms and go off with others to repel an enemy is permitted; but before this one should try to purchase exemption from personal service; if the latter is impossible, it is better to risk scandalizing the weak in faith than to risk the inevitable ruin of oneself and one's family, in addition to scandalizing others by refusing obedience to the government. Wearing a weapon is not forbidden; nevertheless it is better not to do it in order not to increase the risk of abusing the weapon, except when on a journey to frighten away animals and robbers. In the event of attack, one must save oneself by flight or by parrying the blow and not be stirred up to kill the assailant. Obviously, to strike him or to wound him, but not fatally, is not the same as to kill him. It is better to beat or even to wound him than to let oneself be murdered, especially

[5] For the role of the Arciszewskis among the brethren, cf. *Polish Dictionary of Biography*, I, 149ff.

[6] From Cracow, February 15, 1595; *Bibliotheca Fratrum Polonorum*, 1, 438.

if it is not a matter of sacrificing oneself for religion. As for dress, there is no reason to establish definite rules beyond the general principle of avoiding extravagance. Extravagance is to be measured by what is generally used in a given country, for there are lands in which silk is in as common use among the poor as are linen and wool in Poland. It would therefore be a mistake to forbid, for example, a velvet hat where every woman of the better class wears one.

The explanations communicated to Arciszewski undoubtedly mark Socinus' departure from the position held by him in the controversy with Palaeologus. That these were not concessions extorted on the spot is proved by the assertion, in a letter to Smalcius four years later,[7] that a Christian may "govern, rule, reign, and command, and consequently may where necessary strike and punish," provided only that he does not violate the commands of Christ; that is, he may not deprive even a criminal of life. If God promised eternal life to those who repent, it would be contrary to Christian love to deprive transgressors of the possibility of repentance by the death sentence.

Also publicly, in print, the younger generation adopted a position which Niemojewski would not have allowed. When the Calvinistic minister Jan Petrycius among other charges against the Antitrinitarians raised that of their hostile attitude to the magistracy: "the magistrate does not belong to the Lord's Church, and thus not to God, Christ, or eternal life," Stanislas Lubieniecki,[8] younger brother of Andrew, replied to him in 1596, "We receive into the Church of God in which we are any

---

[7] From Lucławice, September 25, 1599; *Bibliotheca Fratrum Polonorum*, i, 462f.

[8] *Odpowiedź na artykuły, które już od kilku lat rozsiewa na Podgórzu, jeżdżąc dom od domu Johannes Petricius z Chomranic minister, oskarżając i niesłusznie udając i chydząc ludzi niewinne (Reply to the articles which for some years Jan Petrycius, minister of Chomranice, has spread travelling from house to house in the Carpathian foothills, accusing and unfairly charging and defaming innocent people)*, n.p. n.d. (1596).

man who is in office and regard him as a brother, unless in his office there is involved some injustice or contradiction of the Gospel." Not much over ten years had elapsed since the time when the Little Polanders had condemned Budny for making such an assumption. Lubieniecki, however, makes haste to explain that the admission to the Church of persons holding offices does not at all imply recognition of the public courts as a procedure allowed for the brethren: "It is true that a magistrate does not belong to the Church in such a way as to have to judge, as a magistrate, parties in the Church, for we ourselves all jointly decide among ourselves by divine statute, by the Christian laws of God . . . and from this decision brother does not now appeal to any court against brother, but is always glad to be content with it; to which court also even the authorities of the land, that is brothers who are in office, belong, yet not as officials but as brethren and joint heirs."

In the following years several successive synods touched upon these delicate questions (on the one hand wars, weapons, and the magistrate; on the other, extravagance and display), at Lublin in 1597, 1598, 1599, at Raków in 1601, 1602, 1603, 1604, 1605. The yearly renewal of these discussions shows that it was not easy to agree on a common position. Resolutions representing a departure from the tradition of the Church and corresponding to the inspirations of Socinus were, however, increasingly arrived at. Thus in 1598, the year of Niemojewski's death, permission was formally given for the bearing of arms "to frighten away enemies and to ward off their blows."

Tradition gives Socinus the credit for purifying the Church from survivals of the Raków inheritance. His biographer, Samuel Przypkowski, in 1631 put the matter as follows: "He removed a heap of superstitions in matters that were (for faith) of indifferent importance, such as laying undue stress on poor clothing, on the prohibition against accepting offices and suing for one's rights without demanding revenge, and like fancies, with which the ardor of first enthusiasm had unreasonably inoculated them."[9] Przypkowski did not wish here to say that even Socinus, in his controversy with Palaeologus, himself defended too eagerly some of the Racovian views which he later toned down and limited.[10] We learn about his slow work in rooting these out from manuscript notes of Valentine Smalcius,[11] taken down from the discussions at the two synods at Raków in 1601 and 1602. Socinus there held a sort of theological seminar with the members of the Synod, reviewing various problems in turn, in lecture form, after which he replied to questions and objections. Among those who were present and took part in the discussions were Czechowic, Moskorzowski, Christopher Lubieniecki, Stoiński, Jan Licinius, and Siekierzyński. In a lecture given in a closed circle and not intended for print, he could express his views more freely. In 1601, of the themes that concern us he

[9] *Vita Socini conscripta ab Equite Polono* (Raków:1636), p. 24, as well as later at the head of the writings of Socinus in *Bibliotheca Fratrum Polonorum.*

[10] The private lectures of Socinus, unpublished, were not known to the world; but even the collection of his correspondence, published in 1618, revealed to readers that Socinus, in his views on the State and the right of the sword, had withdrawn from his uncompromising position since the time of his controversy with Palaeologus. Yet for this very reason he could not be such an authority on this subject as he was on doctrinal questions: "It seems to me," the Dutchman Dominic Sapma complained to Ruar in 1633, "that in his first work Socinus is freer and broader, but in his later ones more restricted, when he allows Christians to hold the office of magistrate, on condition, however, of not using the sword, not condemning to death, not mutilating human members, and not performing other important acts of office—or, in plain terms, on condition of not discharging the office." Sapma considered this an avoidance of the troublesome question, and that Socinus should either have expressly acknowledged the claims of the civil power or else have found decisive arguments forbidding it to Christians. Cf. G. G. Zeltner, *Historia Cryptosocinismi Altorfinae quondam Academiae et M. Ruari epistularum centuriae duae* (Leipzig: 1727), ii, 603.

[11] Ms. 3421 of the Krasiński Library in Warsaw, once belonging to Valentine Smalcius, is a copy of the Raków notes (made in the synod at the time and revised in January, 1608, at Altdorf). The most important of these notes were published by D. Cantimori: *Per la storia degli eretici italiani del secolo XVI in Europa* (Roma:1937) (*Reale Academia d'Italia, Studi e documenti,* VII, 211-277). The manuscript perished in the wholesale destruction of Warsaw archives and libraries by the Germans in November, 1944.

lectured on the question of going to law, on self-defense, and on war; in 1602, on the question of oaths, on capital punishment, property, usury, luxury, and church discipline.

As to *lawsuits*, Socinus maintained that a Christian is permitted to bring a suit in court against his neighbor. The prohibition applies only to complaints that involve heavy punishment or have the character of revenge, but does not touch demands for the return of property. Hence it is permitted me to sue for damages a man who has wounded me, because this is neither revenge nor excessive punishment. Even in matters that should be decided between the brethren, an appeal to the courts of unbelievers cannot be a cause for exclusion from the Church; for not all the commands of Christ which must be observed for Christian perfection are absolutely necessary for salvation. A demand for retaliation is not inconsistent with Christian patience insofar as this punishment really makes good the loss, but in the contrary case it would have the mark of revenge. If, for example, a man tries to deprive me of my honor, I must defend myself publicly even though this would involve the loss of my opponent's honor, which amounts to retaliation. For it is too great an injury to let one's honor be lost, and consequently the honor of all of one's family. In such a case, if the result is the loss of one's opponent's honor, it will not be pure revenge, for pure revenge occurs when one repays injury for injury, without any profit to oneself. Nor is it revenge if one compels a thief to return what he has stolen, even though he thereby suffers a light punishment; only if the loss were unimportant should one endure it.

*Self-defense* is allowed if one does not carry it as far as murder or mutilation. It is not permitted to kill, that is, to be so disposed that one would rather kill another than expose oneself to being murdered. If, however, despite my intention, an assailant should die from a blow or a wound or suffer crippling, the sin is only venial. It is permissible to frighten away an assailant by shooting. Carrying a weapon is permitted, but is not proper in church. It is permitted to repel violence by force, provided one does not break the laws of Christ; that is, provided, in conformity with the Roman law, one can show that nothing is done against fairness or nature for any reason, but only under pressure of violence. It is a grave sin to kill a robber deliberately, but not so very grave if it happens in self-defense. To wear a sword and to draw it is permitted, but to kill, though not deliberately, is always a sin. To cut off a man's hand in self-defense is a sin, but less serious. It is permissible to beat a man over whom one has authority; it is different where a wife is concerned, for she is not only a subject but also a companion: it is permitted to strike her only when it is certain that this will reform her. To beat a man without cause is not permitted. To beat anyone in self-defense to the point of killing him is a grave sin; but less grave in the case of a robber. In general it is a graver sin to kill a Christian than a Turk or a robber.

*War* has not been expressly forbidden, but Christians are not allowed to wage it in defense of their country, for God appoints no country for them on this earth, as in the Old Testament he appointed a Promised Land for the Jews. In the event of a military expedition it is permissible to do anything that does not go against the commands of Christ, and hence to arm oneself, to present oneself armed at a muster, and together with others under arms to join the army. In face of the objection that scandal may result from this, that it will be concluded that an armed man is ready at the moment of encounter to kill the enemy, it cannot be denied that the scandal must be taken into account; but on the other hand one must see from which side greater scandal threatens. Why, if a Polish nobleman refused to take part in a general levy, he would expose himself to a punishment that would lead to the ruin of himself and his family, not only with regard to temporal advantages but also in the future life; for being stripped of everything and reduced to extreme want, he would have to proceed to infamous deeds, as would also his wife, sons, and daughters. Obviously it would also cause scandal that such a man should pass for a deserter and traitor to his country, which must earnestly be shunned, provided only it be without offense to the commands of Christ. Of course, it is always better if a man can buy himself off from an expedition with money.

Also a minister, if he is a nobleman and not recognized by the King or the general public as a minister (such at this time were Moskorzowski, Arciszewski, Stoiński, the Lubienieckis), may appear at a muster and may deliver his horse with harness to the commander-in-chief for the war. But insofar as honor and property are not at stake, a Christian ought not to appear armed at a muster. Finally, all these indications refer to the present period; it would be proper to give other advice if the condition of the Republic were different and many thousands belonged to our religion.

A Christian may be present on a battlefield provided he does not kill anyone. Thereby he harms no one, and it is no deceit— he would be more guilty if he should expose his life to danger. In the defense of fortresses, if a man happens to be given such a station on a wall that he would have to kill, he should not go to it, but risk everything, provided he does not break Christ's command. If, however, a Christian, in defense of his country or during the siege of a fortress, kills enemies, this is a grave sin, but not so grave as adultery or various other things generally hardly regarded as sins. If a brother were to take on himself the regular calling of a soldier and to give himself to it as a profession, he would undoubtedly be doomed to condemnation; and if he should be killed, as a man who finds pleasure in his trade, he would be forever lost. But even in this there is a certain difference between men. A Tartar is worse than a Christian, and it is always a graver sin to kill Christians than Tartars.

One may not take an *oath* in a trifling matter. To swear by God means to invite divine punishment. In answer to a characteristic question as to whether one should rather suffer death than swear to a robber that one will give up one's property to him and then not keep one's word, Socinus replies, better swear and not keep, *durus sermo, durior mors.*

As to *obedience to the authorities,* Socinus teaches that father comes before King, but King before pastor; thus one must obey the King rather than one's pastor, except in spiritual matters. *Capital punishment.* In Socinus' judgment a Christian, whether he is a private person or an official, is not permitted to kill a man. In punishing, he is bound to refrain from bloodshed. Criminals may yet become god-fearing men if they live. Socinus appeals to the opinion of statesmen that the State would fare incomparably better by punishing transgressors in other ways, e.g. with certain tortures, rather than with death; for death, which the transgressor cannot visualize as well as torture, does not so effectually deter from evil-doing. Of himself, however, he makes the reservation that Christian love ought to restrain the authorities from severe punishment of serfs for the lighter offenses. It seems to him, Socinus acknowledges, less of a sin to kill a man in war, for a man does not engage in a defensive war (he does not imagine a Christian taking part in any other) with the intention of killing, but for self-defense. On the other hand, a magistrate issues the death sentence with deliberation. So many men are, however, killed in war that, as a Christian ought not only to refrain from forbidden acts but also from giving occasion to them, it is better to keep aloof from war; although the sin there is not so grave, yet it is always sin.

*Property.* Socinus recognizes private property but is not a fanatic about it. He considers that theft is not a sin if it is committed out of vital necessity. It is by no means allowed to punish theft by hanging.[12] In a case concerning property, a

---

[12] The scandalous cruelty of this punishment was always the subject of indignation in the Antitrinitarian church. The former Secretary of the Danzig City Council, Matthew Radecke, in a letter to Andrew Wojdowicz (Busków:January 20, 1598; in the letters of Socinus, *Bibliotheca Fratrum Polonorum,* i, 495), considers the historical development of capital punishment for theft. Discussing the ordinances of Holy Scripture and of the Roman law, he asserts that the Emperor Frederick II was the first, in a period of the greatest barbarity and cruelty, to decree hanging for a thief,

man should not appeal to the Old Testament, which placed the happiness of the Jews among temporal affairs. Christ transferred it to the life after this. Thus a Christian ought not to be characterized by covetousness, nor to heap up riches more than are necessary for life. A man may indeed possess more if fortune has brought him property, but it is not becoming to pursue excess. The first Christians regarded what they had as belonging to all, not to possess but to use. It is true that different persons have a different understanding of what is superfluous. If they belong to the upper classes, they consider that they must have more carriages and houses, expensive clothing and tapestries. This is a mistake; difference in rank should not be expressed in difference in possessions. A man who has more is bound to give the more away. It is not proper to keep for display more servants than are needed for service; but it is well—here Socinus reckons with the households of the Polish nobility—to keep more boys than are needed if it is a benefit to them. The possession of silver and gold ware does not offend Socinus. It proves cheaper than vessels of poor material which are constantly wearing out and which must often be treated carefully. Here too, however, ostentation should be avoided. Similarly with clothing, Socinus does not find in Scripture that the wearing of fine clothing is expressly forbidden. Usury is not accurately understood in Poland: pledges are not usury, though branded as such. Taking of interest is not *per se* wrong or disgraceful. If a man uses my money, he is bound to give me something from the income that it yields; if, however, the merchant incurs loss, the creditor is bound to make a deduction.

So Socinus step by step removes the exaggerated severity that weighed on the Polish Brethren under the influence of Anabaptism. This, however, does not mean the relaxation of church

---

but only for theft committed with a breach of peace. This penalty was later extended to various laws against all sorts of theft, even when trifling. In Poland Andrew Frycz Modrzewski protested against it in his *de poena homicidii Orationes* (1543-46).

*discipline,* for the observance of which he urgently asks. Men
who sin by covetousness and do not give their surplus income
for the needs of the Church and their neighbours ought not to
be admitted to the Lord's Supper. Socinus is concerned that
"lukewarmness" is tolerated in the brethren: provided a brother
has not committed crimes, though he be not zealous and be not
often at church, this is winked at. In their manner of living
many are not different from the nobility in general: they join
in banquets; if a guest arrives, his host is ready right after
communion to spend time with him in jesting and frivolity. They
take no pains in the education of their sons: out of stinginess
they are not willing to bear the cost of rearing them at home,
and they place them where they ought not (the reference is
certainly to court service). They do not enforce discipline in
their homes, do not hold prayers with the members of their
household. They may not compel their serfs to take part in
the services in church, for they cannot command any man's
conscience; but using now mildness and encouragement, now
severity, they may incline them to it. In short, by energetic
measures the cold and lukewarm brethren must be made over
into fervent and zealous ones.[13]

Socinus' lectures, known to us only from occasional notes
which are certainly incomplete (there is among them, for example, no account of relations to the State and the magistrate),
were designed for private discussion in his own circle. In their
spirit and in agreement with the stand of the brethren, Christopher Ostorodt, minister at Smigiel, elaborated a system of social
ethics in an official publication of the Church, titled *Unterrichtung
von den vornehmsten Hauptpuncten der christlichen Religion,
in welcher begriffen ist fast die ganze Confession oder Bekentniss*

---

[13] From the ministers also, Socinus demands stricter discipline. In
particular, he is displeased when a minister is eager, now by ingratiating
himself, now by begging, to get money and donations from the faithful:
"If he cannot do otherwise, then let him live by some trade or by brewing;
even to support himself by selling brandy is no disgrace, if there is no
other expedient."

*der Gemeinen im Königreich Polen,* etc. (Raków:1604).[14] Ostorodt had no opportunist inclinations and was not directed by
consideration for the nobles in the Church; however, step by
step he purged the ethical doctrine of the extremes with which
it was imbued under the influence of the Anabaptists. Clearly
and distinctly he commands obedience to the authorities: even
if the government commands something contrary to God, a man
may not raise a rebellion, but should rather suffer, or else save
himself by flight or exile. In this, a man must move cautiously
in order not over-readily to consider as contrary to God what
is not so; for so do those who regard war taxes as forbidden.
Every tax must be paid, without regard to the use that kings
make of it. A Christian may hold any office, even the sovereign
one; that is, he may be King. This would be impossible if
government really could not proceed without war and bloodshed. But Ostorodt judges that this is not the case. Punishment
of malefactors may be effected without death sentences: fines,
imprisonment, hard labor, flogging, even torture, can be sub-
stituted. He especially condemns the punishment of theft by
hanging, though "jesters will taunt us as patrons of thieves." It
would be a more difficult matter if the country could not be
defended without war; there are, however, other means, such as
pacts and alliances; yet if an enemy really attacks a country
just because its ruler hesitates to shed blood, one must commit
oneself to God, who will not forsake the faithful.

Oaths are allowed: those who do not recognize them are mistaken, although we do not condemn them for this nor brand
them as heretics and fanatics, for they thereby expose themselves to harm, thinking that they are acting in accordance
with the divine command. It is permissible to be a plaintiff or
a defendant in court, provided it does not bring too heavy a
punishment on the adversary. It is not permitted to kill

---

[14] Ethical problems are surveyed in chapters 25-32, concerning Oaths,
Revenge, the Commandment to Love, the Magistrate, Church Discipline,
Banquets and Dress, Covetousness, Love and Brotherhood.

plunderers or murderers in self-defense, but "we do not forbid the carrying of a weapon on journeys to frighten off murderers and for protection against dogs and wild beasts; for it is not the carrying of weapons that is forbidden, but killing with them, and one must avoid superstition and prejudice in everything, since they greatly injure religion and the true fear of God." Again, therefore, a distinction is made from the Anabaptist views.

As to war, Ostorodt presents two contrary views: the majority regard it as permitted to a Christian; "there are, however, thousands of those who regard it as inconsistent with Christianity, though they are for the most part simple and uneducated people, hence they are laughed at and are regarded as queer by the theologians," yet even among the educated such prominent men as Erasmus and Vives have condemned war. "We agree with those," declares Ostorodt, "who condemn war, though we well know that this gives offense to many who, only because of this one view, irresponsibly reject our whole confession, believing that this view of ours upsets order from top to bottom and causes general confusion." He adds, however, that his Church does not condemn those who, in agreement with the Old Testament, recognize war as permitted, since in general it is not quick to condemn; and moreover the matter is not as clear as that of other transgressions, which are expressly forbidden in Scripture.

Speaking on the subject of banquets and clothes, Ostorodt condemns excess and display, but here too he advises caution against the fanaticism of the sects. It is not well to bar people from church on account of their showy clothing. A man who accepts sound teaching, himself gives up elegant apparel. The exaggeration of the Anabaptists is harmful; of course it is to be wished that the whole world imitated them in plainness and shabbiness of dress; but it is not possible to approve of their making a yoke out of this regulation, frequently without reason exposing themselves to contempt only because of their dress. A Christian may dress so as not to expose his class to scorn, but differences of class and position are allowed. In such things as clothing, gentlemen must be allowed more than the multitude. "We do not say this," explains Ostorodt, "in order to make ourselves agreeable to anyone whatever, but in order to avoid prejudices and not without reason to keep anyone away from the truth because of such trifles.".

Private property does not come under discussion at all. Covetousness, which means trying to get more than is required to support life, merits condemnation. It is another matter to keep what one already has, though it be more than what is needful: "A man who does not spend his surplus for the glory of God and his neighbor's need commits the sin of covetousness. We can assert this unreservedly of profits and revenues, but not of an estate, goods, and capital." Ostorodt justifies himself again, saying that they avow this opinion not to flatter the rich but to remove superstition and to explain in what the good use of riches consists. He repeatedly defends the view that everyone may have what is necessary for health and normal needs, and that a rich man may live better than others, eat more appetizingly, wear better clothes, and the like.

As we see from the above review, Ostorodt in his ethical reasoning is constantly reckoning with the Anabaptists. He is sympathetic to them even where he does not agree with them; however, their strictness seems to him exaggerated, not commanded by Holy Scripture, and harmful in practice, since it frightens away the generality of people by excessive severity. Thus he repeatedly emphasizes his objections to their "superstitions" and "prejudices," which cut off access to the congregations for people of the upper classes. Both Krowicki and Budny would have agreed with his position.

That all Raków by this time shared his views we have evidence in the famous Racovian Catechism.[15] Socinus began to

[15] Stanislas Estreicher's *Bibliografja Polska,* xxviii, 408, admirably shows the fame and importance of this catechism in the theological literature of Europe in the 17th and 18th centuries. Cf. also L. M. Oliver, "An Early Socinian Publication in England," *Harvard Library Bulletin,* VII (1953), pp. 119-121.

draw it up in 1603 with the aid of Stoiński, but when his death in 1604 interrupted the work, it was entrusted to Moskorzowski and Smalcius. It was published in 1605 in Polish and in 1609 in Latin with Moskorzowski's dedication to the English King James I. The catechism taught that a Christian may hold office, provided that in obtaining and occupying it he has not done anything against the commands of Christ; that oaths are permitted; that it is permissible to bring a suit in court and seek redress of an injury provided no desire for revenge is shown; that the taking of interest, if it inflicts no perceptible harm on one's neighbor, is not sin or usury. Its teaching on the subject of food, clothing, and the like is an almost verbal repetition of phrases taken from Ostorodt.[16]

In the course of the seventeenth century, the gulf between the Polish Brethren and the Protestant world widens in doctrine, but grows narrower in the field of social ethics. We see this in the first systematic controversy which was conducted between the Wittenberg theologian Wolfgang Franz and Valentine Smalcius, representative of Raków. In a score or more of university disputations, which he collected in a bulky volume, Franz undertook the defense of the Augsburg Confession against Catholics and Antitrinitarians. The disputation *De rebus civilibus* is aimed almost exclusively at the Racovians. Smalcius replied to it; Franz made haste with a rejoinder.[17] It proved that they agreed in principle on the question of the magistracy and oaths but differed in part on the subject of courts and wars.

Franz defends the unlimited law of the sword: God established capital punishment before Moses, and it will continue to the end of the world. In Smalcius' opinion a Christian government may

[16] *Catechesis ecclesiarum*, etc. (Raków:1609), pp. 136, 159, 171, 174-76.
[17] Wolfgang Franzius: *Disputatio VI de rebus civilibus . . . adversus Pontificios et hodiernos Photinianos . . . respondente Martino Naebio Nidburg.—Borusso* (Wittebergae:1610), several times reprinted in the collection of the whole of the disputation. Smalcius: *Refutatio thesium D. Wolfgangi Franzii* (Raków:1614); pp. 387-96, *De rebus civilibus.*
Franzius: *Vindiciae disputationum theologicarum . . . adversus V. Smalcium* (Wittebergae:1621), in this *Disputatio de rebus civilibus.*

not shed human blood. Both the law of nature and that of
Moses, as well as that of the Empire, must be mitigated to
agree with the law of Christ. The authorities may keep their
subjects in obedience by other means, even very severe ones,
provided they are not deprived of life; for here there also arises
the danger of depriving them of eternal life. To this Franz
replies that a man condemned to death does not lose eternal life,
and protests against carrying the law of love and pity too far:
"It is already difficult today to live peaceably; how disturbed
everything would then be—one would complain at having been
born a man!"

On war Franz also expresses pacifist tendencies, but he considers it inevitable in defense of religion and country. Here
Smalcius is unyielding. No; war, he asserts, destroys religion;
an enemy may command his own religion, but he cannot impose
it by force. A God-fearing man will prefer to sacrifice his life,
but no enemy can get more from him. Better sacrifice life for
religion than lose it in war, for in that case a man does not risk
his salvation. A man may not defend his country by war; through
war many have lost it. He must resort to other means, such as
federations, yielding part of his rights, tribute, and at worst
voluntary surrender; then at least life, religion, and property are
saved. Franz in his reply concedes these arguments, but only
to a certain point. He would agree to abstain from a religious
war if it were a matter of one generation; but if it concerns
posterity, to whom a pure religion must be handed on, the latter
must not be lost "out of fear and a stupid love of peace." In
defense of country it is really necessary to make every concession; but if a barbarian enemy is not satisfied with this,
Christian rulers must be defended, for an exchange of orthodox
rulers for others would be injurious to souls. As we see, in that
age no appeal in defense of country was as yet made to patriotic
sentiments, which were smothered by religious considerations.

The question of trades producing instruments of war was still
a subject of discussion. Franz, recognizing war as lawful, con-

siders the manufacture of swords, guns, cannons, and the like as not deserving of punishment, reminding the Anabaptists that they make celebrated knives, which can also be used as swords. Smalcius admits that laboring at a trade of this sort is not in itself a sin; perhaps also the implement will not be used in warfare. If a man cannot support himself and his family otherwise, let him get his living thus instead of starving; but short of such necessity it would be a disgrace to manufacture implements for murdering men. Thereafter, Smalcius agrees without reservations to Franz's other theses: that every trade is lawful, that commerce is useful, and that traders should not be grudged profits.

# 10  *Raków Restored*

The attractive power of the Church. The revival
of Raków. Foreigners are attracted. Relation to the
rebellion. Gratitude for Sigismund III. Defense
against the Tartars and military service. Influence
of Grotius' *De jure belli et pacis* on the young generation. Szlichtyng's reservations.

With the end of the sixteenth century, in proportion as the
original promoters of Anabaptism withdrew from the stage and
the younger generation yielded to the rationalist influence of
Socinus, the Antitrinitarian movement notably increased in
strength. Calvinism, depending rather on political influences,
was declining and melting away under the pressure of the work
of the Jesuits and the Bishops. As Sigismund III purged offices
and dignities of Protestants, ambitious individuals were driven
to conversion; the internal life of the evangelical Churches,
constantly disorganized, was not intense; their intellectual
powers did not rise above the average; mediocre theologians repeated what they had learned from foreign masters; discipline
was relaxed to an extent which may be gauged by the toleration
in the Church of violent men like Stanislas (Devil) Stadnicki,
a lawless freebooter-magnate. Profound, noble individuals, long-
ing for a more ardent religio-moral atmosphere, yielded to the
attractive power of the Minor Church. Among its more outstanding converts it could now boast of men like Jerome Moskorzowski, a prominent member of the Diet, who did not hesitate

to enter upon the duties of minister with the Antitrinitarians, or Jacob Sienieński, son of the Palatine of Podole, the highly cultivated proprietor of Raków. Successes of this sort led Socinus to publish (anonymously) *"A Demonstration that those men of the Kingdom of Poland and the Grand Duchy of Lithuania, commonly called evangelicals, who are eager for genuine religion ought to join the company of those who in the same nations are unjustly and undeservedly called Arians and Ebionites."* [1] In this appeal, translated from the manuscript into Polish by Peter Stoiński, Socinus compared the austere morality of the brethren with the laxity of the Evangelicals. The Protestants allowed revenge for injuries with the help of the courts; the repelling of violence by force, killing in war, the stirring up of war and the shedding of blood in defense of religion, the killing of heretics, indulgence in luxury and display in clothing and feasts, and abandonment to vain pleasures. Hence their Church was rapidly declining; whereas the Antitrinitarians, on the contrary, were growing, despite the fact that men were repelled from them both by their practice of immersion and by their strict prohibition against bloodshed and resisting force by the sword, particularly in spiritual affairs, and despite the fact that in their ranks there were no magnates and few nobles, and those for the most part of the poorer sort.

The consciousness that their Church was moving along the right path gave the Antitrinitarians added energy in organization and propaganda.[2] After they had won over Sienieński in 1599,

[1] First published (1600) in Polish translation (*Okazanie*, etc.), then in Holland (1610) in the original Latin (*De officio hominis Christiani*, etc.) and at Raków (1611), finally in the *Bibliotheca Fratrum Polonorum*, i, 691-707 (*Quod regni Poloniae*, etc.).

[2] The Calvinists were unable to oppose to the Antitrinitarians a high ethical ideal. Their controversialist, Jan Petricius, pastor at Jodłówka near Pilzno, replied to the *Demonstration* of Socinus with *A brief warning to the brethren of the Evangelical Church against the boldness and impudence of Socinus, and thus of the Arians* (*Krótka przestroga do braciej zbora ewanieliskiego przeciwko śmiałości i niewstydliwości Soceńskiej a toż Arjańskiej*) (1600), in which he argued thus: "Let us go on further in order to look at these delicacies to which they so entice us, promising

they concerned themselves with making Raków, once the seat of chaos and discord, the capital of their administrative, scientific, and educational work. From 1601 their synods, assemblies, and councils met there. Sienieński consented to the founding there of a school exclusively responsible to the Church and administered by scholars chosen at the synods. Established in 1602, under the direction of first-rate teachers native and foreign, it had a long period of flourishing existence, was frequented by youth whose numbers reached a thousand, and won in the world the honorable name of the Sarmatian Athens. At Raków in 1600 there was established a press whose feverish activity filled Europe with a mass of works in Latin, Polish, German, and Dutch which, though banned and burned by Catholics and Protestants, were yet the more eagerly sought and the more zealously circulated in secret.[3] The Church life, previously

---

us something while themselves, poor things, having nothing but dresses and shirts and coarse boots and sad faces for which the Lord God is much indebted to them. And indeed, he needs these things and gladly sees who goes in what clothes and in boots, but without a sword." Jerome Moskorzowski made short work of such shallow gibes in his *Reply to the writing of Petrycius* (*Odpowiedź na skrypt Petrycego* (Raków:1602). An anonymous Calvinist lampoon attacked the Polish Brethren for their neglect of the sixteenth-century rigorous standards of life. The pamphlet, *Żywoty świętych, si credere fas est, to jest O świątobliwości Christianów mniejszego, jako się zową, zboru Dialog* (*Lives of the Saints, si credere fas est, that is, a Dialogue on the Piety of the Christians of the Minor Church, as They Call Themselves*), was discovered by Lech Szczucki and published in the *Studia i materiały z dziejów nauki polskiej*, III (Warsaw: 1955). Szczucki rightly assumes that it originated in 1609 and attributes its authorship to a minister, Jacob Zaborowski. The author of the pamphlet reproves the Antitrinitarians: "Your ancestors wanted to live by manual work; now you rely upon villages where other people work on you, and you give orders only. The ancestors were fond of grey dress; the descendants wear the same dress as other people of their origin and influence." (p. 398).

[3] We have as yet no bibliography of the Raków prints, which form a precious treasure of the largest libraries of the world (the richest collection is probably that of the Czartoryski Library at Cracow consisting largely of copies once belonging to Jacob Sienieński himself). A history of the Raków press is a desideratum. It would certainly be seen that it did not exist at all in the sixteenth century and that the sixteenth century prints attributed to it (even Radecke's *Ursachen*, dated Rackaw: 1593) were printed at Cracow by Rodecki's press, which in time was inherited by his son-in-law, Sternacki, who removed about 1600 to Raków.

exposed at Cracow and Lublin to persecution by the fanatical
populace and students, had now gained a center in which it
developed openly and safely under the protection of the proprietor of the town. Raków became for the Unitarian movement what Rome and Geneva were for the great Churches of
the world. Adherents journeyed almost every year from all
over Poland in order, after their deliberations, to participate in
the common communion of the brethren. Several hundreds sat
down to the Lord's table (in 1611, 400; in 1618, 459). This
communion became a symbolical bond uniting the members of
the Church in one body, the more important since the unpopular
immersion was year by year passing out of practice. Those who
took the communion at Raków felt the unity of the Polish
Brethren, a name that in time displaced the older one of
"Christians." Many of the brethren settled there for their later
years in order to devote themselves in peace to religious conversation and meditation. Such were Otwinowski, Andrew
Lubieniecki, and Matthew Radecke.

The liberality of the brethren for the work of the Church was
extraordinary; funds collected for the common treasury covered
the expense of the enormous productivity of the press, the support of teachers, of the school, and of ministers in narrow
circumstances, and also made possible numerous propaganda
journeys to Silesia, Germany, France, Holland, and England,
where the emissaries from Raków, by means of their publications
and conversations, won secret adherents. In return, adherents of
doctrine made pilgrimages from western lands to Raków, there
to enjoy the free and public confession of it. Sienieński received them as his guests; and the Raków pastor, Valentine
Smalcius, their most distinguished theologian after Socinus and
the son of a Lutheran jurist from Gotha, admitted them into
the Church. Breathing the air of Polish freedom, foreigners
became attached to the hospitable nation, and more than one of
them straightway became Poles.

A noteworthy example of the assimilative power of Raków

is provided by the case of Smalcius just mentioned. Won for the Church by Wojdowicz while a student at Strassburg, he emigrated to Poland as a youth of twenty-one, and there until his death he worked as teacher or minister, first at Smigiel, then at Lublin, and finally at Raków. He married a Pole and brought up his children as Poles. He learned the Polish language so well that he wrote it fluently, composed Polish hymns, and made the entries in his diary in Polish; in his dreams warning voices spoke to him in Polish (Smalcius eagerly recorded miraculous events); and in time it even became difficult for him to write in German. He undertook a bold controversy with the famous Jesuit preacher Peter Skarga. When Skarga attacked the brethren from the pulpit and called upon the King to exterminate them, being especially indignant with the foreign arrivals, Smalcius in a *Refutation* of his sermon included the following "Admonition to the citizens of the Kingdom of Poland":[4]

Be pleased to note this: that as in many other cases, so also in this, the Lord God has honored you above other nations, in that He has granted you to know, with regard to your salvation, that which other States which exalt themselves above you do not have. This great liberty that you have, and many of you employ for ill, the Lord God wisely used and uses for good, and your good for what is better. The Lord God has visited you, sending you His servants and His holy truth. Forbear, then, to reject them and to despise God. Acknowledge the day of His visitation while ye have time, that the Lord God may graciously vouchsafe to turn away His plagues from you. Believe that thus far the Lord God is marvelously gracious to you, chiefly for this, that men of diverse nations, exiles from their homelands, for no evil, only for truth alone and their own conscience, have had and have shelter among you. They have entreated God for you more than once that His judgments may not yet be executed upon you. When you were gratifying the flesh and wallowing in all manner of luxury, then these aliens among you and exiles for

[4] In the *Bibliografja* of Estreicher, Vol. XXVIII, attention is called to the extensive literary activity of Smalcius, and his productions (as also those of Socinus) are treated with impressive thoroughness.

the truth's sake, living on tears, in both public and private sincerely prayed both for those in authority and for this whole Republic. Grasp then this gift of God while the Lord God offers it to you, lest hereafter, having despised the truth of God, and mayhap driven out His servants, ye become like the other States, of whose desolation we hear to our great sorrow; which may our Lord God of His mercy spare you!

Passing over the beauty and force of the splendid language in which Smalcius worthily competed with such an eminent opponent, it is worth-while calling attention to the striking attachment to the Polish Republic shown in this paragraph by a German from Gotha. Smalcius published his attack on Skarga at a time when a stormy rebellion against Sigismund III, an ardent Catholic, unpopular among the gentry, was raging in the Palatinate of Sandomierz, right in the neighborhood of Raków. The rebellion exposed the Antitrinitarian Church to a severe trial. The Polish and Lithuanian Dissenters took an active though not a leading part in it, demanding the protection of the Warsaw Confederation and religious liberty. It did not suit the Antitrinitarians, threatened by the hostile agitation of Jesuits influential with the King and by attacks of city mobs, to withdraw from cooperation with the opposition. Meanwhile their doctrine about the magistrate, so often stressed, did not allow them to offer resistance to violence, to take up arms and raise a rebellion against the authorities. In consequence of this, at the assembly at Lublin Jerome Moskorzowski would not join in the call to rebellion, and thus provoked the dissatisfaction of the nobility. It is true that there Sienieński once took more decisive action, but he was a new member of the Church.

Antitrinitarian writers not only speak no ill of Sigismund III, but on the contrary glorify him in words full of gratitude. The *Poloneutychia* of Andrew Lubieniecki, written some years after the rebellion, has a truly panegyric chapter[5] in honor of the King, sincere and fervent; Andrew extols (as Stanislas Lubienie-

5 *Poloneutychia* (Lwów:1843), especially pp. 138, 153, 162.

cki did later in his *History of the Reformation*) the goodness of the King in not taking revenge on his rebellious subjects (*inter alia,* in not allowing himself to be pushed into destroying Raków, as those around him would have persuaded him to do). Lubieniecki tries to pacify the Protestants, who held the King responsible for attacks upon their churches, by an assurance that Sigismund is trying to keep his oath to support the Confederation: "Although here and there," he adds, "damage has been done to church buildings by lawless persons, yet considering what has been done in foreign kingdoms, where rulers are not bound by such oaths, careful people will not consider this any very great injury." [6] If attacks and outrages were made by the community upon the brethren, they undoubtedly had no cause to blame the King, under whose rule they were enjoying a period of brilliant development. It was a quite natural thing that foreigners, finding shelter among the Polish Brethren, should recognize the tolerant behavior of the King; indeed at that time Smalcius, having set out for his native Germany, had to flee from its dangers. The towns and petty states of the Empire were imprisoning anyone suspected of Socinianism, while Protestant Holland did not suffer Antitrinitarians even to spend the night in an inn.

The increasing influence of the nobles attached to the Church movement reacted characteristically upon the political ideals of the Church. The Tartar incursions into the border territory of the Republic, repeated more and more frequently after the death of King Stephen Batory, together with the danger of a war with Turkey, necessitated a more precise definition of the relation to the State. The Jesuits accused the Antitrinitarians of siding, in the depths of their hearts, with the Mohammedans, and in 1595 they reproached them outright with beseeching God to

---

[6] Jan Stoiński in his *Modlitwy nabożne* (*Devout prayers*) (1633), p. 308, expressed his sorrow before God at the death of Sigismund III: "We perhaps did not know how to thank Thee for him as was meet, nor to consider as we ought what we had of Thy grace, until Thou didst take it from us."

arouse in the Sultan the wish to conquer Poland. The Church
could not let this pass in silence. Under the name of "a loyal
subject," Jerome Moskorzowski then published an address to
the King and Senators[7] with a refutation of the calumnies.
"Thus, should we," he asked in agitation, "we who were born
and bred in this Kingdom, who have here the memorials of our
ancestors, here most precious hostages in our children, here our
estates and dwellings, should we have desired to push this
Kingdom, our dearest land, our children and wives, into such
danger and utter ruin, and for such a wicked purpose have abused
the name of the immortal God and our Lord Jesus Christ? . . .
Even if you should expel us from the country," he turned to the
Jesuits, "you cannot weaken our devotion to the Republic.
Wherever we are, we shall not deem that we are driven out by
our Lord the King, or by our dearly beloved native land, but
only hunted out and driven away by you."

In view of the incursions of the Tartars into Podole, the
synods at Raków in 1604 and 1605 consulted how to behave in
the face of "the public enemy" who was laying waste the land
—whether it was permissible to resist him and take the field
against him. In accordance with the private teaching of Socinus
already known to us, they passed the important resolution that in
principle it was permissible, though they hedged this decision
round by reservations that they might not kill or wound anyone, and if it were not possible to avoid this, that then it would
be better to emigrate from the threatened districts and to seek
residence elsewhere. This resolution, however, gave offense to
the extremists. The chronicler Radecke, in reporting it, insisted
that it was accepted by a small group.[8] It was, however, of out-

---

[7] *Oratio qua continetur brevis calumniarum depulsio, quibus premun-
tur . . . ad Regem et Senatores Fidelis Subditi* (1595).

[8] *Nieznana kronika arjańska (An unknown Arian chronicle), Reformacja
w Polsce*, IV (1926), 172. This synod, however, adopted extremist resolutions on other matters. It forbade playing at cards and dice, taking part
in wedding or funeral gatherings of other confessions, marriage with too
worldly women or Catholics, and even forbade marriage with Protestants
without consent of the Church.

standing importance: it opened the way to bearing arms and, indirectly, to service in war. In view of the friendly attitude of the Antitrinitarian nobility to Sigismund III, it more and more often happened that brethren served in the army. At Raków in 1619, Kasper Sleszyński inscribed himself in the autograph album of Andrew Lubieniecki[9] as "Captain in the Cavalry of His Majesty the King," a thing not to be thought of in the sixteenth century. The venerable Lubieniecki allowed him to do this, although he certainly did not approve such a calling. In this album there is also the signature of Mathew Wojnarowski, who fell in 1621 at Chocim. Lubieniecki, who himself had once taken part in the wars with Muscovy under Batory, at this time adorned Wojnarowski's page[10] with the characteristic little poem:

You had promised your Lord to be His soldier,

A knight fighting with the world, the flesh, and the Devil,

But following the world you have undertaken

Not a spiritual war, but an earthly one.

There from the sword of the Turk you have won a like prize
    with murderers.

Such is the end of your knights, O cruel devil.

The younger generation was less and less bound by doctrine. Christopher Arciszewski, who, it is true, was excluded from the Church for murdering a man who had wronged him, went in the service of Holland to another hemisphere and won fame in the navy. After the tolerant Ladislas IV ascended the throne, members of prominent Antitrinitarian families, Moskorzowski, Kurosz, Buczyński, Samuel Przypkowski, fought on the King's

[9] Czartoryski Ms. 1403, p. 222.
[10] *Ibid.*, p. 161.

side at Smoleńsk. *The Diary of the War with Muscovy in 1633*[11] is actually a collection of their accounts and letters. They took part in the campaign without scruples, yet at the same time not denying their faith. One of their group, the son of Samuel Gołecki, "died of fever at Smoleńsk, steadfastly holding to his religion and confessing it at the moment of death." [12] From the field of battle they sent their eminent fellow-believers Andrew Moskorzowski, Martin Ruar, and Jan Stoiński detailed accounts of their hardships and victories. They manifested unusual devotion to the King (wrote Moskorzowski: "the King, whom one may justly call the darling of the human race"), and they rejoiced that by their bravery they were winning his confidence in them: "As far as we are concerned," wrote Samuel Przypkowski,[13] "our labor is not employed uselessly, since to the anger of those who pretend that the King can not regard us, he not only regards us kindly, but even before many others, for it happens that he plainly shows us undoubted marks of his favor and grace, and almost noticeable kindness. For he sees that after all not only our toil and labors but frequently also our dangers are borne for him and the fatherland. In the recent battle at Góra Zaworonkowa the Lord God enabled us to furnish proof almost in his very sight that we are able in the face of imminent dangers to hold out and endure for our native land not only equally with others, but even at the front before others."

We have unfortunately no sources which would make it possible to look into the inner life of the Polish Brethren and explain this important evolution in greater detail. It must undoubtedly have been preceded by many passionate discussions. Undoubtedly it was influenced by political considerations—the consciousness of the complete consolidation of society behind the banner of intolerance which, at first breaking out sporadi-

[11] *Dyarjusz wojny moskiewskiej 1633 roku*, published by A. Rembowski as vol. xiii of the *Bibljoteka ordynacji Krasińskich* (Warsaw:1895).

[12] *Ibid.*, p. 119.

[13] In camp at Upper Bogdanowa, November 20, 1633; *Ibid.*, p. 61.

cally, threatened to root out everything that passed for heretical.
Foreseeing a difficult period, the Polish Brethren endeavored to
get rid of provocative points in their doctrine which gave grounds
for accusing them of lack of patriotism and of disloyalty to the
government of the King.[14]

But along with these practical considerations there were also
ideological factors leading to a radical revision of the relation
of the Church to the State and to war. The outstanding influence here was the epoch-making work of Hugo Grotius *De
jure belli et pacis* (1625). The brethren found the author
personally sympathetic, both as a member of the only denomina-
tion in the West (the Remonstrants or Arminians) which in
spite of dogmatic differences maintained friendly relations with
them, and as a celebrated victim of religious persecution. Apart
from this the great writer took a lively interest in the movement of the Polish Brethren; although he wrote against their
works, he behaved towards their universally condemned confession with good-will, corresponded with their leaders, and
was glad to see Polish Antitrinitarian youth in his circle.[15] The
brethren could not suspect their friend, the fervent defender of
religious toleration and pacifism and the apologist for Christianity, either of militarism, of flattery of the warlike tendencies
of the monarchs of the time, or of distorting the spirit of
Christianity; and yet at this time Grotius brought forward the
thesis of the lawfulness of defense against violence, as well as of
defensive war. The justification of self-defense in a private
sphere and in that of the State he based on the law of nature,

[14] During the war in Prussia against Gustavus Adolphus, Catholic opinion
charged them with praying in the church at Raków for the success of
Sweden. Andrew Moskorzowski complained in the Lublin Tribunal that
"in spite of the fact that no accuser was present, his honor the son of the
Palatine of Podole (Jacob Sienieński) and his honor Paul Lubieniecki were
without investigation ordered to take oath that they did not offer prayer
in the church for Gustavus." Speech at the Diet of Opatów, August 30,
1627; Ossolinski Ms. 647, p. 26.

[15] Cf. L. Chmaj, "H. Grotius wobec socynjanizmu" (H. Grotius and
Socinianism), and Kot, "H. Grotius a Polska" (H. Grotius and Poland),
in *Reformacja w Polsce*, IV (1926).

which is directed neither by revenge nor by a wish to annihilate the enemy but by a positive tendency to preserve life and property, and was not abolished by the divine law. The teachings of the Gospel, he declared, limit the law of nature, yet mostly they are not commands, but only counsels and suggestions.

Here Grotius faced the arguments of the literature which condemned war and any kind of resistance to evil. He did not, indeed, mention by name any of the writers of this group, but he undertook to attack their proofs.[16] Discussing the passages of the New Testament cited by them, he shows that they took these in too partial a sense, pushed them too far, and applied them too generally, taking no account of their substance and circumstances. Turning the other cheek to an assailant, giving a cloak as well as a coat, and similar teachings aim at the cultivation of patience, the restraint of quarreling and strife; but the very choice of trifling matters in these examples shows that they cannot be applied to great crimes in which life or all one's property is at stake. It does not follow from the command to love one's enemies that one should love criminals more than innocent men and refrain from defending the innocent against attacks of wrong-doers whether private or public. It is from love for the innocent and the peaceable that courts and the principal punishments and righteous wars come. Private administration

[16] Stanislas Estreicher, in a brief tract abounding in information of the highest value taken from the original sources (*inter alia*, relating also to the history of Catholic pacifism) and entitled *Pacifism in the Poland of the sixteenth century* (*Pacyfizm w Polsce XVI stulecia*) (Poznan:1930), asserts that "the whole first part of the famous tract [of Grotius] is a veiled attack on Socinus." After comparing the two works, I should modify the statement as follows:

Socinus was not the only one whose proofs had to be overthrown. Grotius knew the arguments of various writers who condemned resistance to evil, courts, the death penalty, and war, both humanists (Erasmus, Ferus), and also sectarians, e.g. the Dutch Mennonites and Anabaptists. He grouped the arguments systematically and, without taking account of their origin, discussed them critically. Among them one may find refutation of Socinus' interpretation of various passages of the Gospel. In many instances Grotius wholly accepts the position of Palaeologus.

of justice is forbidden, for one can resort to the judge; but resistance to assailants in urgent cases is not an expression of revenge. It is permissible to defend not only life but also property; however, Grotius considers that in the matter of property in the course of history the interpretation of Holy Scripture has been too much adapted to contemporary customs: thus, for example, the divine law nowhere requires that a thief should suffer death. As courts are to private injuries, so war is to quarrels between States, which have no judge to whom to resort. Here the injured State's right or self-defense functions. At the call of the government, to which its subjects are bound to give obedience and pay taxes, they must also rise to repel a foe. Although the enemy were to make war in good faith, the party attacked may fight for justice with the help of force. The foe is struck, not to punish him for an injury or a crime, but to preserve the defender's existence. The law of nature leads to and authorizes this; the law of God does not forbid it, although it calls for the most far-reaching patience and concessions.[17]

In his work Grotius also wished to lead nations and monarchs to christianize their policy. He endeavored, through binding them by certain rules, to check the increasing cases of violence occasioned by the undertaking of unjust wars conducted by barbarous methods. This tendency of his was so obvious and the appropriateness of the methods indicated by him so convincing, especially in view of the wars that were then raging, that even the Polish Brethren could not but acknowledge the reasonable and humanitarian character of his proposal. It is true that they immediately replied to his work with a fresh edition of Socinus' *Ad Jac. Palaeologi librum responsio* (Raków: 1627) and also they appealed to Grotius personally for a discussion with him on "whether it would not be possible to avoid

[17] The justification of defense against force, of punishments and courts, as well as of lawful warfare, is contained primarily in the Prolegomena of Grotius' work, Book i, chap. 2 and 3; Book ii, chap. 1.

the death penalty, as well as what are the just causes of war," [18] but to a marked degree they yielded to the influence of his arguments, especially the vindication of lawful war.[19] By this is partly to be explained their first collective participation in the war against Muscovy in 1633; Samuel Przypkowski, who took part, was under the particularly strong spell of Grotius.

That Raków was, however, unwilling officially to withdraw from a position held for so many years, and that it tried to defend the old doctrine and indirectly to oppose that of Grotius, is witnessed by the action of Jonas Szlichyng of Bukowiec. As though waiting for an opportunity, he undertook the defense of his confession against a criticism long out of date, for it had been published in 1619 by the Wittenberg professor, Balthazar Meisner[20] and in his *Quaestiones duae contra B. Meisnerum* (Raków:1636) devoted an unusual amount of space to judicial punishments and the death penalty, and in particular to the shedding of blood.[21]

Szlichtyng defended the teaching of Socinus but displayed much readiness to make concessions in favor of the new currents. Strictly speaking, he nowhere limits the established rights of the civil power, but only from the standpoint of religious morality makes severe demands upon the Christian in the field of

[18] *Grotii Epistolae* (Amsterdam:1687), p. 280, letter of May 10, 1631. In 1638, Grotius again replied to a letter from Jan Stoiński, defending his position, *Epp.*, p. 1057.

[19] "I recognize," declared Martin Ruar to Brenius in 1627, "that a Christian may hold office, inflict corporal punishments and even the death penalty upon criminals, and also repel invaders by armed force and defend his innocence by war if it cannot otherwise be made safe. Arguments in support I shall not cite, since I am content with those brought forward by Grotius, though they do not all seem to me equally strong, and some indeed quite weak." Zeltner, *Historia Crypto-Socinianismi*, ii, 366.

[20] Meisner's *Brevis consideratio theologiae Photinianae, prout eam Faustus Socinus descripsit in libello suasorio cui titulus: Quod Evangelici omnino deberent se illorum coetui adjungere qui falso Ariani atque Ebionitae vocentur* (Wittenberg:1619), as may be seen from the title, was a reply to the work of Socinus already mentioned, which, in the author's Latin original, did not appear until 1611.

[21] Pp. 334-460.

individual ethics. Hence he regards it as inadmissible for a man to make a complaint in court against a wrong-doer insofar as it is not aimed at prevention of or restitution for an injury; the number of remaining cases in which only punishment could be in question is not really so large. Szlichtyng naturally does not deny the State the right to intervene in these cases; he only judges that the person wronged should not proceed to drag the guilty person from office but should forgive him the injury. In the matter of defense against attack, Szlichtyng submits to the thesis of Grotius that it derives from natural law, but he judges that it is not consistent with the calling of a Christian. The government has the right to inflict capital punishment, but a god-fearing Christian ought not to serve as its instrument. The government has the right to declare war, but a pious man ought not to enlist in military service.

Not denying the authorities the right to wage war, Szlichtyng nevertheless submits that advantage should not readily be taken of this right. It is unbecoming in a Christian State to start a war over a broken agreement, over an insult however serious, over reception of deserters or the loss of any possessions; it should rather offer peace to an enemy on condition of Christian love. In these reservations we feel an echo of conditions in the Thirty Years War, when varied reasons were seized on to stir up new wars. Szlichtyng especially holds it against the evangelicals that they seek glory in military courage instead of exercising patience. Better perish under persecution, he is convinced, than in war. Do not let them try to save religion through war, which stirs up so much evil, for they do not live in the Republic of Plato, and have to do not with ideas of war, but with its terrible crimes—the medicine is worse than the disease. Even if wars bring some advantage to those who survive them, what happiness do they give the mass of those that are slain! War with fire and sword is not an effective defense against pillage and desolation. Better let oneself be banished or killed without resistance; this happens only to individuals, and the rest escape. Besides, God and religion have no need of their weapons. It should be noted that Szlichtyng carefully passes by the question of a defensive war of the sort that Poland was waging, and hence directs his exhortations at the German Protestants and German religious wars.

The different character of the Polish wars must have been the subject of discussion between the brethren and Grotius, since the latter replied as follows to a Dutch Mennonite who questioned the right of the State to make war: "Pray consider whether the Polish King is bound to submit to the Tartars murdering great numbers of children, thereby, according to the opinion of some who oppose wars, excluding them from the heavenly Kingdom, which they might enter when of age through a godly life; and whether he must consent to permit outrages worse than death against women, when he can prevent this by repelling the robbers' violence by the royal power?" [22]

[22] Letter to Nicholas de Bye, May 4, 1641; Grotius, *Epistolae*, p. 919.

# 11   *Decline of Social Radicalism*

Negotiations with the Mennonites. Communistic
experiment of the Moravian Brethren at Węgle. Return of Ostorodt to social radicalism. Völkel and Crellius in defense of private property. Last effort at
communist propaganda among the Polish Brethren.
Ruar's controversy with Zwicker.

The Polish Antitrinitarians from the very beginning had a
sense of the independence of their religious position. In the
profound conviction that they were the first to carry the reforming movement of the age to its logical conclusion, they cherished
an ambition to bring together in their Church those men of all
nations who were near them in thought and faith. The resistance
of the Moravian Anabaptists, of which we have already spoken,
for some time made them waver in active propaganda, which
was also checked by friction with the brethren in Lithuania and
Transylvania. Quite early, however, they turned their attention
to the Germanic element in the borderlands of the Republic, to
the Dutch and German settlers.

In an age of religious persecution, Polish Prussia was regarded
as a blessed land in which a man might both freely confess his
faith and find work. Thus, as early as 1526 members of Dutch
sects gathered there, artisans and laborers who were gladly
employed in the district at the estuary of the Vistula, about
Danzig, Elbing, and Marienburg. Most numerous of all were

the Mennonites, whose leader, Menno Simons, had himself been in Prussia about 1546. They were sometimes persecuted by Danzig, or again by Elbing, but as a result of commercial competition the bishops of Kujawy and the Palatines usually gave them protection, in consideration of their ability to farm marshes and lowlands. Though not admitted to East Prussia by the Lutheran administration, in Royal Prussia their sect enjoyed toleration.

They were a simple people, without educated leaders, choosing their religious teachers from among artisans; they lived modestly and observed a strict morality. They were divided into several religious sects, which agreed in practising adult baptism and refusing to take oaths, to bear arms, or to hold office.[1] Obviously, both as foreigners and as humble people they could proclaim their abstention from state activities without any danger to themselves, since they had no occasion to come into conflict with the demands made on aristocratic society. Poland respected their objections against military service. When, for instance, in July of 1571 detachments were organized in Gdańsk (Danzig) for the defense of the port of Puck, threatened by the Danes, "a number of the suburban inhabitants who declared themselves Anabaptists refused to take part in the expedition to Puck, declaring that they were Christians and not warlike people and did not possess arms, since it had been written that if slapped in one cheek, one should offer the other." Such was the message from the Danzig City Council to their delegate at the Polish court, Matthew Radecke (who himself soon after-

[1] On the Mennonites in Prussia, cf. W. Mannhardt, *Die Wehrfreiheit der alten preussischen Mennoniten* (Marienburg:1863); A. Brons, *Ursprung, Entwickelung und Schicksale der altevangelischen Taufgesinnten oder Mennoniten* (Norden:1891); W. J. van Douwen, *Socinianen en Doopsgezinden, 1559-1626* (Leiden:1898); B. Schumacher, *Niederl. Ansiedlungen im Herz. Preussen* (Leipzig:1903); E. Randt, *Die Mennoniten in Ostpreussen und Litthauen bis 1772* (Königsberg:1912); H. G. Mannhardt, *Die Danziger Mennonitengemeinde* (Danzig:1919); H. Wiebe, *Das Siedlungswerk niederländischen Mennoniten im Weichseltal bis zum Ausgang des 18 Jh.* (Marburg:1953).

wards became renowned as a fervid adherent of the Polish Brethren).[2] Nobody was punished for this refusal.

Having learned from a certain Jew that in Little Poland there was an Anabaptist church, the Mennonites in 1582 sent a delegate to the synod at Lucławice. In return, Martin Czechowic, Alexander Witrelin, and Matthias Krokier went to Danzig to reach a closer understanding, which, however, was not achieved because of doctrinal differences.[3]

The brethren from Little Poland did enter into relations with scattered followers of their Church at Danzig, notably Matthew Radecke, the Danzig town clerk, who began to organize a secret gathering of Anabaptists among the German element. When Danzig made it impossible for him to work within the city limits, he organized a church hard by at Busków, the estate of Paul Arciszewski, and from there he came into active relations with the church at Smigiel in Great Poland, of which Germans also constituted an important part.

Independently of the brethren in Little Poland, the Moravian Anabaptists began to carry their propaganda into the same territory. In 1579 they sent four missionaries to the Silesian border of Great Poland. *The History-book of the Hutterites*,[4] gives a full account of the fate of this expedition, which remained without result. In both the villages of Kowalewo and Attendorf (Dryżyna) in the district of Wschowa (Fraustadt) missionaries were at once arrested and lodged in the common jail. Their

[2] Published by S. Bodniak in *Pamiętnik Biblioteki Kórnickiej* (1946), p. 170, from the Gdańsk Archives. Such a refusal of military service happened several times, and Polish Kings used to exempt Anabaptists from it and to take them under their protection against the Protestant authorities of the city of Gdańsk. These facts are not mentioned by Johann Driedger in his paper "Farming among the Mennonites in West and East Prussia, 1534-1945," *Mennonite Quarterly Review*, XXXI (1957). Moreover, by stating that from 1534 on, "the political sovereignty of the area at that time was in the hands of a strongly clerical and intolerant Poland," Driedger implies that Polish Kings persecuted the Mennonites.

[3] These relations were given in detail on the basis of the synod records by F. S. Bock, *Memorabilia Unitariorum acta in Prussia* (Königsberg: 1753), pp. 13ff.

[4] *Geschicht-Buch der Hutterischen Brüder*, pp. 392-99.

fearless reasoning made such an impression upon the noble proprietors that in spite of threats they were set at liberty; the people, however, did not receive their teachings gladly.

After the failure of this attempt, the Moravians turned to the Prussian Mennonites, and Peter Walpot himself went and formed a loose connection with them. This caused dissatisfaction among the Antitrinitarians at Smigiel, who regarded themselves as the special friends of the Moravian Anabaptists. Christopher Ostorodt, minister of Smigiel, explained this to the Strassburgers in 1591 in an epistle already cited in part:

We know that sectarianism is just as much the work of the flesh as other sins are; therefore we willingly tolerate others and do not avoid them for a difference of understanding, provided only that they be obedient to the Lord Jesus and acknowledge us as brethren. For this reason two of our brethren made a journey to Moravia in Lent of the present year to confer with the Baptists at Slavkov (Austerlitz) and Pouzdrany (Pausern), and to lay before them our confession; but to this they have had no reply. As for communion with us, they decided to take it under consideration and first to make proof of our congregation, to which we have no objection. Would to God that both you and they had been as careful before you approached the Mennonites, among whom there are yet gross faults, such as boastfulness, greed, usury, a madness of constant excommunications and exclusions from the Church, etc.

Ostorodt's wish was not realized. The Moravians evidently persisted in the distrust of the Polish Antitrinitarians which they had conceived twenty years earlier. It is also possible that the chief obstacle was again their insistence on communism. Perhaps they had undertaken some agitation in this direction at Smigiel, as Ostorodt came out with a tract in German, *Against the Hutterites or Moravian communists*.[5]

The simple Mennonites seemed to the Moravians better allies than the independent Antitrinitarians and, approaching them,

[5] We unfortunately know neither the further circumstances nor the date of the appearance of this tract (cf. Sandius, *Bibliotheca Antitrinitariorum*, p. 91).

they also turned to Prussia at the time when the forward march
of the Imperial armies began to threaten the Moravian communities. Hearing that "in Polish Prussia religion is free to
everybody," they sent there in 1603 several brethren headed by
Joseph Hauser, who was familiar with languages, to explore the
situation. Having concluded an agreement with the Mennonites
of Elbing, a considerable number of them came in 1604 and re-
quested of the Elbing Town Council permission to establish their
community. Surprised at being refused, they settled in two
Mennonite villages near Marienburg, in Węgle and Marcushof.

Here disagreeable times began for them, during which they
were thoroughly offended by the Mennonites. At great cost they
leased for ten years the manor-house and land at Węgle in order
to establish a communistic society after their custom. Though
received into the community, the Mennonites proved to be a
burden: they wished only to hold continual discussions and to eat
and drink well. They swallowed up a great deal of money, and
would have consumed more, as the *History-book of the Hutterites*
indignantly says,[6] if they had been indulged in every case of
pride, quarrel, or insult. In addition, they scoffed at the Moravians because of their simple dress, calling them gypsies, and
praised their own Mennonites, whom the communists on the contrary reproached, as Ostorodt had done before, for their pride,
usury, deceitfulness, and harlotry and for the manufacture of
guns and powder. The situation was made worse by the chicanery
of the bailiff of Marienburg and the threats of the tradesmen of
Elbing, who stirred up a hundred journeymen to burn the communistic settlement. The Moravians were at last rescued by a
certain German nobleman who bought up their lease, so that they
were able to abandon their unfortunate enterprise, Prussia, and
the Mennonites.

After a stay at Węgle in August, 1605, Joseph Hauser composed
*An Instruction that community of temporal goods is the doctrine*

---

[6] There is an account of the whole expedition to Prussia on pp. 470-
472. Cf. also L. Neubaur, "Mährische Brüder in Elbing," in *Zeitschrift für
Kirchengeschichte*, Vol. xxxiii (1912), and Beck, *Geschichtsbücher*, p. 338.

*of the New Testament and is binding upon the faithful.*[7] Propaganda of this sort must have reached the German members of the Antitrinitarian Church, for in the following year Smalcius, now settled in Raków, prepared in German a *Writing against the Hutterites or Moravian communists, for the use of Georg Hofmann, a citizen of Smigiel.*[8] Unfortunately, neither Smalcius' nor Ostorodt's manuscript has been preserved; thus we cannot learn their arguments against the Anabaptist communists.

The extreme radicalism of the Moravians did not, however, pass without leaving some trace among the German Antitrinitarians of Danzig and the vicinity. Christopher Ostorodt, a man on whom Socinus once counted and who was himself formerly engaged in controversy with the communists, succumbed to it. Transferred in 1605 from Smigiel to Busków as minister of the church, he found himself in an environment purely plebeian and began to stir it up against what was in his view the excessively aristocratic leadership of the Racovians. He attacked in particular his old friend and fellow-laborer at Smigiel, Smalcius. When the latter, adapting the doctrine of the Church to the demands of Polish conditions, interpreted the rules of the Gospel in a moderate sense and taught that not all the doctrines of Christ and the Apostles are necessary for salvation, Ostorodt adopted the opposite position; and he who in 1591 had so strongly criticized the sectarian spirit now called for the breaking of fraternal relations with those who thought differently. He set forth without compromise the questions of war, office-holding, resort to courts, oaths, and the owning of property, and excluded from the Church those who did not meet his demands.[9] When he also came out in writing against the Racovians, the synod in 1610 voted that a formal

[7] *Underrichtung, dass die Gemeinschaft der zeitlichen Güter ein Leer des N.T. sei und von allen Gläubigen erfordert werde, geschrieben auf Wenglen in Preussen von Josef Hausser aus Mähren den 12-ten Aug. 1605.* Ms. in the University Library at Budapest (Cod. V. d.).

[8] We know of this Ms. of Smalcius only from Sandius (p. 101), who wrote down the title in its Latin form with the date: *Racoviae, a. 1606, 28 Aug.*

[9] Bock, *Memorabilia Unitariorum acta,* p. 19; and Zeltner, *Smalcius' Diary,* pp. 1187f, 1192f.

delegation be sent to Danzig to remonstrate with him. Under the leadership of Sienieński, the ablest Raków theologians, Moskorzowski, Smalcius, Gosławski, Wojdowicz, and Völkel, set out and were joined by deputies from the young German church at Międzyrzecz (Meseritz). Ostorodt at first gave way, but after his death, which occurred soon afterwards, it appeared that he was preparing for a cleavage. A fresh delegation composed the dispute, receiving back into the Church those expelled by Ostorodt.[10]

A letter of January 15, 1612, written in Olomouc by a young Pole who had travelled through the country, gives us an idea of what could reach Poland about the life and institutions of the Moravians at the beginning of the seventeenth century. The addressee was Philippe du Plessis Mornay of Samur, the head of the French Calvinists. The writer, his pupil and a Calvinist as well, was the future Polish Senator and diplomate Andreas Rej, a youth of fine education and wide horizons, and a grandson of the eminent Polish writer Nicholas Rej.[11] After having described the political and ecclesiastical atmosphere of all the other denominations in Moravia, he passes to the Moravian Brethren:

The barons suffer the heresy for high profits. The King has no power at all; they rule over themselves and their subjects in the

[10] Moskorzowski and Smalcius took advantage of these journeys to carry on conversations with the Mennonites about union. A part of the Dutch at Danzig favored this idea, and in Holland itself one branch of the Mennonites, the so-called young Flemings, at whose head stood Jakob Outerman, preacher at Haarlem, also supported the plan. But the settlers at Danzig, chiefly laboring people, distrusting their own judgment, sent the proposition of the Racovians together with their letters to the fatherland to Hans de Ries, leader of the moderate branch. Out of dislike to radicalism in doctrine and fear of persecution on the part of the dominant Reformed Church, he brought about the rejection of an alliance with the hated "Socinians." On this, cf. in detail van Douwen, *Socinianen en Doopsgezinden*.

[11] A letter from the Sorbonne Ms. 369, pp. 170-173, published by František Hruby, "Filip du Plessis Mornay a Karel Žerotin (Morava v zrcadle hugonotskeho zpravodaje)," in *Pěkařův Sbornik* (Praha:1930), II, 66-69. The same author published about the Moravians "Nove Přispěvky k dějinam moravskich novokržtenců," in *Českou Minulosti. Prace žakou Vaclava Novotneho* (Praha:1932), and *Die Wiedertäufer in Mähren* (Leipzig:1935).

old, secular way. There are certain kinds of Anabaptists, not much distant from Arianism. Many of them form communes, buying houses from their common purses and assembling them into a block in order to live together. In the same way they buy lands from which to draw their subsistence, as well as from manual work and crafts, which occupy them most and because of which their patrons keep them.

They live niggardly, which is, according to them, in keeping with piety. The child when it is three years old is taken away from its mother in order not to impede its parents' work, and is reared collectively together with other children. Men and boys capable of work have their meals together; women eat separately.

They do not punish anybody by death, and they do not defend themselves when beaten.

They say that they believe in the Apostolic Symbol and that it is the basis of their faith. They admit that our faith is not wrong, provided we live a life similar to theirs. They claim that outside their community there is the world corrupted and the children of the world. They neither allow to be read nor read any book, except the Bible translated into German by the Helvetics.

Moreover, the externals of their life are irreproachable; but they are conceited in the fact that they despise and consider infidel and un-Christian all and sundry.

They live in communes in about twenty localities, all in all about sixty thousand people of both sexes. Once or twice a year they contract marriages in a fixed place announced from the pulpit, where everybody who wants to marry, men and women, have to report. They make their mutual choice at first sight with the help of a minister. Thus, a man choses one out of three women who, no matter how she is disposed, has to accept the marriage; and sometimes a young man has to accept out of the three an old hag who wants him. If neither side wants to choose anyone from among the people presented, they have to wait for six more months. . . . Then they match; but men take their meals with men, and women with women, and afterwards each one accompanies his wife.

In each house—that means commune—there is one who rules and whom everybody obeys unconditionally. To each elderly woman they assign twelve children, who are fed by her, sometimes two or three hundred together, in great fetor and filth, so that a number of them often perish.

During the Lord's supper they take a whole loaf of bread; each
of them breaks off a fraction and then passes the bread, as well
as a small vessel with wine, to the next one.

They have their settlements only in the most fertile lands.
Outside of Moravia nowhere can one find such a way of life.
They pray for the office but they do not recognize it for their
own. They claim God to be the sole office. The Kings are
bestowed by God's anger. None of them participates in any way
in the business of war, since, as they say, "We should not be the
cause of bloodshed." When force is applied to them, they
resign themselves to depravation by force. Although there are
excellent craftsmen among them, they do not produce anything
that would be of use either in war, or for self-defense, or for
the purpose of striking at an enemy. No luxury or super-
abundance is to be found among them.

Social radicalism found no sympathizers among the Polish
Brethren. They stood definitely for private property, laying upon
it the duty of ample aid to the poor and liberality to the Church.
Consequently they rejected the communism of the Moravians.[12]
The problem of property was discussed fundamentally by Johannes Völkel of Grimma in Meissen, who was baptized in 1585 at
a synod at Chmielnik, was teacher at Węgrów and later minister
at Filipowo and Smigiel, and was author of the work *De vera
religione*, which contained a systematic account of Antitrinitarian
doctrine. His great work was written about 1612 but was not published until 1630, long after his death.

Christ, argued Völkel, did not do away with private property,
nor did he command the holding of it in common; moreover, communism does not follow from the command to love one's neighbor.

[12] But they tried to keep up certain contact with them. Jan Amos
Komenský (Comenius) mentioned the impression made upon him in his
youth by a group of Polish nobles who in 1608 came to the school at
Przerów, and, having enjoyed the hospitality of a teacher, left him as a
gift a Racovian Catechism. It afterwards transpired that they had come as
envoys to the Moravian Anabaptists, in order to establish closer relations
with them. It is also fairly certain that they brought with them the
German edition of the catechism published that year (letter of Komenský
to Wolzogen in 1659; cf. J. Kvačala, *J.A. Comenius*). (Leipzig:1892), p.
10.

This love demands that a man share his own with his neighbor; it is, therefore, necessary to have something in order to give some of it to another. Moreover, even those who have nothing ought to try to get some property for this purpose. Community of goods is doubtless, at the moment it is realized, a sign of love of neighbor, but it is considerably weakened by the fact that admission to the Church is dependent on this condition. In the continued existence of the community, however, love of neighbor simply disappears, for there is no possibility for individual distribution of alms. Members of the community, personally possessing nothing, cannot give the hungry food or drink, clothe the naked, or take in the stranger. This may, indeed, be done by the elders to whom the management of the community is entrusted; but that is not the same thing. Charity, performed under the direction of others, is rational, cold. A Christian should bear witness to it in person, out of gladness of spirit and ardor of love. Christian kindness does not depend upon establishing joint ownership of property in a community whose members mutually profit by their investments: in the first place, members cover all their living expenses, often gaining rather than losing; in the second place, by constant work they increase their common property, and it is quite impossible to consider them poor. Christ commanded something wholly different: generous alms for the need of poor neighbors. This command can be fulfilled while personal property exists, if in use it becomes in a certain measure common. The first Christians in Jerusalem certainly did not sell off everything, did not dwell in common in one establishment, did not form a communistic Church. But even if such a Church had existed in Jerusalem, would it follow from this that others were bound to found one similar? Communists appeal to the fact that Christ possessed no personal property, for he had not where to lay his head. Is this an argument for a communistic Church? Its members certainly have where to lay their heads. We acknowledge a real community, based on liberal assistance to those in want and on their admission to the enjoyment of our property. A communistic community, embracing only a definite number of persons, rather stands in the way of this obligation.[13]

The greatest theologian of the generation after Socinus, Jan Crellius, rector of the school and minister at Raków, codifier of the ethics of the Polish Brethren, completely agreed with Völkel in rejecting Moravian communism; instead, he recommended as worthy of a Christian two forms of community of goods. One, the more perfect, which the first Christians practiced, consists in selling and distributing one's goods to one's neighbors. This was possible under the eye of the Apostles, in the heroic days of Christianity. It was characterized by a splendid fervor, but it is hard to require it today; he who distributes what he has must afterward become a burden to others; only a man who has no children and is able to endure poverty bravely may live thus. The other sort of community of goods, less perfect, is better suited to ordinary life. It consists in readiness to give assistance to one's neighbors from one's property; for example, loans of money, of tools, of servants, of oxen, and the like. This is practical communism, consistent with the demands of reality, and therefore more lasting.[14]

The outbreak of the Thirty Years War paralyzed the attraction of the Moravian Brethren; and confessional hatred and exaggerated rumors of their riches drew to their settlements predatory bands of mercenary Imperial soldiers. In the years 1620-21, Polish Cossacks tormented them cruelly. The chronicles of the Anabaptists[15] abound in descriptions of the violence that they underwent. *Die Pollaken* committed especially savage murders

[13] Johannis Volkelii, *De vera religione libri quinque* (Raków:1630), pp. 288-95.

[14] *Commentarius in Act. Apostol.*, chap. iv; written before 1633, in *Opera Crellii*, iii, 140-48, in *Bibliotheca Fratrum Polonorum* (1656). For Crellius, cf. article by M. Wajsblum in the *Polish Dictionary of Biography*, IV, 101-104. For the part played by his son Christopher and his grandson Samuel in propagating Unitarianism in England, cf. S. Kot; "The Activities of the Polish Brethren in England," *Reformacja w Polsce*, VII (1935-36), 235-44.

[15] Beck, *Geschichtsbücher*, pp. 380-405; *Geschicht-Buch*, pp. 549-59.

at Przibice. However, manifestations of humanity on the part of the Poles are also noted. In April, 1621, three thousand Poles were quartered on the community at Čejkovice. "And although they were formerly wicked and satanic, they were moved with pity," relates the chronicle,[16] "when they saw our honesty and uprightness; especially their colonel gave our people protection so that no one suffered any violence or injury. Some of them said that had they known what sort of folk we were, they would not have behaved so harshly with us at Przibice." Indeed, when fire broke out in the community house, the Poles helped earnestly to fight it, as if it had been their own home. In 1622 the communists were expelled from Moravia by Imperial command, and remnants took refuge in Hungary, while the majority increased already existing congregations on the border at Sobotište and Wielkie Lewary, and one group formed a community at Alvintz in Transylvania.

In the middle of the seventeenth century, there occurred the last attempt to bring the communists and the Polish Brethren nearer together. In 1648, Andrew Ehrenpreis, an energetic elder of the community, sent three brethren to Prussia for propaganda. At Danzig they entered into relations with the oculist Dr. Daniel Zwicker, who some years before had joined the Polish Brethren. Zwicker, a restless spirit and inclined to radicalism, became enthusiastic for communism, seeing in it a genuine example of imitation of the poverty of Christ, and he began to correspond with Ehrenpreis. The latter convinced him of the faults of the Antitrinitarians, whom he knew from Transylvania, from Kolozsvár (Cluj). "If a man observes the fruits of your religion," he wrote to him in September, 1650,[17] "he finds among your members indulgence in delights of the eyes and the flesh, an ostentatious life, riches and worldly pleasures, and among many the mask of all sins—a miserable pride and arrogance, as well as the root of all evil—greed, which is idolatry;

[16] *Geschicht-Buch,* pp. 558f.
[17] Beck, *Geschichtsbücher,* p. 488.

among some usury taken even from brethren, also hardness of heart toward the poor; the sword and arms."

Zwicker began to raise a ferment among the Polish Brethren by showing that the possession of private property was not in accord with the Gospel. At that time there was living at Straszyń near Danzig, Martin Ruar, an emigrant from Holstein, from his youth attached to the Polish Brethren, and their chief ambassador to western Europe.[18] He composed a text in German in which he examined Christ's command to sell what one has and defended the right to accumulate savings against the hard times of life, provided one does not attach one's affection to them.

Zwicker did not let himself be moved from his view and decided to investigate the communistic system face to face. Hence he repaired with three Danzigers to Slovakia, and staying for ten days (from May 31 to June 8, 1654) at Sobotište, was confirmed in his attachment to it. He became acquainted with their way of life, thoroughly studied Riedemann's *Rechenschaft*, and decided to enter the community. Although an Antitrinitarian, he closed his eyes to their doctrine of the eternal divinity of Christ conceived of the Holy Ghost from the Virgin Mary and subscribed to their confession of faith, only reserving for himself freedom on the question of two natures in Christ and on the obligatory character of communism for all brethren. The communists, who were already in decline and losing their attraction, eager to gain an energetic member and a prolific writer, agreed to these reservations, received Zwicker as a fellow-member by the laying on of hands, appointed him a "minister of the word," and entrusted him with the mission of forming communities in Poland.[19]

Returning to Danzig, Zwicker actively set about carrying out his mission. His plan was to induce the whole organization of the Polish Brethren to recognize the moral superiority of the

[18] Cf. W. Sobieski, "Marcin Ruarus," *Reformacja w Polsce,* I (1921), 137; L. Chmaj, *M. Ruar,* pp. 132-35.

[19] Beck, pp. 486-92; *Geschicht-Buch,* p. 643.

Moravian Brethren and to admit communists to carry on propaganda and preach sermons in the Polish Church. It was not to be a union: the communists did not regard the Antitrinitarians as their equals in evangelical perfection, and promised to receive into their organization only those who, at first retaining their private property, bound themselves to give over their surplus incomes into the communists' hands for the benefit of the Church and the poor. Zwicker believed that despite such humiliating conditions the Polish Brethren would open their churches to the propaganda of the Moravians. He began by trying to convince the two leading brethren with whom he was most intimate, Wolzogen and Ruar. To Ludwig Wolzogen, theologian and philosopher, formerly an Austrian baron, he addressed a memorandum arguing that the Church of the primitive Christians in Jerusalem was communistic, and then he considered the reasons why communism had not been introduced into other Churches. We do not know this document, nor do we know how it was received. We know, however, his correspondence with Ruar, which throws an interesting light on the mentality of these circles.[20] Under the influence of his sojourn among the communists, Zwicker informed Ruar as early as July 18, 1654, of the mission he had undertaken, whereupon for several weeks an active correspondence went on between them. Each letter is a sort of pamphlet, filled with arguments, taunts, and erudition. Zwicker in his enthusiasm soon exposed his naiveté; Ruar, old and mature, overwhelmed him with his experience of life and with quiet irony.

Zwicker, not wishing to risk exclusion from the Polish Brethren and to be deprived of access to their churches, did not admit to accepting the trinitarian confession of the Moravians. He presented the matter as though in adhering to them he had obtained their consent to his acknowledging and defending the Polish confession; and he gave an assurance that the communists, universally known for their ruthless sectarian spirit, had agreed to

[20] Cf. Zeltner, *Historia Cryptosocinianismi,* ii, 250-302.

recognize non-communists as brethren so long as the latter did not oppose their conception of evangelical poverty. Hence he proposed concluding an agreement with the communists and establishing a peace, during which they would draw nearer each other and became ready to unite; if, however, during this time the Polish Brethren found fault with Christian perfection and did not renounce wars and lawsuits, the responsibility for breaking off the union would fall upon them.

Ruar did not reject this proposition, but he brought forward so many doubts and reservations that after discussing it for several weeks, Zwicker became convinced of the impracticability of his plan. At first Ruar expressed his gratification that the Moravian Brethren had withdrawn from their uncompromising position, for hitherto their absolute insistence on communism had been a hindrance to their coming together; yet at the same time he regretted that Zwicker, during a too short stay among them, had not come to know the bad sides of their organization, which they concealed from guests.[21] Ruar considered that the fact that they allowed brethren to be received without taking from them all their property, demanding only that which a man had above his needs—could only be taken into account after the definition of the extent of those needs. Men who, in their effort for perfection, are ready to give their property to poor brethren deserve praise; but it is impossible to allow the duty to be forced upon one of working for brethren who through their own fault fall into poverty. The Moravians have bound themselves to communism too readily if they consider it a crime to assert that it cannot be deduced from the words of Christ. They are also too ready to regard the Polish Brethren as idlers:

[21] Ruar referred to the testimony of persons who knew the internal conditions of the Moravians well. In those years, the idea of property in common had already notably weakened; individual brethren secretly possessed money, and great offense was also caused by a tendency to luxury, manifested especially in the dresses of the women. Thirty years later they formally abandoned community of goods and allowed each of the brethren to have his own money, house, and furniture. Cf. L. Müller, *Kommunismus der mährischen Wiedertäufer*, p. 107.

"To each one we recommend honest labor; yet we do not force all without distinction to do heavy manual labor, from which even among them their elders are free, and despite this are not worse nourished."

In answer to charges against the life of the Polish Brethren, Ruar has no doubt that the Poles are equal in piety of life to the best of the Moravians, which is the more praiseworthy, since not being confined to a compulsory workshop, it radiates abroad. It shows greater faith in Providence when a man is left alone to himself and a hundred hands are not working for him. When property is held in common, there is no possibility for the individual to perform works of mercy. A man cannot disdain pleasures if he has no opportunity for them. How is a man to lead a just life, giving everyone his due, if he possesses nothing personally? There is no merit in modesty in dress if a man wears only garments that are prescribed. If he sleeps, eats, drinks, and works at another's command, there is no place for free will, which is the condition of virtue. It is not possible to glory in victory over the world while living wholly outside the world. If a man practices all these virtues outside the community, are they worthless only because he possesses something from which he can support his family without troubling his neighbor? The communists do not distribute their property among their neighbors, but save their incomes so that they may have security for the future. All sound men among them work, sell dearly, live frugally, and hence must have a considerable surplus (Christ laid up nothing!). Why do they reproach others for managing their own individual households with equal prudence?

It seems to me very unfair that, while they would indeed leave those of our number who enroll with them some private property, they yet require the surrender of everything a man has beyond immediate needs. But if illness comes, or infirm old age, which does not permit me to work, must I then starve or beg because I have saved nothing for such a case? You will say perhaps that

I am to turn to the brethren in Hungary. Why, before word reaches them of my need, before aid from them arrives, I shall starve to death. Why may I not retain in my own hands what they will keep for me? And if I die and leave little children unprovided for, must they write letters to Hungary to the Moravian Brethren and, hungry, wait for aid? Pardon me for not wishing to buy myself admission into their community under such severe conditions.

And Ruar would prefer to admonish his neighbor not to tempt God needlessly by asking him to work miracles, but to secure his family out of that which God has given him. The Christian religion does not command us to reject the dictates of sound reason.

Ruar also rejects the communists' assertion that they took the poverty of Christ for their model. Christ nowhere commanded all Christians without distinction to imitate the poverty in which he himself lived. To follow his example strictly, a man would have to give up house, furniture, and his way of earning his living. He would be improvident who thus impoverished himself without reason. The mission of Christ had a basis different from that of our duties. It is not permissible to scorn the means of support that God gives and to look to others for charity:

If the Moravian Brethren regard their chimerical poverty as perfection and should wish to impose it here in Poland, when they do not observe it among themselves; if they should still wish, under the pretense of poverty, to sweep the property of others into the net of their elders, we beg leave to oppose their scheme. In spite of this we do not cease to be lovers of peace, ready to bear their teachings and customs, not perverse indeed but colored by superstitions, ready also to amend our own, wherever they appear not in accord with the teaching of Christ.

The above paragraphs show clearly enough the line taken by Ruar, so we pass over the rest of his arguments and attacks, contained in three long letters, against which Zwicker was no match. It is true that Zwicker did not withdraw from his position and stuck to his communism stubbornly, although this exposed him to expulsion from Danzig in 1656. Having settled in Holland, he wrote in defense of the communism of the Moravian Brethren until late in life, confuting the treatise of Smalcius against the Hutterites, or bringing together citations from the Church Fathers against private property in a little book on the revival of Christian poverty. The Polish Brethren, engrossed in the tragic fortunes of their Church, did not respond to the utterances of this enthusiast;[22] while among the Moravian Brethren themselves, communism was disintegrating.[23]

[22] Sandius, pp. 155f.

[23] It is worth-while in passing to mention the later fortunes of the Moravian Brethren. The Empress Maria Theresa compelled them by violent means to go over to Catholicism. The police confiscated many of their chronicles, hymn-books, and manuscripts which, thanks to this, were preserved in the Church archives of Pressburg and Esztergom (Ostřihom), and in the libraries of Vienna and Budapest. At Sobotiště and Leváre Velké some buildings of the old community have been preserved to this day. The descendants of the brethren, nicknamed *habani,* have become Slovaks.

But a group of the more stubborn, chiefly from Transylvania, reinforced by an influx of heretical laborers from Carinthia, still cherished the idea of communism, and in 1781 emigrated to the Ukraine, where they organized for themselves a community at Vishenka on the Desna on the estate of Count Rumiancev. In 1802 they removed to Radichava; after the burning of their community house they settled in the Crimea in 1842, where they founded, in 1857, a model community under the name of Huterdorf. After compulsory military service was established in 1874, they left Russia and with the remnant of their books set out for America, where they settled in the State of Dakota. Today there are about three thousand of them, and they have five communities in the United States and twenty-four in Canada (Macleod, Alberta). In spite of these moves they have preserved their German nationality, they still keep to Riedemann's *Rechenschaft,* and they hold to the religious foundations of their communistic organization. Through their efforts, the great historical book of the Hutterites, which they keep as a relic, was reprinted in 1923, thanks to which we have been able to recreate the primitive stage of their relations with the Polish Brethren.

# 12  *In Defense of the Duties of Citizenship*

Brenius' sectarian doctrine of the State. Wolzogen supports it. Jonas Szlichtyng defends the power of the State. Controversy between Szlichtyng and Wolzogen. Relation to the State. Self-defense. Lawfulness of war.

The perennial discussion among the Polish Brethren about their relation to the State was settled in principle by a positive decision appearing in the Racovian Catechism and making possible, at least in theory, a way out of the sectarian position. A number of years later, however, a similar dispute broke out in the West, in Holland. There the Mennonites had long since taken a negative stand, but this confession, which had spread among artisans of the large towns and among laboring people in Frisia, had no learned theologians to go into so intricate a problem scientifically.[1] The radical wing of the Remonstrants, which was in contact with the Polish Antitrinitarians, took it up. A member of this group, Jan Geesteranus,[2] presented to the

---

[1] The greatest resonance found Jacob Jansen (Kist) with his sixteen arguments against the authority of the State. They started a debate in his own camp which lasted for about twenty years. Cf. also N. van der Zijpp, *De Vroegere Doopsgezinden en de Krijgsdienst* (Wolvega:1930) and *Geschiedenis der Doopsgezinden in Nederland* (Arnhem:1952); W. J. Kühler, *Geschiedenis der Nederlandsche Doopsgezinden in de Zestiende Eeuw*, 1932.

[2] In 1622 he received an invitation to be head of the school at Raków, but he did not go to Poland (Sandius, p. 114), deciding to support himself by manual labor.

famous synod of Dortrecht (1619) a declaration denying to Christians the right to accept office under the State, thereby arousing indignation against the Remonstrants. Then Simon Episcopius, the most prominent theologian of the camp,[3] came forward with a different view, but he met with opposition from his own pupil, Daniel de Breen (Brenius).[4]

Brenius henceforth unweariedly propagated his own uncompromising views. First of all he sounded the Polish Brethren through Ruar,[5] won adherents in a secret group of Dutch Anti-trinitarians, the so-called Rijnsburg Collegiants,[6] and finally published a thorough discussion entitled *De qualitate Regni domini Jesu Christi* (1647). Here anti-State sectarian ideology found its most consistent expression.[7]

To the organization of the State Brenius opposes the kingdom of Christ existing on earth as the Church. These are two worlds, completely different in structure and aim. The Kingdom of

[3] *An homini Christiano conveniat officium magistratus gerere* (1620).

[4] Episcopius himself had encouraged Brenius to study the question. Cf. his letter of 1623-24 in *Praestantium ac eruditorum virorum Epistolae* (Amsterdam:1684), p. 637. A letter of Brenius, written undoubtedly to Episcopius from Harlem on November 2, 1626, and preserved in Ms. III E 2 of the Remonstrant Collection of the University Library in Amsterdam, discusses at great length the problem whether it is possible for a Christian to hold offices and disputes to a certain degree the views of his master. Brenius' treatise was published without the author's knowledge in a Dutch translation in 1639 and 1646. The Latin original appeared as late as 1651 (*Opera*, II, 71-95).

[5] Cf. letter to Ruar from Amsterdam, August 26, 1627; and Ruar's reply in Zeltner, *Historia Cryptosocinianismi*, ii, 576, 365.

[6] On mystics-spiritualists in Holland cf. J. C. Van Slee, *Rijnsburger Collegianten* (Haarlem:1895); C. B. Hylkema, *Reformateurs*, II (Haarlem:1902), pp. 71-82 deal with the opposition against wars and armaments); Stanislaus Dunin-Borkowski, *Spinoza*, I, 2 (Münster:1933); L. Chmaj, "De Spinoza a Bracia Polscy" ("Spinoza and the Polish Brethren"), *Reformacja w Polsce*, III (1925), 54ff; as well as papers of H. W. Meihuizen and R. Friedmann in the *Mennonite Quarterly Review*, XXVII-XXVIII (1953-1954).

[7] Both treatises, Episcopius' and Brenius', circulated early in manuscripts and provoked discussion. They were published at first in Dutch: *Van de hoedanigheid des rijks Christi* (1640, 1641), then, in 1657, in Latin: *De Regno Christi glorioso* and *De qualitate Regni Dei;* reprints in 1664 and 1666 in the collective *Opera Theologica*.

Christ is composed of the faithful, who govern themselves strictly according to the laws given by him, and therefore cannot submit to other laws. They are called to another sort of greatness than the rest of humanity. Their greatness lies in the fact that they serve others, are patient and obedient, love their enemies, do not countenance murder, wars, resistance to evil, or self-defense, and ban all courts and public punishments. The subjects of this Kingdom are found all over the world, in various communities, everywhere feeling themselves one. The supreme good for them lies not in property or in government, but in contempt for these earthly goods. They do not disturb the foundations of society, for they recognize the authority of parents over children, man over wife, master over servant, and all differences of class. They are forbidden to take part in the government of the State, but commanded to yield obedience to every authority, though it were evil and unjust, though acquired by wrong and force. Under each the believer is strong (after the pattern of Christ) in his own submission and service; but he does not bear a sword to exterminate evil men, for he has turned it into plows and pruning-hooks. Defenseless, God defends him and inclines even pagan powers to mildness toward him for his obedience.

The State has a quite separate existence. It is not condemned, but subjects of Christ cannot govern themselves by its laws: enough that they are obedient to it. They do not need the protection of government. They derive no advantage from its justice, for they cannot lower the teachings of Christ to the demands of natural justice. The civil power has to restrain evil men; in this the faithful cannot aid it. They cannot accept office, for they are not allowed to behave according to earthly laws. Unable to defend good or to punish evil men, an official from their group would deprive the people of laws granted to them by divine providence. Their withdrawal from the functions of government threatens no harm, for enough men will always be found willing to administer punishments.

Brenius' stand made a deep impression among the Polish Brethren. His ideas, as we see, were not striking for their novelty. They were the same as those developed in the beginnings of the Antitrinitarian movement by Peter of Goniądz (Gonesius), Gregory Paulus, and Czechowic. The difference is perhaps this, that in those pioneers we observed what was rather an escape from the State as a dangerous temptation for the Christian, and in Brenius we feel a great self-confidence and pride in the little Church of God, proceeding from a sense of its superiority to the State. It surprises us, the less expected since, in the period of the Thirty Years War and of confirmed absolutism, the mutual relations of Church and State were already settled to the advantage of the State, whereas about 1572, when the religious wars broke out in Europe, this could not yet be taken for granted. And yet sectarian dreaming appears in Brenius with a program and arguments strangely reminiscent of the mediaeval campaign of the Church against the State at the period of the greatest power of the Papacy.

The Polish Brethren, among whom the dust of oblivion had concealed the radical writings of the first Racovians, and who in the last generation had accommodated themselves to the existing social system, expressed themselves in very lively fashion. Brenius roused their thoughts and pens; their concealed doubts found expression. Two contradictory views appeared, the one represented by the German members of the Church, the other by the Polish nobility. The Germans, taking no part in the political life of the Republic, taking no account of the evolution of society towards violent intolerance, not thinking it possible to gain anything by an opportunist adjustment to society, contented themselves with being able to confess their faith in a closed company, in secret groups that escaped public notice. The Poles were not willing to let themselves be relegated to such a rôle. In spite of decrees by the tribunals destroying their churches, in spite of the destruction of Raków with its press and school (1638), they made heroic exertions to retain even a fragment of the rights that they had enjoyed since Sigismund Augustus. This difference in point of view called forth two separate lines of discussion on the step taken by Brenius.

Advocacy of the ideas of Brenius was undertaken by Ludwig Wolzogen, an Austrian baron settled among the Polish Brethren, who devoted himself to theological and mathematical studies.[8] During his visit to Holland—he lived mostly in Gdańsk (Danzig) —he became friendly with Brenius and translated into German his *Van de hoedanigheid des rijks Christi.* Together they prepared a treatise *On the Church Triumphant,* now lost. His treatise *De natura et qualitate Regni Christi ac religionis Christianae*[9] surpassed in extent and in the extremity of its views the Dutch work which had inspired it. "In Christ's Kingdom," runs Wolzogen's thesis, "there is no place for worldly powers, kings or magnates, who rule by force of compulsion not only over goods and estates but also over the lives of their subjects, and who use others' services not only out of necessity but for show and worldly ostentation." It is of the essence of government to have authority and obedience; but the mark of the Christian is submission, hence Christ's command is opposed to the essence of authority; Christians cannot meddle in the affairs of earthly government. Although Christ did not do away with States, he forbade his followers to participate in them, calling them to a higher dignity. It is not, to be sure, necessary to deprive kings and officers, ruling in a Christian world, of hope of salvation, so far as they rule in good faith, govern justly, care for their subjects, and do not violate consciences, but as caring for bodily welfare they are lower than those who care for salvation. Thus even the best of them cannot be admitted to the Church.

But the nobility? In so far as they fall in with the evil customs of the world, e.g. the bloody revenge of injuries, they

[8] Cf. L. Chmaj, *Wolzogen przeciw Descartes'owi* (*Wolzogen versus Descartes*) (Cracow:1917).
[9] Inserted in Wolzogen's *Opera,* in *Bibliotheca Fratrum Polonorum,* ii, 241-96.

cannot belong to the Church. But noble, count, and the like, these are outward titles, worn like clothes, according to the custom of the neighborhood. Better dress in accordance with the general custom than wear unfashionable garments. If admission to the Church were made dependent upon laying aside one's nobility and going over to the common people, this would arouse aversion to religion. Moreover, even a noble may live modestly, without luxury. But the Christian commoner is not allowed to strive for nobility, for that is an indication of pride. Also, a man ought not to go armed, though customs are today so depraved that it is hard to forbid it. The nobles do not wish to be treated as commoners, hence they may keep their arms if they pledge themselves not to wound anyone with them. But if the weaker brethren should be scandalized by this, love for the latter must be placed higher than regard for carnal honor.

It is forbidden to seek the punishment of a wrong-doer even through the court, nor may one forcibly defend oneself against an assailant. A Christian may not acknowledge the State courts which inflict corporal punishment upon malefactors, for he ought to love the latter and repay them with kindness. Good men may be at peace though they do not defend themselves; likewise, evil deeds do not escape without punishment. Although natural justice inclines a Christian to take part in the administration of justice, God forbids him to do this. As Christ shields his own from the violence of evil men, so he defends the whole nation against the army of a foe. Wars do not come by accident, they are the judgments of God upon nations, thus the faithful do not interfere in wars. If God pronounces a decree against a country or a town, let them flee lest they suffer the punishments of God; God will make this easy for them. In the midst of disasters the Christian is happy, for he knows that they will turn out for his good. Wars are not allowable even for so-called freedom of conscience. Conscience is always free; but such wars have in view essentially physical peace, not peace of conscience.

But with Christians behaving in this way, will not States

and civil order fall, crimes flourish, and the Turks become masters of Europe? They will never fall into a state of anarchy, Wolzogen asserts, for they have the best court and King in the person of Christ. It would be worse if Christ did not restrain earthly kings in their greed and stupid purposes.

And yet Christ, in judging the world, does not dispense with some organs, which are the offices of the State; is it then possible to withdraw from fulfilling the rôle of an instrument of God? Here Wolzogen replies by comparing the world to an enormous garden in which a beautiful flower sometimes appears, though the whole is full of nettles and tares. So in the world now and then a true Christian is found, but the generality are absorbed in worldly pleasures. Christ permits the political order, officers and judges, to exist in accordance with the wisdom of the world, and in order that this system also may serve his followers, even against the wish of men of the world. The faithful are a little group, but in a strict sense even monarchs must serve them. The elect themselves do not have to turn their hands to worldly affairs; they should regard them as a comedy, or perhaps a tragedy, performed on the order of kings by their servants. Through his instruments God punishes the wicked, but He does not employ His faithful as instruments for such lowly acts; He performs them through meaner servants, through the tares of the garden. Hence no chaos or impunity is to be feared. If a man does evil, the Church cuts him off; and then the sinner dies by the sword of the executioner or on the gallows.

But will so revolutionary a doctrine destroy the authority of government? No, replies Wolzogen, for we have to be obedient to the authorities; and withdrawal from office-holding in no way prevents this. For at a king's court one is not contemptuous of the office of marshal or chancellor if one asserts that it is not fitting for the son of the king to hold it.

It would have been impossible to go further in withdrawing from all influence in society, from the possibility of real action and open measures by the congregation, or on the other hand to go further in exalted consciousness of the mission of the sect, as compensation for this withdrawal. The violent position of Wolzogen provoked a reaction. The man who took the field against him was at the time the most prominent member of the Church, Jonas Szlichtyng, a pupil of Crellius, the chief champion of the doctrine of the Brethren against the Protestants (Clementinus, Vechner, Meisner, Grotius). Although he was descended from the county nobility, he filled the office of minister at Raków because, in the words of Andrew Moskorzowski, "laying his gifts at the feet of the dear Savior, he preferred to endure the contempt of the world rather than enjoy the world to the very great damage of his conscience." [10]

In the controversy with Meisner mentioned above, Szlichtyng adopted a fairly extreme position, but in time he modified it, and in his Commentaries on the Epistles of St. Paul he declared decidedly for participation in the life of the State. He knew no reason, he declared, why others could hold office but Christians could not.[11] Who could be better for the purpose than the Christian, who more temperate and just in the use of authority and the right of the sword, who more zealous in the defense of good men and especially of Christians? If all became Christians, would it be necessary to entrust the authority of the State to a foreigner in order that a Christian should not exercise it? Even in a purely Christian society, secular power will clearly be necessary, for there are always wicked men, and the office of the sword will always be needed. And if authority is a good thing, efforts should be made to see that Christians exercise it, that Christians are chosen as kings, or that kings become Christians. If the office of king is consistent with faith, who could deny a Christian king the right to the sword, and

[10] Speech at the marriage of Szlichtyng's daughter to Łaziński in 1643; Krasiński Library Ms. 311, p. 286. In 1647 Szlichtyng was by decree of the Diet condemned to banishment for his Confession of faith, after which he lived in hiding among the brethren in the Carpathian foothills.

[11] *Comment. in epist. Pauli ad Romanos, cap. 13* in *Bibliotheca Fratrum Polonorum, Opera Schlichtingii,* i, 302.

to soldiers and the employment of them, when the public welfare of the people requires it? "I should fear," wrote Szlichtyng,[12] "to restrict the Christian religion to private persons only, to common people and the rabble. Things stand thus today, but this is due to human blundering and error; nevertheless in my view the Christian religion may include kings and emperors, for it brings to all classes and callings God's grace, which inclines all men to a godly and sober life and kings to a benevolent exercise of their power."

Having arrived at this conviction, Szlichtyng could not keep silent in face of Wolzogen's anti-State doctrine, and he wrote against him *Quaestiones de magistratu, bello, defensione privata.* This work is lost, but we know its arguments from Wolzogen's reply, *Annotationes ad Quaestiones Jonae Schlichtingii.*[13] Not acknowledging himself beaten, Szlichtyng answered him in his *Annotationes oppositae memoratis J. L. Wolzogenii Annotationibus,* which again we know only from Wolzogen's *Responsio ad Jonae Schlichtingii Annotationes in Annotationes,* which closed the dispute.[14] Instead of summarizing these four stages of the controversy step by step, we shall present the leading thoughts in the form of a dialogue between the authors on the several main subjects of the dispute.

Thus on the question of relation to the *State:*

SZLICHTYNG (*Quaestiones*): It is necessary to strive for the ideal that kings should be Christians, or else that Christians should become kings. Why contest this today, when the godly are so few and those who are astray so numerous and powerful? Christ does not exclude from the Church kings and rulers of the people, but summons to true greatness the great as well as the small, leaders and ministers as well as subjects. He would not have kings resign their rule, but behave properly in order that they may serve the people, even as he sacrificed himself for

---

[12] *Comment. in I epist. Pauli ad Timotheum, ibid.,* II, 243.
[13] Wolzogen, *Opera,* in *Bibliotheca Fratrum Polonorum,* iii, 63-78.
[14] *Ibid.,* iii, 91-132.

the people. A king must care for the welfare of his people, and even sacrifice his life for them.

WOLZOGEN (*Annotationes*): Are we to long for public peace under our own kings? Is peace happiness? Better suffer oppression under un-Christian kings than devote oneself to luxury in peace. We shall never have Christian kings, not because there will always be only a little handful of us, but because our Kingdom is not of this world, and there will never be place in it for an earthly king; a substitute for Christ would be only a usurper. Better not rouse such expectations, for the weaker brethren are ready to think that the happy times in which a Christian may rule over his brethren are already at hand. Some of the younger ones who think thus are today already uttering shocking things, and the latest sad examples (certainly he here has in mind utterances in the manner of Samuel Przypkowski) condemn this view. It would bring about the ruin of the Church if a majority should today admit into the Church a king or potentate who acknowledged the truth.

SZLICHTYNG (*Annotationes in Annotationes*): Everyone has the right to enjoy earthly goods. Oppression is a cure for luxury, but still the medicine is not better than the disease by the fact that it cures it. A good Christian king would be the best restraint on crimes, for it is really Christ who rules when godly kings rule. Increase in the number of the faithful is not brought about without State organization. Only fanatics or madmen can desire the abolition of authority, for then even the Church could not exist. The Church has always flourished when the ruler was a member of it. We know how much benefit Jan Zapolya brought the Christian Church in Transylvania after he came to power; also in Poland the magnate Jacob Sienieński afforded the Church protection. The death of each brought disaster to the faithful. Poor is the Church that is incapable of receiving rulers into its company. The Church should not be confused with the State, but it should be remembered that both organizations are created by Christians endowed with thought and reason. You concede coercive authority to Christ, and yet you abhor it and condemn it as sinful. One may condemn the mistakes of kings, but not their office. It does not follow from the fact that Christ did not exercise secular authority that it is forbidden to his followers. They hold Christian truth in too low esteem who think it designed only for the common people. You retain the distinction of classes, you admit to the Church tradesmen and innkeepers, you consent to a Christian being master over his serfs, why not then a king? For there is no fear that the admission of rulers would at once rouse an impulse to aspire to this dignity and excite tumults. The dislike of the office of the sword is unreasonable; and what would happen if wicked men did not fear the executioner? Moreover, who can rule with the sword and the gallows more justly than a Christian ruler? Even Christians must not be allowed to commit crimes, robbery, theft; thus even in a Christian State the office of the sword may not be condemned.

WOLZOGEN (*Responsio*): Let us look above all to the good of the faithful. Outsiders will have prosperity enough even without Christian kings. God does not wish Christians to be free from persecution. Lasting peace is a very great foe of godliness; hence it is proper to hate it. Moreover, even a Christian king is powerless against pride and greed, for secular authority does not cover transgressions of the higher commandments of Christ; on the contrary, his court would of necessity become an example and an occasion of pride. Increase in the number of the faithful through the instrumentality of kings we do not wish, for that would be spreading the faith by the sword. The Church assuredly could not exist without any State organization; but it can exist without Christian rulers. A Christian king would do away with real martyrdom, and the place of Christian courage would be taken by martial courage. The faithful would resort to any means to extricate the truth of God from oppression, which would cause a multitude of revolutions and disturbances. The history of Jan Sigismund Zapolya is quite obscure and cannot be appealed to. It is no matter for pride if, to win his favor, many went over to his religion; it is, moreover, doubtful whether piety was the gainer in this. The present state (in Transylvania) would indicate that it did not derive much advantage thereby. Sienieński, again, was not a ruler; few of the nobility, and they not too powerful, may be in the Church. Misfortunes have come not because of the loss of important patrons but because piety is decaying in the Church and scandals are increasing. If holiness had prevailed in it, patrons would have been found, even outside the Church. Church and State are strictly separate. The Church does not need a Christian State and can exist without it. God is author of the political order; these people may exercise their authority not among Christians but among the rest of the population. The Church can develop under an outside power, as hitherto in Poland, where Christ has for so many years invisibly defended his lambs among wolves, although their foes are ready enough and strong enough to destroy them. Religion is not degraded if the multitude profess it; those insult it more in whose opinion earthly kings do not have to resign their thrones and palaces for its sake. The occupation of trader is not opposed to the Christian profession; innkeepers may be reformed, and if not, then expel them. To hold serfs is not opposed to Christianity, but one may not exercise over one's brethren the full rights of a master: "I doubt, however, whether one may be a Christian and such a master as the Poles who hold serfs, not only because they load their serfs with excessive labor and do not set them free every seven years as God commanded, but also because they allow them no appeal from their masters, nor any refuge or right to complain of grievances." Today the world is filled with so many crimes that it is hard to restrain them by sword and gallows. Let the State then rather have for king a Turk, a Jew, or a pagan, who would be warlike and pay heed to external justice. But the punishment of criminal brethren does not belong to the State; Christ entrusted this to the Church with the proviso that it is to inflict only spiritual punishments and is by no means allowed to mete out such punishments as would leave the sinner no possibility of repentance. Today even erring Christians recognize that they must not cut off evil-doers from the way to salvation; even those on the way to the gallows they comfort with the hope of salvation. The Christian Church must pardon the sinner everything, if he shows repentance.

The discussion on *self-defense* produced no unexpected arguments:

Szlichtyng (*Quaestiones*): Love due to an assailant has limits (the argument is borrowed from Grotius) in the love that we owe ourselves or the innocent victims of an attack. In both love and hatred we must observe moderation. It is a mistake to regard as virtue what is so regarded by honest churls (an allusion to the Anabaptists and Mennonites): resistance in defense of one's own life is just; petty injuries should be forgiven but one must defend one's property, the loss of which sinks a family into misery. One ought not to tempt God to do miracles; and therefore in the face of dangers it is better to go armed.

Wolzogen (*Annotationes*): Murder of an assailant is always murder and conceals within itself a vengeance which is the worse for being carried out before the assailant has managed to commit the sin. If one lets oneself be killed by an enemy, it is not out of love of him but for the sake of showing Christian patience. One should not place defense of property on a level with defense of life. If a believer will not go armed, God of a surety will not forsake him. More men have perished in the world when armed than when unarmed, nor can we ever know when God wishes through an evil-doer to punish us for secret sins. Otherwise, let us be consistent, let us educate our youth in another way, let us exercise it in shooting and wielding weapons.

Szlichtyng (*Annotationes in Annotationes*): We cannot deduce a prohibition of capital punishment from the commandment: "Thou shalt not kill." If killing a man can *per se* be just, it does not become unjust through being done by a Christian. If an assailant gets killed when attempting the life of an innocent man, he himself will quite justly meet the same fate as he was planning for the innocent man. Away with such virtue as bids us spare a robber! The longer a bandit lives, the more crimes he will commit. Where robbery prevails, there is no harm in exercising youth in shooting instead of calling on angels from heaven to defend us, for that is an absurdity contrary to reason. Flight is often impracticable. In the Ukraine bands of Tartars repeatedly appear and unexpectedly raid the heart of the country. Similar murderous bands appear in the Carpathian foothills, where nobody would expect them. To love bandits means only to pray God to melt them, nothing more; but what Tartar or brigand mountaineer will repent? One may of course pray God to pardon a murderer, as some of our brethren did at the time of the Cossack invasions (in 1648 many of the Antitrinitarian families in the province of Kiev were slaughtered by the Cossacks), but above all one must value one's life higher than that of the bandit.

WOLZOGEN (*Responsio*): If my opponent recommends youths to practice shooting, it is best to encourage them to enter the army, for nowhere can one better learn the use of weapons! The argument about Tartars and bandits is not convincing. Let Christians not dwell in such districts, especially in isolation where there are no others to defend them. To dwell there only means to tempt God. If Tartars raid the heart of the country, then either buy them off or take advantage of the fact that others will drive them away. But if this also fails, bear in humility the visitation of the Lord God, without whose will nothing takes place. In time of war, behave like a traveller, retire by degrees to places of safety, and when those are wanting, remove to another country. It is Szlichtyng who is tempting God when he finally urges that the brethren should not flee from Poland but should stay there at the risk of their lives, confident that either God will save them or their troubles will contribute to the glory of God.[15]

We proceed lastly to the controversy on the lawfulness of *war*.

SZLICHTYNG (*Quaestiones*): Even a Christian kingdom cannot be denied the right to maintain soldiers, for no State can exist without forces. War, abstractly considered, is reasonable, if pious people wage it. Evidently it is somewhat otherwise today, when wars are crowded so full of abuses and crimes. If even now, however, a man goes to war at the command of the law or when carried off by force, but not for pay or a career, and if he participates in it only in body, not in spirit and behavior, God grants His help in combating evil. A man should not, however, voluntarily prepare for war with the idea of killing the enemy. Defense of country does not absolutely require this. A man can serve his country in other ways also, such as providing the army with food. Those who remained in the rear have often done more for their country than those at the front.

WOLZOGEN (*Annotationes*): War is usually God's punishment on the wicked, among whom few of the elect dwell; therefore the faithful ought not to defend themselves against the anger of God along with unbelievers. To the former God indicates flight or some other way of escape. Defensive war is today the same as offensive, and in a Christian State it would be no better than in that of today. Nothing forces the Christian to go to war; the civil laws of the Republic are not binding upon his conscience; thus it is not these, but the flesh, worldly goods, the esteem of men, the temporal privileges of the nobility that push him into war. It is hard to renounce these good things; we make money, we buy villages, and we shelter ourselves by pleading the com-

---

[15] For lack of any date in the polemical tracts under discussion, we do not know to what danger Szlichtyng's summons referred: to the Cossack or Swedish wars, or to the verdict of expulsion from Poland. He himself, as we know, was condemned to banishment in 1647 and lived in hiding in the country until at length, on the withdrawal of the Swedes in 1656, he was compelled to emigrate.

pulsion of the law. You say you are going with the others, but will not kill. It is just then that you are breaking the law, which commands you to kill the enemy. You pretend that you are free to fight, and yet you know that you are not. I know the wealth of arguments in the discussion of this subject, for example, that our religion will be threatened. Of this I am not certain, but even were it to be so, a Christian can be saved without external worship; and indeed he is not subject to human authority who with a pure heart professes religion. Those who go to war without any intention of killing must be regarded as weak and imperfect Christians; the laudable custom of debarring them for a certain time from the Lord's table should be adopted, and it should be continually insisted that in this respect a Christian is not at liberty to obey the public law.

SZLICHTYNG (*Annotationes in Annotationes*): It is no sin to offer forcible resistance to an enemy's attack upon the kingdom. The believer may possess worldly goods; their increase, so far as it is done without greed or injury, is, after all, taken for a gift and a blessing of God, hence he may not give them up to be seized by enemies. Similarly he may not surrender wives and daughters to be outraged. Men must take care of these goods, unless they are willing to be themselves the cause of their own ruin. God does not act by miraculous means if natural ones exist. Otherwise we ought not, for example, to stir when a fire is ruining a fellow-man. The fact is, moreover, that according to public law, to be a Polish noble and a soldier are synonymous terms. To flee before the enemy is the sign of a coward and a traitor to his country, and not of a true Christian. If all should flee before the enemy, who would defend it? For a man to defend his country by sacrificing his blood and life is indeed a really Christian thing to do. If he must wage war, let him wage it, provided he do so in a Christian way. The faithful, who do not regard the repulse of an enemy as contrary to the teaching of Christ, who regard it as their duty to die for their country, and in a war conduct themselves as Christians, cannot be condemned. Those who, of their

own choice, rush into military service and into war-making are
different. But a man who takes part in a just war, as bound by
law to do so, should not be kept from the Lord's table.

WOLZOGEN (*Responsio*): A Christian has no country on earth.
Therefore the bit of this earth on which we are born is not worth
the risk of one's own or of another's life. Better defenders are always furnished by those who have their country and their highest
good on this earth and live only for military glory. Of such there
is never any lack; there will always be on earth more mud than
gold; others will always take the place of the Christians who keep
aloof from war in order to save their lives for the glory of Christ
and the salvation of their fellow-men. Strictly speaking, my opponent is inconsistent in not approving of voluntary service in the
army; if war is good, then a man ought to go to it without being
compelled by the laws. The good patriot, sound and strong,
ought to undergo the most difficult exertions; especially would
youth, apt for war, have to be urged to it. A man does not surrender family or goods to the spoiler when he does what he can
without offense to his religion and therefore removes them from a
field where they are threatened, or compromises with the enemy,
and the like. Does nobility indeed demand military service? The
privileges of nobility are too much exalted in Poland. It is true
that our churches can thank the nobility for their existence thus
far, but it does not follow that a man is allowed to be a Polish
noble at any cost. Would the churches be unable to exist without
this? Why, the Jews, communists, Mennonites, Remonstrants in
various countries do not depend upon the privileges of the nobles!
"Our ancestors would have helped our churches and the truth of
God in Poland much better had they either resigned the privilege
of nobility or made some other arrangement with the Republic by
which they might have retained their nobility and freed themselves from the burden of war as well as from swearing by the
Trinity and the crucifix." Christian discipline teaches us to
emigrate from our country if we cannot live a godly life within

it, and to choose one where we may serve God and live in His
fear.

We do not know the exact chronology of the dialogue between
Szlichtyng and Wolzogen, but it began in the peaceful years under
Ladislas IV and ended after the storm of the Cossack invasion
burst in the reign of John Casimir, perhaps about 1650. Wolzogen,
sojourning in Poland as a religious immigrant, not sentimentally
bound to it, from beginning to end held an attitude indifferent to
its fortunes, inexorably anti-State and sectarian. Szlichtyng, on
the other hand, in the course of years and the misfortunes of the
Republic, became more and more inclined to compromise, more
and more withdrew from the doctrine of Socinus and, although
he endeavored to keep up certain basic appearances, at bottom
yielded to the demands of good citizenship. Let us not be aston-
ished by his condemnation of voluntary participation in military
affairs; from the experiences of the Thirty Years War it was well
known to what brutalizing influences the soldiering element was
then subjected. Wars were waged by methods not to be distinguished from private banditry. A man who voluntarily enlisted
did so largely for the sake of booty and plunder.

Martin Ruar, distinguished for his deliberation and experience,
defended the lawfulness of the Polish wars against the Turks and
the Tartars.[16] When, however, Abraham Mierzyński asked him
for a recommendation for his brother, who was preparing to
volunteer for the French army (which in 1656 was carrying on
war with Spain) and trying to get the rank of ensign, Ruar condemned the plan: "I cannot," he wrote Mierzyński,[17] "condemn
a man who under the compulsion of danger to himself or his
family takes up arms for necessary defense; but voluntary military service, undertaken for pleasure or for glory or gain, I
regard as totally opposed to the rule of life that the Savior and

[16] Zeltner, ii, 268.
[17] *Ibid.*, pp. 302-04.

his Apostles prescribed for us." If we are to love our enemies, then certainly we should not except those who have given us no offense in either word or deed, and should not attempt their lives and property. Even in a just war, according to today's customs, many injuries are inflicted upon the innocent, and this is quite unavoidable if a man would not expose himself to the anger of his commanders. It will be hard to acquit oneself of this before God, but behind what excuse shall a man shelter himself where the question of the rightfulness of the war itself is not clear?

# 13  *Przypkowski on the Relations Between Church and State*

Przypkowski versus the doctrine of his sect. Relation of Church and State. Limits of the two jurisdictions. Defense of coercive authority. Unfavorable
results of sectarianism. Palaeologus' defense against
Socinus. Lawfulness of defensive war. Duty of defense against an invader. Criticism of utopian pacifism. Controversy with Zwicker. Reaction of sectarian
spiritualism. Expulsion of the Antitrinitarians from
Poland. Bayle on the possibility of influence by the
Socinians.

The sectarian views of Brenius must have spread devastation
among the thoughtful if, independently of Szlichtyng, the most
highly talented writer of the Polish Brethren, Samuel Przypkowski, undertook to confute them. His *Animadversiones in Libellum
cui titulus De qualitate Regni Domini nostri Jesu Christi, ubi
inquiritur, an Christiano sive Regni eius subdito terrenae domina-
tiones conveniant*[1] (written probably in 1650) in the arrangement
of its chapters and contents follows step by step the work of
Brenius. Out of consideration for the Dutch and German members of the sect, it is written in Latin, in elegant language and a

[1] Pp. 619-81 in the collection of Przypkowski's works entitled *Cogita-
tiones sacrae . . . nec non tractatus varii momenti, praecipue De jure
Christiani magistratus* (Eleutheropoli-Amsterdam: 1692).

clear and lively style. It is one of the most acute philosophico-
theological treatises that came out of the Antitrinitarian camp.
Przypkowski does not wish to beat his opponent by erudition or
by irony, but by close reasoning, thus he himself states his positions in the form of syllogisms, which he then develops. Despite
this apparently forbidding form, one reads his work without
growing weary. A writer of high culture, he avoids the usual
polemic devices and treats his opponent with genuine courtesy,
however much he objects to the absurdity of his theses.

The *Animadversiones* of Przypkowski is the most original and
exhaustive Polish work on the mutual relations of Church and
State. The Kingdom of Christ, not in the broad conception as embracing the whole world, but in the narrower one, that is, as the
Church, exercises a spiritual authority, to which men are subject
of their own will. An earthly kingdom, or State, on the contrary,
rests on its coercive authority. Membership in the Church does
not exclude the exercise of authority, even sovereign authority
in the organism of the State, but a subject in a State cannot
possess any kind of sovereign authority or independence of the
State. When Christ established the principles of *Church* government, he did not forbid its members to take part in civil government, but only removed some members of the Church from earthly
rule. He forbade dominion and coercive authority in the Church,
but this prohibition does not reach beyond spiritual and ecclesiastical government. Political government is very useful and indispensable for the people of Christ in the temporal life. The witness
of many ages teaches that the same people who in the Church
submit to the new order of Christ may in the State maintain the
eternal order of God as to coercive authority. Neither in the
economic nor in the political order has the teaching of Christ set
aside the positive law which annulled or limited natural freedom
and equality; on the contrary, it commands submission and due
obedience to officers and masters according to the flesh also for
conscience' sake, not only for fear of punishment. It did not do
away with the differences in rank and social class established on

the basis of general agreement, nor abolish any laws derived therefrom, only limiting their use by the requirements of Christian justice. The fact that men are by nature free and equal is not opposed to the necessity of authority, just as the possession of estates and the existence of serfdom are not prevented by the fact that when a man is born, he possesses nothing. Christianity, which in its ecclesiastical discipline knows no difference between persons, in secular affairs rather acknowledged and confirmed differences in laws and positions, sovereigns and subjects:

Hence also in the same Christian society there may and actually do exist parallel systems, different and apparently contradictory. One is founded on equality of persons and the absence of coercive authority; the other on difference between persons and the existence of compulsion. The one system is that of the Church, the other that of the State. The Church did not take the place of the State, but strengthened it. The rise of the authority of the Church did not set aside the secular authority, but brought about the establishment of such mutual limits that the one did not encroach on the sphere of the other. Both when the State with compulsory authority encroaches on the government of the Church, and when the Church takes the sword which God himself has entrusted to it out of the hands of the civil authority, there is a violation of justice.[2]

In view of this, Brenius' thesis that there would be no place for the civil authority among a people which belonged to the Kingdom of Christ, with its quite different, ecclesiastical system, collapses.

The spiritual society, or Church, ensures the salvation of the soul and its eternal welfare; the civil society, or State, ensures temporal welfare. The fact that we long for the eternal is no reason why we should neglect the temporal—except it were contrary to the other, which does not always happen—for access to eternal life is possible only through the present earthly life. Similarly, it is as absurd to exclude a man from the State because he professes a certain religion as it would be to drive a man from

[2] P. 629.

a religious union because he was bound by certain ties to the State. The opponents of this community life have no strong proofs; they employ only figurative phrases or equivocal expressions in a strained sense. For example: they whose kingdom is not of this world may not meddle with earthly government, the kindgom of Christians is not of this world, hence Christians, etc. The only drawback to simultaneous adherence to Church and State would be a confusion of jurisdictions, but that does not arise here:

There cannot exist in the same society two State organs, independent of each other, if one does not have jurisdiction above the other; for both possess authority of the same sort, that is, coercive, and from their rivalry war must result. But kingdoms so different in kind as a spiritual one without compulsion and a secular one with coercive authority may exist in the same nation without conflict of jurisdiction; if both authorities, so separate, remain within their own limits, each may exercise its functions without hindrance. The spiritual authority with gentle bridle guides the thoughts, the consciences, and the inner man toward the most perfect kind of virtues. But authority endowed with compulsion with harsh bridle leads the outer man not to virtue, which it is impossible to compel, but to refrain from offenses and to observe the political order. Another object, a different method of direction, ensures that neither authority can get in the other's way. On the other hand, it is not at all necessary that they should have no points of contact or that one should not in a measure be dependent upon the other. It is true that because the spiritual authority, even if only in consequence of the nature of its object, is more noble, it is fitting that the political should serve it, just as in a man the outward acts and powers of locomotion should be subject to the orders of the spirit and the reason. The political authority does not, however, have to be subject to the spiritual in that which would destroy it, that is, in the application of compulsion to outward acts, nor in that which would undermine the spiritual authority itself, whose essence it is to direct the inviolable freedom of minds. But political authority can be of service in this, that restraining coarser offenses by a coarser bridle, it makes it easier for men to avoid those which are less flagrant; further, by securing to

each his rights, it safeguards the precious goods of the human
spirit, peace and liberty, especially of conscience, and the defense
of the noble against the oppression and injury of evil men, who
often render it impossible for truth, and consequently also for
virtue, to prevail in the thoughts of men; finally, by the fact
that, in secular legislation, it admits of nothing opposed to
spiritual laws, which would be contrary to the laws of Christ.
On the other hand, it is inconsistent with the nature of spiritual
jurisdiction that the secular authority should command anything that properly concerns observance of the laws of Christ;
in this respect religion not only does not ask help from the State,
but defends itself against it by every means, as against the inter-
ference of an outsider in another's sphere. From this it follows
that the spiritual Kingdom of Christ not only is compatible with
the existence of organized government among the same people,
that is, with authority in the strict sense of the word, but that
without it it could not even exist, nor could it in any case
successfully grow and spread, save only if it rested on miracles or
a fresh recollection of them.[3]

We have quoted Przypkowski's basic argument *verbatim* in
order to show how he cleared the way for the modern conception
of the relation between State and Church. The epoch of the Reformation did not, fundamentally, settle this relation. In general,
theoretically, the mediaeval doctrine was retained within the
limits set by the newly created actual situation. The Catholic
Church did not change its doctrine, although life was out of
harmony with it. The increasing power of civil government in the
period of absolutism scoffed at the pretensions of Rome; but
there was no quick legal formulation of the changed state of
things (the Gallican declaration in 1682 and the edict of Louis
XIV in 1695, in the matter of ecclesiastical jurisdiction). The
reformed churches jealously guarded their own influence on the
State, where they had achieved a State character. On the contrary again, the Augsburg Confession conceded the State a widely
extended influence on religious and ecclesiastical life. Everywhere, therefore, the situation hovered between domination of the

[3] P. 634.

State by the Church and of the Church by the State. The sects, in general averse to the authority and organization of the State, in their own way acknowledged the supremacy of the Church. From this ideological background there could not have emerged the modern theory of the coexistence of both organizations with independent jurisdiction, which was possible where the State, un- limited in its authority in the temporal sphere, consented in spiritual matters to freedom of religious unions. To proclaim such an ideal, one would have had to come from a Church so extreme and small that it could not aspire to influence the civil government, but at the same time to free oneself from the sectarian spirit far enough to be able to recognize the State's *raison d'être* and its ends. These two conditions were found in Przypkowski who, thanks to his patriotism and his devotion to the State, was able to overcome the low esteem in which his camp traditionally held the State, but who derived from his sect a profound attachment to independence of thought and absolute religious tolerance. The uniting of these two ideological elements at length, in the nineteenth century, was to form the foundation of the coexistence of Church and State in the same society without disputes and encroachments on each other's jurisdiction. How great a service thinkers from the camp of the Polish Brethren rendered in the development of this principle it would be possible to determine by detailed studies of the history of their influence, in the second half of the seventeenth century, on politico-ecclesiastical thought in Holland and England, out of which sprang the rationalism of the Age of Enlightenment.

Przypkowski persuaded those sectarians who were averse to the State that the authority of the State, if it is Christian, may cooperate excellently with the Church for the welfare of the faithful. The authority of the Church consists in overcoming and reinforcing the weakness of god-fearing people; the authority of the State, in breaking down the arrogance of criminals—another field of influence, other methods of action. The spiritual law of Christ penetrates to the deepest fibers of the inner man in order to cultivate his good impulses; according to it a man is already sinning who has the intention to sin. Meanwhile, according to secular law, a bare thought, so long as it does not issue in an act, harms no one. Thus there is one standard of transgressions in the Church, another in the State; the criteria of ecclesiastical life cannot be transferred to the State.

Christ did not prescribe principles of politics, just as he did not lay down principles for agriculture, trading, or for earning a livelihood. But it does not follow from this that he was opposed to the State; in this respect he left mankind freedom, since organizations must vary, depending upon the preferences of peoples and the demands of the time. It is absurd to treat government only from the standpoint of display and enjoyment, for it does not exist to satisfy the ambitions of private persons, but has social tasks to fulfill. The absence of compulsion in the Church cannot weigh unfavorably on the State. If compulsion is necessary with regard to animals, or with children, then it is all the more so with regard to those people who do not trouble themselves about heaven, in whom the sense of right has not stifled criminal impulses. If the command to love one's enemies ensured evil-doers impunity for their crimes, or enemies impunity for plundering, then it would disarm the honest and give the peaceable over to plunder. God never promised immunity from secular courts; Christ only promised forgiveness to the repentant who have broken the commands of the Church. The author does not approve the exceeding readiness of the criminal law to shed blood; but he insists that religion cannot shelter evil-doers for fear lest they should lose eternal life. Indeed, a bandit who runs the risk of being shot by the man whom he attacks deprives himself of the possibility of repentance; however, the awakening of regret—a pretext under which the Protestant sects do not allow capital punishment of transgressors—does not require a long time.

It is absurd to deny a public judge the right to punish crimes on the ground that a private individual is not permitted to avenge himself: the sentence of the court is not revenge but punishment. Moreover, why should there have been any courts if the rigors of punishment were to be taken from them? As the existence of spiritual food does not exclude the use of food for the body, so the sword of the spirit is not opposed to the employment of a material sword. It is proper to despise life and property, but only when they cannot be kept without offense to God; compared to Christ they are of little importance, but it is a different thing to give them up to the lawlessness of enemies or bandits. Christian virtue may be shown in breaking the bonds of the natural feelings (an allusion to the duty of defending one's family from an enemy); but breaking them is not always a manifestation of virtue, it is often simply an escape from duty. A man may pardon injuries he has himself received, but to pardon injuries inflicted on others is a yet greater injury. Let us do good to the evil— granted; but above all let us do good to those who are good! It is impossible to justify indifference to the State by the example of the Jews; the Jews feel themselves foreigners, living in other peoples' States, whereas Christians are inhabitants of their own countries and do not acknowledge a fatherland elsewhere beyond them; feeling need of social organization, they do not separate themselves from the State whose benefits they enjoy.

Przypkowski speaks peaceably, but he is unable to conceal his irritation when he passes to the assertions of sectaries that, despite the abolition of punishments and courts and every form of State coercive power, society will not fall to pieces, for God will preserve it by extraordinary means. In this cause he has no inclination to have recourse to Holy Scripture and proof-texts lest, as he says ironically, "a good cause be buried under a mass of excellent quotations artfully pieced together"; he points out the naked truth in accordance with the dictates of sound reason, considering that it is allowable to explain the words of Christ in their natural sense, for native reason is guided by a light bestowed by God. Thus Przypkowski condemns a naive expectation of miracles. Would God himself destroy the natural way of acting in human society, that is, that men have to be judged and punished by men? By the inspiration of God for the good of men, economic and political forces have limited man's natural freedom and equality. Seeking for miracles, a man breaks down earthly society. With the introduction of immunity from punishment, perhaps little groups of perfect people would preserve their own society, but millions of weaker ones would be driven into a horrible existence, as the prey of criminals. Would God, who does not forget even the ravens, care only for that handful and look on the masses with indifference? It is a delusion to build on the hope that criminals will themselves care for public order; the assurance of impunity would attract all the most horrible criminals as a sign attracts men to a tavern. Przypkowski warns the naive, who take all men in good faith, by the witness of history, by the bloody outbreaks in Westphalia, that the perverse sort misuse the watchwords of religion to palliate the worst crimes: "under the alluring cover of perfection, the Rothmanns and the Knipperdollings [the protagonists at Münster] can always sneak in unexpectedly." Criminals will assume the pretense of genuine Christian perfection, will fanatically defend their freedom of transgression, will glory in their martyrdom, terrorize the minority of pious persons, inflict terrible damage on religion; and it is a great question whether God will at that moment interfere to defend the righteous.

It is better to avoid such confusion by obedience to the authority of the State. The latter will always be necessary; even a general conversion will not remove the need of it. Its possession is a benefit to the faithful; even the gaining of only the ruler himself might already assure the faithful peace and freedom. The Church has no need to fear peace: peace may indeed bring many corruptions, but in itself it is not evil. When we pray in the words, "but deliver us from evil," do we not really pray for peace and for cessation of persecution?

In the dispute about relations with the State, Przypkowski[4] distinguished two kinds of opponents: the one absolutely fanatical, regarding all political sovereignty and compulsory authority as incompatible with religion; and the other in theory recognizing the authority of the State, but depriving it of an essential condition, that is, "the sword, war and peace." He settled matters with the fanatics in the above summarized *Animadversiones*; but this work, evidently out of serious scruples, he did not issue in print.[5] Instead, he prepared for publication another work, aimed at the other camp, *De jure Christiani magistratus et privatorum in belli pacisque negotiis*, for he deemed that by proving from the religious standpoint the lawfulness of punishing criminals and of public defense, he would undermine the foundations of the doctrine of the maximalists. This new work, he designated as a first book devoted to refuting a false view; he meant to work out a further part with a positive interpretation of civil law considered from the standpoint of the Polish Brethren: we do not know, however, whether circumstances allowed him to undertake this work.

The most effective medicine for the chronic diseases of the Christian world, as Przypkowski explains his idea, might be the doctrines, laws, and institutions of the Church of the Polish Brethren. Not forcing belief in anything beyond the minimum contained in Holy Scripture and the Apostles' Creed, generally

---

[4] P. 690.

[5] Sandius (p. 124) gives 1650 as the date of the composition of the *Animadversiones*. It must have been known in Holland from a manuscript, since Jan Hartigsveldt came out against Przypkowski in defense of Brenius. He was an important person, son of the Burgomaster of Rotterdam, in his youth a member of the court of William II, Prince of Orange, and later a wealthy merchant. He was one of the leaders of the group of Rijnsburg Collegiants and was a friend of Daniel de Breen. He sent to Kreuzburg, to the brethren exiled from Poland, a considerable sum for relief (cf. van Slee, *De Geschiedenis van het Socinianisme in de Nederlanden* [Haarlem:1914], p. 240). We do not know the date of his Dutch work in defense of his friend's thesis against Przypkowski and entitled *De recht weerloze Christen*, published at Rotterdam in 1678 soon after the author's death, by Franz Kuyper, the publisher of the *Bibliotheca Fratrum Polonorum*.

acknowledged for centuries, the Church removes the possibility of the propagation of heresy. Not requiring belief in anything that would be contrary to the light of reason, it sets a bar against atheism. Not basing the hope of salvation on the merits, sacrifices, or expiations of another, but only on a man's moral life, it forces believers to lead a godly life. Limiting faith to the simplest articles, and in the more difficult questions leaving freedom to individuals, it ensures peace, tolerance, and harmony.

On only one thing the Polish Brethren never took a definite stand: on the question of defense, whether by individuals or by the government of the State, against an injury, that is, on the question of war, court, and punishment. In the beginnings of the movement, wishing to avoid abuses committed in this respect throughout Christendom, the majority ran into fanatical views, not knowing how to find a middle way between irreligion and superstition. Even Socinus inclined to the opinion prevailing at the time, apparently in spite of his conviction. In his *Reply to Palaeologus,* he in fact combated his opponent but not his views (here Przypkowski repeats word for word what Budny had once said of Socinus' work). Extremes of this sort kept many from the Church, made many ill-disposed towards it. It is hard to require of people that they should place love of an enemy or a criminal above the interests of their family, brethren, and country. It is contrary to reason. Those who held to the absurd view, feeling that it could not be defended, pleaded Christ as an excuse in order to compel the blind obedience of the Church for themselves. There would have been no misfortune in this if a purely contemplative question were at stake; but meanwhile its vital importance provoked incessant conflicts with conscience. For wiser persons, not sharing this view, did not conform to it. The doctrine is extreme, not only because it is socially dangerous and absurd but because it renders it impossible to enlarge the membership of the Church. Its adherents said in plain terms that it was better for the Church not to grow than to admit a crowd of the "called"—thereby restricting it to a handful of the "chosen." What is such "purity" of the Church worth when, in order to provide a shelter from the influx of evil men, institutions are formed which do not admit even good men? There results a narrowness after the monastic pattern. If tyranny rules in the contemporary world, violating truth and conscience, then it is necessary to endeavor that the Church may reach a certain influence on the State, and to this end it is necessary to leave aside doctrines which exclude from the Church those exercising authority and which cut the roots of all government.

Desiring to lead the Polish Brethren out of their sectarian back-street, Przypkowski declared war on opinions which, by means of religion, ruin the State and hence, in his view, religion itself along with the State. He arrived at the conviction that they grew out of a misunderstanding of the words of Christ, and he resolved critically to examine their Gospel justification. Because he stood on the time-honored ground of recognition of the State and its rights and deemed that the teaching of Christ did not weaken them, he saw no need to demonstrate his view positively, but chose a negative way: that of overthrowing the arguments that the extreme school advanced. Przypkowski did not wish here to drag in any of his contemporaries, in order to avoid giving the discussion a topical character; he therefore drew on the man who was now regarded as the father of the doctrine of the Church, that is, on Socinus, and subjected to analysis the arguments put forward by him in his controversy with Palaeologus. Thus Palaeologus now at length received satisfaction, and from an impartial pen, that of a writer who was such an admirer of Socinus that the Church had entrusted to him the preparation of a life, to be prefixed to Socinus' collected writings. This formulation of the theme by Przypkowski, who restricted his argument to theological polemics, releases us here from the obligation to summarize his work *De jure Christiani magistratus*. In a question so many times discussed, we can expect no fresh arguments; however, we may note how far Przypkowski differed from Socinus in his interpretation of the Gospel.

Przypkowski argued that the command to love enemies refers to private individuals; further, that Christ did not forbid wars and took account of the fact that enemies will exist even after his teaching is accepted; he forbade only hatred; and we know that wars are often conducted without hatred, out of unavoidable necessity. Revenge is not to be identified with all resistance to injury; minor injuries should be borne, and one should not exploit one's rights in a violent way, but insistence on impunity for crimes destroys all justice. It is absurd to lose one's life rather than expose an assailant to harm, as it is also to expose the whole of society to lawlessness for fear lest one contribute to the loss of a criminal's soul. Obviously it would be better to change the death penalty to other modes of punishment, provided they were severe enough to frighten men from committing crimes. While condemning the lawlessness and excesses of war, it is impossible to deny the State the right to defend itself against an enemy. Also one may not interpret the words of Christ about loving one's enemies in the sense of love for a foreign foe, "which is impossible without injuring one's fellow-citizens, betraying one's native land, and treachery to the State and to the supreme government." Indeed, greater love is always due to one's native land and its government than to foreigners, although they were not enemies. It is impossible to extend one's submission indefinitely; we are in general not bound everywhere and in everything to give up our rights.

The possession and defense of both private property and the goods and institutions of the State are lawful. It must be understood that what fate has brought to a people, through their being born in a certain territory or by other right, has been awarded to them by the will of God, and that they possess it by as good right as the Jews once did their own land. All nations have a natural right to possess their own dominions in peace, hence also to defend them in case of need by the right of arms and war. A man who does not venture to resist an enemy should not blame God for his defeat. Socinus maintained a cautious attitude on the question of war waged by the State, and his prohibition of war-making referred to private persons. In this he was inconsistent. Would Christ allow the authorities to do what he forbade a private person to do, or forbid a private person what he allowed the authorities?

In these two controversial works, the *Animadversiones* upon Brenius and the *De jure Christiani magistratus* against Socinus, Przypkowski expounded his doctrine about relations with the State. He left us no hints for fixing their chronology;[6] even the *De jure Christiani magistratus* did not appear in print in his lifetime. The cause of this was undoubtedly the unbroken series of wars, first with the Cossacks, then with the Swedes, and rising against that background the hatred of the brethren which culminated in their banishment. An assertion in the face of public opinion by a prominent member of the Church that views hostile to war and adverse to the State were so rooted in its heart would at once have been exploited in bloody fashion against the brethren, already accused of lack of patriotism and of sympathy with, and even of joining, the enemy.

To several prominent members of the brethren who shared his view Przypkowski gave his discussion on the *De jure Christiani magistratus* to read through; and hence knowledge of it spread, making a deep impression. The period of invasions roused patriotic feelings and constrained men to defend themselves; many of the Polish Brethren, having found in Przypkowski's opinion absolution from the scruples long ago inculcated in them, took their places in the ranks of the armies of the Republic. This shocked one of the younger ministers, Joachim Stegmann, a German by birth who, having for some years served churches in

---

[6] Neither work makes any allusion to the other. If the *Animadversiones* upon Brenius was written in 1650, the *De jure Christiani magistratus* also need not be a later production; nothing in their contents would stand in the way of placing them some years earlier.

Volhynia, after the overwhelming invasion of the Cossacks withdrew to Czarkowa, and thence to Danzig. Having certainly got Przypkowski's manuscript from his father-in-law, Ruar, he replied to it in a controversial treatise.[7] Stegmann was not an extreme fanatic like Dr. Zwicker; indeed, he opposed Zwicker's maximalist arguments, though he remained under the influence of Wolzogen, whose German writings he translated into Latin; and from him he got his aversion to war. Although he held Przypkowski in high regard and habitually called him "a great man," he reproached him for coming forward with a revision of doctrine at such an inopportune moment; by his authority "he had opened the window" to elements that were too eager for war and arms and the corruption of morals connected with that way of life. He also criticized him for disrespect shown to the memory of Socinus, reiterated all the arguments against military service already known to us, and was certain that the Church would not follow Przypkowski but that all worthy brethren would condemn his untimely utterance.

Przypkowski was unwilling to leave the attack unanswered. In order finally to overwhelm the position held by his sect and to cut the old authorities to pieces, he composed a work of large dimensions,[8] entitled *Apologia prolixior tractatus de jure Christiani magistratus*. In it he is no longer careful to observe such restraint of tone as in the original work. His *Apologia* abounds in taunts, malicious remarks, and sneers at his opponent. For us it has not very great interest, for with the greatest exactness he destroys and reduces to absurdity the arguments of Stegmann, who had really contributed nothing new. But various passages are notable for their temperament, especially those in which Przypkowski indulges his irritation. He would not, he protested,

---

[7] Stegmann's manuscript is lost. We know its contents only from extensive quotations in Przypkowski's reply. In this controversy an important rôle was played by the authority of Grotius, on whom cf. L. Chmaj, "Przypkowski a Grotius," *Księga pamiątkowa ku czci profesora W. Heinricha* (Cracow:1927).

[8] It fills 112 folio pages in fine print in the edition of his collected works, pp. 737-851, not less than Socinus' *Reply to Palaeologus*.

let himself be hounded out of the number of "worthy men" by
fanatics and sectarians, and would combat views dangerous to
religion and the State. He did not admit the reproach that he inclined the more eager persons to corruption of morals. He did
not, he declared, encourage anyone to choose a soldier's career;
besides, not so many had made haste to enlist even for defense
against the enemy: "In this storm of war which is shaking our
country, military life has no such attractions nor does it so gratify
the flesh as to draw the generality to it. It may once have been
more attractive in time of peace, when the foe ran away from
even the shadow of our armies. But today, when one gets in
return only wounds, death, and chains of bondage among bar-
barians, hunger and want, loss and ruin caused by so many
disasters, who would not be frightened away from war more by
his own danger than by our poor arguments?" [9]

Not wishing to let himself be cut off from the Church, Przypkowski mentioned that there was no law of the Church opposed
to his opinion, and it was impossible for him to agree to allowing absurd views to hinder the progress and spread of their
confession. Some purposely did not consent to an increase in the
numbers of the Church, for they could the more easily keep control over a little handful. They would answer to posterity for
hindering the progress of the truth. Stegmann considered it only
possible for the brethren to hold the lower offices, while forbidding the higher as connected with the right of the sword. To
whom then would they leave the government of the State, asked
Przypkowski; would it be to unbelievers, or perhaps only to the
preachers? For if eternal punishment was foretold for those who
did not wish to be Christians, and likewise for all Christians who
might be willing to guide the State in peace and war, then evidently the direction of the affairs of the State should be given
only to those who were appointed to preach the Gospel.

Przypkowski employed his irony against opponents who im-
agined that it was possible to defend the State without war. You

[9] P. 742.

are ridiculous, he sneered, when you allow war to be waged by others' hands; is a Christian then permitted to kill an enemy if he does it through a hireling? Do you advise hiring one of your neighbors with money to defend your State? Is it not more sensible with the same money to prepare your own army? You advise a man in an extreme case to give himself up voluntarily into captivity rather than risk his life in an uncertain war; that is like following the example of a sick man who prefers passively to surrender to death rather than try a cure that might save him. Granted that one must submit to the will of God, who transfers the kingdom from nation to nation; yet where is the certainty that an armed invader is really the representative of the will of God? Christian resignation has sense when a moderate and just enemy is concerned; but to surrender voluntarily to an absolute enemy means to accept in advance the frightful conditions of captivity. We know, for example, that the Turks cut down Christian nobles and carry off their sons to be bred as janissaries; we know also that the Spanish yoke takes away all freedom of conscience. A man who gives himself up to captivity to an invader, in order not to look on the steel of his sword, is wholly unworthy of freedom. What is the use of buying one's life with such obstinate patience, since the life of men who have at so mean a price sold every reason for living has after all no meaning? Besides, even one's life is not usually saved by such submission. The inhabitants of the "islands of the Atlantic ocean" found out in dealing with the Spaniards[10] how much surrendering without resistance to the mercy of an enemy is worth.

Let no one compare such patience with Christian courage, of which only a noble mind is capable: "Suppose that in the conflict at Piławce [battle in which the Cossacks defeated the Poles in 1648], disgraceful unto all ages, there was a man who took to flight in good faith, in consequence of a patience which shrank from slaying his enemies; who will say that from his action the glory of God or the edification of men resulted? Only God knows

[10] P. 753.

whether in his soul there lay any noble thought, but the public shame involved all in a common disgrace.[11] Wars are condemned because in them men kill one another and commit violence; but Przypkowski asks whether the anti-war doctrine of his opponents protects men from murders and violence. By no means; by ensuring impunity for them it tends to multiply them still more. It is not necessary to yield to the rhetorical suggestions of writers like Erasmus of Rotterdam, who in any case did not condemn necessary and lawful wars; only when watching how kings make war in order to gratify their ambition and win lands and booty did he attack this militaristic tendency with his characteristic virulence.[12] War will not be checked by slogans about non-resistance to the enemy; only when the enemy perceives our firm determination to defend ourselves and the sword in our hands with which we can repel him and in the event of battle destroy him, is there hope of assuring ourselves peace.[13] "Obviously the ideal state of things would be if wars were removed from every corner of the earth," is Przypkowski's comment on the sequence proposed by Stegmann: first disarmament, then the making of peace.

Unfortunately, however, the necessity of wars will not cease through this alone because, with freedom of motion in no wise impeded, such a state of things cannot be brought about or afterwards maintained except only by way of war and by putting a powerful sword on guard. If the illnesses raging today among humanity were allayed by some universal remedy, it would appear at the first glance that medicines were no longer necessary, and that even this miraculous means could be dispensed with, for the diseases were banished. And yet, upon reflection, we cannot deny the need of them as long as that condition endures in which diseases can return in consequence of a fresh impairment of human health. In just the same way, if those injustices and wrongs were done away with which are the immediate cause of

[11] P. 741.
[12] P. 762.
[13] P. 764.

wars, wars would be unnecessary for only so long as their causes
were removed; but if they revived again, which must be expected
with freedom of the human will, the necessity of wars would at
once return with them.[14]

We have quoted this rather long paragraph *verbatim* since it
shows that in the middle of the seventeenth century a Polish
thinker was weighing more than one of the arguments repeated
in the twentieth-century discussions on disarmament.

In the posthumous edition of the works of Przypkowski we find
one more work[15] devoted to the cause for which he fought, entitled *Vindiciae tractatus de magistratu contra objectiones
Danielis Zwickeri.* It would thus seem to be a defense of the *De
jure Christiani magistratus* against Zwicker, who certainly appeared with his reproaches independently of Stegmann. This work
of Przypkowski, however, although it refers to the last-named
work, and was therefore composed later, had a quite different
origin. Dr. Zwicker, already known to us, had written a certain
tract of his own on the magistrate, which Przypkowski severely
criticized. Against this criticism Zwicker came out with objections, and only now the *Vindiciae* answered these objections. It
is thus the fourth item in a controversy between them; the first
three we do not know—no serious loss, for Zwicker's tracts, of
whose contents an idea may be got from Przypkowski's discussion,
were muddled and illogical. They were marked by the boastfulness of a sectarian who condemned the government of the State
as a purely pagan institution and by anarchist tendencies. According to Zwicker, every Christian society ought to dispense
with the power to punish, for threats of punishments were not
necessary for its members. No magistrate could exercise dominion
over the brethren, for they were entitled to steer by the royal
Kingdom of Christ. Still less could any Christian hold office.
After Przypkowski's criticism, Zwicker changed his view so far
as to exclude only perfect Christians from office, permitting it to

[14] P. 815.
[15] Pp. 853-80.

men who did not aspire to one of the higher places in heaven. In addition, as might have been expected of an adherent of communism, a social note was struck in Zwicker's tracts. For example, he deduced from Holy Scripture a command against the holding of serfs, and denied masters the right to punish their servants. He also demanded the restoration, following the example of Christ, of the custom of washing the feet of the poor, on which Przypkowski maliciously remarked that it was not for that age, since even the poor went in boots and not barefoot. In general, Przypkowski treated Zwicker with indulgent disregard, which sometimes turned into irritation, as when he touched on the latter's presumptuous and arrogant tone: "Your pride," he scoffed, "is certainly more opposed to Christian humility than is the authority of the magistrate." [16]

The campaign carried on by Przypkowski was looked at askance by many members of the Church. They took offense at it, not being large-minded enough to reach Przypkowski's horizons, and disavowed him. The memory of this dislike still persisted long after his death in 1670. The Dutchman Frans Limborch, who published his writings, noted an echo of it in the preface to the collected works in 1692:[17] "They dismissed from the world [he was describing Przypkowski's opponents] "kings, magistrates, all civil authority, wars, and capital punishment, in general all obstacles restraining the outbreak of a deadly irreligion, and built a State out of their own chimerical ideas, neither Platonic nor Christian, but such as no one could reach with either

[16] The warlike Zwicker also carried on a lengthy dispute in manuscript with Stegmann who, under the influence of the Cossack massacres, following Szlichtyng, changed his uncompromising position with regard to the State. Zwicker ended the dispute in a print entitled *Ecclesia antiqua inermis seu Responsio ultima Annotatoris anonymi ad Collectoris itidem anonymi Collectiones XIII de magistratu, vi coactiva, suppliciis capitalibus et bellis Christianis licitis* (Amsterdam:1666). A copy was in the University Library at Königsberg. It appeared also in Dutch under the title *De weerlose oude Kerke* (s.a.l.).

[17] Preface to the reader, folio **3.

feet or eyes, or even in thought. These errors, which brought inevitable hatred upon the poor wretches, he [Przypkowski] endeavored with delicate and careful hand to root out; and in return for this he suffered the jealousy sowed by the Papacy in the minds of all theologians." Limborch then recalled the passionate attacks upon Przypkowski and the venomous vexations, as well as the kindliness and patience with which he parried them, never letting himself be thrown off his balance.

We do not find in the sources any explanation why Przypkowski laid such great weight on the utopian theories of his opponents and devoted so much energy to combating them. Indeed, it would seem that they were merely repeating what Czechowic, Gregory Paulus, and Niemojewski had proclaimed in the sixteenth century, which in the following generations was limited and modified as unrealistic and to a considerable degree even removed from the Church. It would be impossible, however, in this way to explain the vigor and enthusiasm that mark the new advocates of a position aloof from the State. It must be supposed that they drew their inspiration from a fresh source, from the new stage in the sectarian movement in the West, in Holland and England, the so-called spiritualistic tendency, which took form about 1640 and increased in the following decade. The spiritualists, under the influence of a breath of mysticism, turned their backs entirely upon the outer world and its forms of organization; they recognized only the spirit, its freedom and inner movement. They rejected all the order, system, ceremony, and organization of the visible Church. They were content with the Church invisible, in which everything was done by the spirit alone. This loose conception of the religious life contributed to the decay of even the most radical sects which survived the epoch of the Reformation. The latter sects were reproached for compromising too much with the world by the spiritualists, in whose eyes both the Mennonites and the Polish Brethren were too little spiritualized, attaching too great importance to the demands of the outer

world.  Thus the spiritualists set up in opposition their own
spiritualistic "Kingdom of Christ," decidedly remote in its essence
from the freest of the Church groups.  Daniel Brenius evidently
based his ideas on this foundation; and undoubtedly Wolzogen
also accepted it in his doctrine—the close relations between
Danzig and Holland permit this supposition.  Przypkowski, who
was striving to get the Polish Brethren out of their old narrowness
and wished to fit them for active propaganda, for expansion,
realized the great danger of spiritualistic mysticism, and therefore fought so strongly against its chimaeras.  Probably also those
Remonstrants who, twenty years after his death, collected his
controversial treatises and printed them in Holland appreciated
their timeliness and appropriateness for Church life on Dutch
soil.

When the Swedish invasion of Poland began, Przypkowski was
forced to interrupt his activity.  The inundation of all Poland by
its enemies compelled the Polish Brethren to settle their quarrel
practically.  Many of them stood by John Casimir, arms in hand;
others, together with a large part of the army and dignitaries of
the Republic, acknowledged the success of Karl Gustaf without
feeling themselves guilty of treason.  Only attacks on their homes
and families in the Carpathian foothills and murders committed
on them by fanatical bands forced them to seek refuge under
Swedish protection.  Condemned to banishment by a resolution of
the Diet in 1658, they left their native land in 1660 in a few
companies, of which the most numerous found shelter for a time at
Kreuzburg in Silesia.

Stanislas Lubieniecki wrote down the following rules of conduct
for a group that was going to seek refuge among the Unitarians of
Transylvania: "To procure exemption from any military service,
the general levy included, and to give up the noble title and the
rights to citizenship rather than to be obliged to go to war for
them.  Our people should not accept offices either in towns or in

the country, because different activities connected with the office constitute a danger to one's conscience." [18]

Even in their exile, discussions about war and the magistrate did not quiet down. They disputed about them the more warmly as they sought for the causes of that hostility of public opinion towards the brethren, which had led to their banishment from a most tolerant State. A trace of this discussion has come down to us in a letter to the brethren sent in 1666 from Kreuzburg by Jeremias Felbinger, a Silesian from Brieg, formerly a minister assisting Ruar at Straszyń near Danzig. Among the chief errors of Socinus, which had a fatal effect on the fortunes of the brethren, he reckoned the prohibition of holding office and engaging in war.[19] At the same time, on Dutch soil, one publication after another bore witness to the vitality of this question in sectarian circles.

It is hard for us to comprehend how, after their expulsion from Poland, the scattered and dwindling handful of Polish Brethren could still both delude themselves and engross public opinion with the hope of holding their own and even of spreading their views.

---

[18] *Observanda Fratribus Polonis Unitariis in Transylvania receptio* (1660), Ms. K 30, fol. 68, in Uppsala.

[19] *Ad Christianos . . . epistola, in qua Socini et ejus discipulorum errores graviores . . . succincte refutantur* (Kreuzburg: Feb. 21-22, 1666), printed in 1672, and again at Rotterdam in 1681. In an earlier work, entitled *Politicae Christianae compendium* (Breslau:1648; a Dutch translation by Antonius Van Koppend, Amsterdam:1660), Felbinger had already taken a stand opposed to the doctrine of Socinus, and in the spirit of Przypkowski he wrote, "If any believe that Christians are entirely apart from the government of the State, I do not condemn nor hate them for their view; indeed, it is well for States if they have as many citizens as possible who hold aloof from public offices; but I warn them as a friend not to backbite secretly those who differ from them in their understanding of the Gospels and not to bring them into hatred by cunning tricks." Similarily, Georges Niemirycz, an eminent member and patron of the Polish Brethren community in the Ukraine, reproached them for not having taken a positive stand in the matter of war and the office of the sword, while their coreligionists in Transylvania accepted offices and took part in wars. Cf. S. Kot, *George Niemirycz et la lutte contre l'intolérance réligieuse* (The Hague, to be published in 1958).

Meantime a competent judge of the atmosphere of that time, Pierre Bayle, assures us that at the end of the seventeenth century it was still generally believed that the Socinians were secretly spreading and that Europe might all of a sudden become Socinian if some of the powerful rulers were publicly to accept this heresy, or at least to abolish the disabilities that lay on those who confessed it. Others, however, discounted these fears, pointing out that no ruler would go over to a confession which condemned war and the holding of office; besides which, this would frighten away private persons too, for there was seldom a man who could bring himself to renounce ambition and arms.[20]

Bayle himself acknowledged the correctness of this last view. He considered that the powers of Europe, which hired their armies for money, would be exasperated if their subjects became Socinians; it would undermine their finances. Rulers love to take a hand in the military quarrels of their neighbors, and it is important for them that it should be known that they cannot be attacked with impunity. Hence subjects whose religion forbids bearing arms are of little value to them. Besides, men cannot adhere to the Socinian confession because the majority, from various motives, like war and are eager to obtain offices and honors: "Thus the Socinian religion is not for the multitude; only certain exceptional natures can accept it. If it is true that one of the Popes prophesied, on the news that Protestants did not tolerate adultery or licentiousness, that they would not last long, this prediction of his would certainly be more applicable to a sect that abstains from wars and honors." In Bayle's view, the Socinians are more absolute than any other Christians in forbidding revenge and worldly honors, and they do not try to interpret figuratively the passages of the Gospel which prescribe strict morality but, in the spirit of these directions, have revived the customs of the primitive Church. Their prohibition of revenge is not so severe, for it is always possible to get around it by means of interpretation; but in the matter of war and offices there

[20] Pierre Bayle, *Dictionnaire des lettres* (Rotterdam:1697), *s.v.* Socin.

is no escape; practice cannot be separated from theory, action must unconditionally follow teaching, and that is a very heavy load.[21]

[21] Bayle, with characteristic skepticism, alarmed the public with the suggestion that the Socinians might change their views on the subject of war and the magistrate; for this was not an article of their faith. Indeed, in Transylvania they made no scruples about offices, and they would certainly take up arms if they had a ruler of their own religion. He also recalled that the Antitrinitarian Polish nobles often went to war, even when they were not legally bound to do so.

# 14  *From Radicalism to Humanitarianism*

Relation of the ideology of the Polish Brethren to the teaching of the New Testament. From social radicalism to humanitarianism. Evolution of their relation to the State. Moral level of the Polish Brethren. Their significance in Europe.

Among the Polish Brethren the discussion about their relation to the State and to society lasted for a hundred years, from the appearance of Peter of Goniądz (Gonesius) to Samuel Przypkowski. We know only the more important published manifestations; the warm deliberations at meetings and synods and the disputes carried on among members of the Church privately, are not open to us. The chief question which rallied the Church and maintained harmony was not the relation to the political and social order of the time but primarily the Unitarian doctrine; nevertheless, in no other Church of that time did matters of life and social morality play such a rôle as among the brethren, and just for this reason caused so much discussion and excitement. Their ideology may be criticized as utopian, for they were only a handful in a society on which they were unable to impose their views. But it must not be forgotten that despite this their opinions had no merely theoretical character, for it was their principle to live as they thought and believed.

The social and political ideas of the Polish Brethren were developed on a strictly religious basis derived from the sources of

Christianity, which they limited to the teaching of Christ and the Apostles. At first glance, then, it may seem hard to understand why there were so many changes and hesitations, ranging from the social and anti-State radicalism of the "anarchists" of Raków to Przypkowski's complete approval of the State and the social order. Why did Krowicki, Palaeologus, and Budny derive from the same sources different indications from those derived by the Moravians and their Polish sympathizers; why did Brenius, Wolzogen, and Stegmann extract different indications from Przypkowski? Here the same factors were at work by virtue of which the Roman Church, starting from the same religious basis, treated the practical problems of public life so differently from the medieval heretics, or the Protestant Churches so differed from the radical sects that grew out of them.

The teaching of Christ did not set up a program for the social reconstruction of the world.[1] It only commanded absolute love of one's neighbor, including even one's enemy; for only such broad love awakens a real understanding of God and opens the way to Him. One's way of life, one's work, are only important as they are necessary for life, but have in themselves no proper moral worth. The economic life plays no rôle in it; care for the morrow should be left to God. Wealth is not forbidden, but it is dangerous to the soul. God gives man his work, and in time of need charity will come with help: that is the real test of piety. In order to be able to perform an act of charity, the existence of labor, income, property must obviously be assumed. There is not a word on the question of the State. Imperial Rome is treated as a lawful institution under the providence of God. The faithful are to remain in the existing social and political order and to wait for the Kingdom of God on earth.

The Apostolic Church rallied about the teaching of the Sermon of the Mount and began in the spirit of its recommendations to

---

[1] Cf. Troeltsch, *Die Soziallehren der christlichen Kirchen und Gruppen* (Tübingen:1912); English translation, *The Social Teaching of the Christian Churches* (London:1931), Vol. II.

draw up a certain social order, binding only upon the members of the Church, not upon the whole of mankind. In the Apostolic Church, poor at it was, communism based upon community of consumption developed. There is no trace of the organization of community of production, nor in general of an organization of any sort which took account of technical considerations. The existence of private property and income was a condition of mercy and charity. No idea of social equality was expressed. In the Apostolic Church there were also no courts or magistrates. In the poor handful gathered together there appeared no need of defining relations to the State. In this system the germ of revolution was undoubtedly involved, though as there was in it not the least conscious wish to raise a revolution, it passed away without any struggle to maintain the principles on which it rested.

The missionary activity of St. Paul dampens what was revolutionary in the Gospel idea and strengthens the conservative character of Christianity. The idea of equality is defined: it will be an equality of all men before God, not one of claim and pretension, but equality in the sense of uniform littleness and unworthiness, which is fulfilled when all have an equal share in the worship of God and in love. With this religious basis the rationalistic idea of equality, which would fain be extended to earthly relations, has nothing in common. The principle of appointing men to different vocations, or of calling them according to the will of God, stands in the way of bringing these two ideas together. Hence God in his unsearchable purposes has introduced inequality in social and civil life. This inequality is to be the incentive to love one's neighbor, to active mercy and aid for the weak. Nothing is said of reforming existing relations, but of bearing them in patience and of using them for the inner purposes of man. The early Church is the more readily reconciled to this inequality since men attribute unchangeability to the conditions of contemporary Rome. The Christian congregations, organizing their internal life and their new worship, and at the same time rapidly spreading, adapt themselves to the usual demands of

social and economic life and reject communism. Missionary work
proves impossible without agreement with the State; thus its
existence is acknowledged and its value is even raised as an institution concerning itself with law, order, and outward decency.
Upon acceptance of the State, the social order bound up with it,
with its division of classes and temporal goods, is approved. With
the claim to its own laws evangelical resignation is forgotten
and the germ of its own jurisdiction is formed.

So a conservative basis is established in the Christian world;
however, it consists not in an inner sincere attachment to the
institutions of the time, but in a combined feeling of contempt
for them, submission to them, and relative acknowledgment of
them. The souls of the faithful are closed to the ideals of the
State, are disposed to be hostile to earthly authorities and to
nationalistic and imperialistic tendencies. There is no awakening of understanding for the ethical values of law, the State, and
economic life, nor of any desire to transform them to suit their
own ends. Social and political institutions are a product of the
hated paganism; hence, it is possible to be inwardly independent
of them, and alongside them to organize the proper life of the
Christian Church, but it is necessary to recognize their outward functions and to adapt oneself to them. So, in the main,
primitive Christianity hands down to posterity in Holy Scripture
two different inter-penetrating currents in relation to the political and social order: the conservative and the revolutionary.

We must remember this in order to understand how the New
Testament could furnish food for both conservative and subversive tendencies, depending on which passages were assigned
decisive weight and on what was sought in them. If the Racovian
radicals relied on the Sermon on the Mount, their opponents
looked for support in the epistles of St. Paul. If the communists were provided with the Apostolic Church at Jerusalem,
the conservatives appealed to the organization of the Churches
of a Christianity spreading over the Roman Empire. Even if in
discussion (which happened rarely) they took into account

the succeeding centuries of the Church, the third and fourth, there also they found the two currents, the one socially radical (Tertullian, Cyprian, John Chrysostom), citing the tale of the rich young man, and the other moderate, trying to reconcile the obligations of mercy with private property and economic demands; one politically hostile to the State, to courts, and to war, the other, with the domination of Rome by the Christians, more and more deeply compromising (the synod at Arles in 314 decreed excommunication on soliders deserting from the Roman army).

Simpler minds, less keen, less cultivated or one-sided, were blindly attached to those teachings of Holy Scripture which fell in with their inclinations; the opponents of the doctrinaires were compelled to use more subtle reasoning to detect and explain contradictions, to interpret them by external circumstances, by the choice of audience, by the historical factor, thanks to which they sometimes arrived at an acute analysis of the texts and at apt historical criticism.

As in the very beginnings of Christianity the demands of reality called forth display now of a hostile, now of a compromising attitude toward the political and social order of the time, until in the end there ensued a harmonization of religion with life; so in the century of the history of the Polish Brethren we have witnessed a like evolution. The first generation of our Antitrinitarians was distinguished by an uncompromising radicalism. All of them, born in the Catholic Church, swallowed up in the whirlpool of the Reformation, passed through the doctrine of Luther, of Calvin, of Zwingli, or of Łaski, more and more violently withdrawing from the old Church and more and more uneasily seeking realization of the "pure doctrine." There grew up in them an impulse to reject all the compromises that centuries of the Church's history had accumulated, and to put into practice the highest ethical ideals which spoke to them from the Gospel. Keeping to a strictly religious basis, they did not proclaim a revolution either social or political, but wished to apply absolutely the commands of love both with their social consequences, even to resigning privileges, and with their political consequences, even to denying the law of the sword.

Social radicalism very quickly lost force. Various factors tended to quench it. First was its religious origin, which did not favor its transformation into a broad program of social action. It was motivated not by economic misery nor by the social wrongs of the lower classes but by absorption in the command to love one's neighbor. If Jan Przypkowski freed his serfs from servitude, he fulfilled his personal obligation of love toward "creatures of the one Creator," but he did not adopt the notion of abolishing servitude altogether and conferring freedom upon the peasants in the whole Republic. If Niemojewski and Brzeziński sold their fertile estates in Kujawy and used the proceeds in assisting poor brethren, thus satisfying their own consciences by following the advice given to the rich young man of the Gospel, they by no means made a like demand on nobles who did not belong to their group. Subsequently, heroic acts of this sort of renunciation of earthly goods did not prove economically desirable. Even Niemojewski conceded that it was impossible to command charity which swallowed up all the property of a rich man, for it involved the owner in poverty, condemned him to beggary, and even so did not permanently ensure against want the poor who had been given alms, but at most only caused a transfer of wealth to other hands.

They did not know how to develop for themselves a conception of the economic reconstruction of society which would have allowed them to combine the demands of religion with those of economics. They rejected the communism of the Moravians as not strictly answering to the commands of Christian mercy; they saw in it only a proof of the efficiency of "managers," who condemned their brethren to heavy labor and exploitation. Belonging in the main to the gentry, the Polish Brethren could not follow in the footsteps of the radical German or Dutch groups, which were composed of laborers and artisans. Thus the attempts at first made to impose on members of the Church the obligation of manual labor, for which they were fitted neither by education nor by experience, did not gain acceptance among them. Dutch and English sectarians, accepting the Calvinistic doctrine of trade ethics, plunged into work, thrift, and the accumulation of wealth, and in time became a strong pillar of capitalism; in commercial and colonizing lands on the seaboard this was possible. The economic system of the Republic, which was founded on agricultural production and the labor of a feudal peasantry, did not furnish such opportunities, and the Polish Brethren were unable to separate themselves from this system. Thus even by the end of the sixteenth century they had become reconciled to it and practiced active love of neighbor only by making the circumstances of peasant life easier and by refraining from exploiting their serfs. Their radicalism was transformed into humanitarianism.

The following is placed in the mouth of an Antitrinitarian noble as a characteristic prayer, in a prayerbook composed by Jan Stoiński:

Let me, O God, set such a watch upon my conscience, that my land may not cry out against me, and its fields also may not weep together for my unjust treatment of my servants, that I put them to labors beyond their duty, heavy and hardly to be borne, or do not grant them what is their due, or withhold their just wages from my hired men.

Am I more deserving than those who are under my authority? Art Thou, who didst create each of them, not the One who didst create me also? Didst Thou not form them also in their mother's womb like me? Let me then, remembering this, not stretch too far the extent of my rule over them, and not put them to unfair work. Let me be content with what their duty brings; and indeed let me sometimes yield my rights and, where I can, indulge them, rather than in view of my power and authority prey on their poverty, who cannot escape me, and lay on them burdens unbearable. Let them not work for me like cattle, but let me remember that they are yet men, created in Thine image, in nature like me. Let them have no cause to complain to Thee against me, that Thou hast not heard them and hast not avenged their wrongs upon me.

And as to the common people of the towns, Stoiński put into the mouth of an Antitrinitarian noble this vow:

May I never encroach on their right, and never abridge that freedom which they have from me or from my ancestors; nay, let me rather enlarge it when there is need. For as I love myself in my greater freedom as a noble, so also do they in their freedom, narrower though it be; and what I do not like, it is not becoming in me to do to another.[2]

Similarly, out of the initially absolute condemnation of criminal judicature there developed in time a more practical humanitarian demand for a relaxation of the extreme severities of the criminal law, and in particular of the penalties for theft. In general the Polish Brethren tried to minimize the wrongs of the social order by Christian mercy and brotherliness. As far as they could, they abolished among themselves all distinctions of class, birth, and property. Within the sphere of the Church, nobles and commoners lived and were recognized as equals. Their restraint of greed, luxury, and display diminished outward differences; the rich, moreover, did not flock to such an extreme confession, and the wealthier members of the Church distinguished themselves by their great liberality, which made it possible both to aid the poor and to support ministers in the poorer congregations, and to carry on an immense publishing and missionary work.

If the social ideology of the Polish Brethren soon passed its crisis and reached a basis of compromise, it was more difficult to settle their relation to the State. They began their existence as loose private groups averse to the State, which they regarded as an unavoidable result of the existence of evil in the world, although, by strongly emphasizing obedience to the civil government, they were able to defend themselves against charges of

[2] Jan Stoiński, *Modlitwy nabożne* (*Devout prayers*) (Raków:1633), pp. 695, 393, 389.

sedition and tendencies to revolution. They did, however, frighten away from themselves all elements that were not willing to renounce active participation in the life of the Republic. It proved that in a gentry-State one could not survive without fulfilling certain obligations to the State, especially when it was threatened by the pressure of eastern barbarism. Absolute abstinence from civil life could in the West be practiced only by little groups of sectarians, drawn from the poorest stratum. It was impossible in Poland to imagine the existence of organizations of the common people not based on any guarantee in the public law; it was at most admissible in the case of groups of foreign colonists like the Mennonites on the bottom lands near Danzig. The Polish Brethren, who scandalized all Churches by their Antitrinitarian doctrine, could shelter themselves only under the privilege of the rights of the nobility, and it was necessary to pay for their enjoyment of the rights by discharging obligations to the State. As the experience of history shows, every religious group, insofar as it is united in a church organization, acquires a tendency to spread if it does not wish to die out, and hence is forced to enter on the path of compromise with the existing order. Various sects succumbed to this same fate, even those as radical as the Mennonites, Baptists, and Quakers. Among the Polish Brethren the process began with the acknowledgment of elementary duties to the State; then came the turn of warmth of patriotic feelings, and even of patriotic devotion, in proportion as the conviction grew that the State secured them certain values of a higher order. The Republic, which allowed them to enjoy the great treasure of freedom of conscience, aroused, despite all their scruples, a fervent attachment of which we have proofs, for example in the *Poloneutychia* of Andrew Lubieniecki, or in the *Chocim War* of Wacław Potocki (an epic poem on the Polish victory over the Turks at Chocim in 1621).

It is obviously impossible to apply to the political ideology of the Polish Brethren criteria that were not developed until the

eighteenth century. They were not striving for the political
freedom of the citizen in the sphere of the State, nor for the
influence of the will of serfs on the course of State affairs. On
the contrary, they themselves withdrew from these affairs, seeking no honors or offices. "Having equal liberties with you gentlemen *cum paritate juris,*" said Andrew Moskorzowski, addressing
the Estates of the Republic on behalf of the Antitrinitarian
nobility at the electoral Diet in 1632, "we have left the move
to you gentlemen in all honors and dignities. We run after none
of them; we do not try to seize anything before anyone else;
yet sitting in our solitude we do not hinder others." [3] They
asked of the State only that its laws and institutions should not
violate the requirements of their religion, asked of it above all
freedom of conscience, for all confessions as well as for themselves. Even when they were being persecuted in violation of
the law, they did not raise the standard of rebellion. They
complained, tried to persuade, protested, and finally, in face of
the harshest violence, when forbidden to confess their religion,
they left their native land and went into banishment, misery,
and exile. Their native land repulsed them; they did not disown it.
They placed the cause of God and of conscience above any
worldly goods and affections, in this respect true sons of the
era of the Reformation, whose spirit the Jesuit Peter Skarga
expressed in his memorable cry: "Defend the Church and the
souls of men before the fatherland! If the temporal fails, let
us hold fast to the eternal."

In Polish society during the sixteenth and seventeenth centuries the Polish Brethren represented not only great intellectual
but also great moral values. They gave profound consideration
to the commands of Christian ethics and tried in all strictness
to conform their lives to them. The moral level of their Churches
aroused the enthusiasm of impartial observers. The Scotsman
Thomas Segeth related [4] that when he found himself at Raków

[3] Ossoliński Ms. 647, p. 39.
[4] Cf. Ruar, *Epistolae,* p. 379.

in 1612, "it seemed as though he had been transported into another world, for whereas elsewhere all was full of the noises of war and tumults, here it was quiet; men were so trained to frugality and calm that you might think that they were angels."

In spite of the fact that they were hated and passionately opposed by all the confessions, we find no complaints against their morals whether collective or individual. Even the Jesuit Martin Łaszcz, not at all fastidious in his choice of calumny, found himself at a loss when he desired to render them morally odious. He did not succeed in discovering anything against them, and he had to fasten upon them slanderous lies current about the Moravian Anabaptists.[5] It was just this moral level, based on concord of life with faith, which ensured them such strong solidarity that they were able to endure for several generations, and even the severest test of banishment from their native land resulted in but few desertions among them.

Uniting in themselves a lofty morality with profound knowledge, the Polish Brethren, despite their numerical insignificance, constituted an influential and attractive center. The whole world of that time was interested in them. The Raków prints, though everywhere banned, were in demand and were snapped up, especially in Germany, France, Holland, and England. The pens of theologians of all the Churches were sharpened against them. A considerable library could be formed of the literature

---

[5] Szczęsny Zebrowski, *Recepta na Plastr Czechowica* (*Prescription for the Plaster of Czechowic*) (Cracow:1597), p. 15: "And if there [in England] there is as yet little of this stench, you have more than enough among your Immersers, among whom *omnia sunt communia,* and they have their wives in common, and like cattle, making no distinction, they borrow one another's wives. Without going far, you have enough of this filth in Moravia, where children do not know their own parents, nor parents their own children. When they say in meeting *Crescite et multiplicamini,* these are your little brethren, you have to deny them in vain. Although you here with us do not do mischief so openly, but somewhat secretly, your servants can tell [!], and yourselves stink through your skin with this stench, and you pretend to be great Christians, though you live like beasts." Even inquiry through the servants did not bring the Łaszczes any weapon!

called anti-Socinian in the seventeenth century. By their doctrine they raised a ferment in distant regions. For want of detailed investigations in this field, it is impossible as yet to pronounce how important an influence they exerted on the history of religious thought and on the intellectual development of the second half of the seventeenth century. It is certain that they placed their mark on the religious movement of the radical Dutch confessions and, in part through them, in part directly, on the English sects. Voltaire in his time was still aware of this when, for example, he emphasized in his *Lettres anglaises* the sympathy of Newton for the Polish Brethren. No attention has, however, been called by historians of political ideas to this Polish contribution to the important intellectual work out of which the European Enlightenment sprang.[6]

The Polish Brethren did not live to see the time in which their ideas, principles, and methods of thought began to exert an influence on the intellectual life of the world. They died out while dispersed as exiles, grieving that their own nation had rejected them, although to them its spiritual and moral elevation was of the greatest consequence. Only after centuries of oblivion have students of the Polish past discovered them. But the consciousness is precious to us that in the remote past such an unusual flower grew up on Polish soil, that the nation produced within itself a group of such moral elevation, such critical spirit, and such gravity of life.

[6] Troeltsch's fundamental work, *Die Soziallehren der christlichen Kirchen und Gruppen* (Tübingen:1912), while defining the position of petty German and Dutch groups in the history of the political ideology of Christianity, does not even mention the Polish Brethren.

# Index

Adult baptism, 30, 49
Albinus, 51
Alciati, Johannes Paulus, 19
Anabaptism, Ostorodt's separation from, 123–126
"Anabaptist plague," 20
Anabaptists, and adult baptism, 30; aims, solidarity of, 14; and Antitrinitarians, compared with, 46–49; banishment urged, 23; Budny's dispute with, 97–109; Calvinist views on, 16–17; Catholics oppose, 95; Danzig group, 148; first reactions to, 9–16; in Germany, extermination of, 3; and Holy Trinity, 40; oppression of, 12–13; Poland, expelled from,' 11; in Poland, wanderings of, 11–21; political ideas of, 3, 7–8; Protestant dislike for, 14–16; and Racovians, differences with, 33; social ideas of, 3; Socinus supports, 91; and Thirty Years War, 156–157
*Animadversiones*, 183, 196
Antitrinitarians, and Anabaptists, compared with, 46–49; and *De primatu*, effect of, 19; Dutch, 165; at Iwie, synod of (1568), 24; least-known period, 110; life among, 111–112; nobility and, 77; at Pelsznica, synod of, 25; Poland, expelled from, 205–206; and radicalism, 20; and religious radicalism (1569), 26; rise of, 130–131
Antitrinitarian Church, and rebelion of Sigismund III, 135
*Apologia prolixior tractatus* . . . 197

Apostolic Church, 209–210
Arciszewski, Christopher, 138
Arciszewski, Elias, 114, 115
Arciszewski, Paul, 148
Ascherham, Gabriel, 9
Augsburg Confession, 127, 187

Balcerowicz, Jan, 83 *n*
Baptism, adult, 30, 49; infant, 18–19; rite of, at adult age, 2
Baptista, John, 33
Bartholomew, 33
Batory. *See* Stephen Batory
Bayle, Pierre, and spread of Socinianism, 206–207
Belzyce, synod at (1569), 25–26
Bernard of Lublin, 10
Berzewiczy, Martin, 95
Bielinski, Daniel, 33, 77–78, 96
Blandrata, Giorgio, 21, 51, 93
Brenius, doctrine of the State, 165–168; Przypkowski on, 196; Szlichtyng against doctrine, 171–182; Wolzogen on doctrine, 167–170
Brog, 69
Brzesc, synod of, 21
Brzezinski, Lawrence, 28
Brzeziny, synod at (1565), 19
Buczynski, 138
Budny, Simon, 110; on Anabaptism, 16–17; and Anabaptist dispute, 97–109; as apostate, 108–109; at Belzyce, synod of, 26; and break with Little Poland Church, 98; condemns synod of 1584, 108; conservatism of, 17–18; and *De primatu*, 18–19; expelled from Church, 108; at Iwie, synod of, 24; at Losk, synod of,

# Date Due

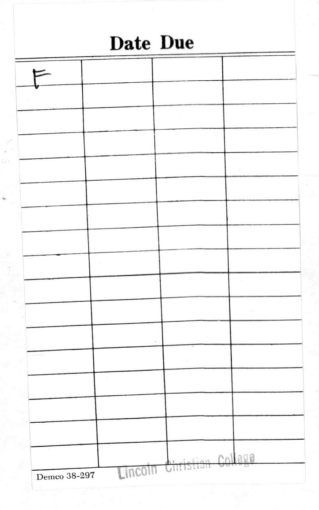